Harriet E. O'Shea

RORSCHACH RESPONSES

OF

ELEMENTARY SCHOOL CHILDREN

RORSCHACH RESPONSES
OF
ELEMENTARY SCHOOL CHILDREN

A Normative Study

by

NETTIE H. LEDWITH, Ph.D.

Chief Psychologist

Pittsburgh Child Guidance Center

UNIVERSITY OF PITTSBURGH PRESS

Library of Congress Catalog Card Number: 58-59653

© 1959, University of Pittsburgh Press

Lithoprinted in U.S.A.

EDWARDS BROTHERS, INC.

Ann Arbor, Michigan

1959

Foreword

The impetus for the investigation reported in the following pages came as a result of an attempt in 1944 to introduce the Rorschach Inkblot Test into the psychological test battery which I was then using in my work with emotionally disturbed children at the Pittsburgh Child Guidance Center. A review of the Rorschach literature, including at that time more than two decades of investigation following the introduction of the technique by Hermann Rorschach in 1922, revealed a dearth of satisfactory norms for children's Rorschachs. Although there was an increase in the number of Rorschach studies with children during each succeeding year of this twenty-two year period of Rorschach history, there were so many differences in sampling, scoring, and interpretation among the reports in the literature that it was difficult to integrate this published material into usable form. There were a few early attempts to summarize and coordinate this diversity of investigative effort, but as the studies grew in number, such attempts tended to become increasingly less comprehensive and were of little practical value to the Rorschacher inexperienced in the children's field. Stumbling blocks, other than this lack of integration, seemed to prevent further the development of adequate normative material. For example, there was a controversy over calling the Rorschach a *test* since some workers felt that it "revealed" rather than "measured" personality characteristics. Other workers who believed that objectivity would jeopardize the effectiveness and even change the character of the test opposed any standardization procedure. Such views served mainly to discourage and discount normative studies.

No attempt will be made here to give a detailed review of the early Rorschach literature, since many excellent reviews have been published through the years. Suffice to say at this point that in 1944, when I was searching for help in applying the Rorschach to emotionally disturbed children, I found in the literature general agreement as to the value of the test as a diagnostic tool and an increasing recognition of the need for additional normative material at all age levels. As a result of the literature survey, I concluded that a Rorschach study of normally functioning children was the first important step in learning how to use the test with emotionally disturbed children. And so the project reported here was initiated.

Beginning in September 1946, I selected, during the succeeding school year, a group of one hundred and sixty first grade children from the various school systems of Pittsburgh and surrounding county. Through their six years of elementary school experience, I studied these children annually, obtaining a series of six yearly Rorschach records from each child. Other psychological as well as historical data were also collected about each child through the years. At the conclusion of the six years of investigation, one hundred and thirty-eight children from the original sample remained as subjects in the study. The use of control groups, to be described in the first chapter, increased the number of children studied to two hundred and ninety-one.

In the years following the initiation of this investigation several studies involving the children's Rorschachs have been reported in the literature. Mary Ford's Monograph, *The Application of the Rorschach Test to Young Children,* published in 1946, analyzed the Rorschach responses of a highly homogeneous group of young children in terms of age, sex, mental ability, and various other aspects of personality. In 1949, "Through Adolescence with the Rorschach," by McFate and Orr appeared in the *Journal of Projective Techniques* as the first of a series of three articles analyzing the Rorschach protocols of one hundred and ninety-four adolescent children, ages eleven through eighteen years. "Genetic Aspects of Some Rorschach Factors," a paper presented at the American Orthopsychiatric Association meeting in 1950 by Rabin and Beck, reported the age changes of Rorschach factors in the protocols of one hundred and thirty-one preadolescent school children of average intelligence.

In 1952 Ames and others from the Gesell Institute of Research published *Child Rorschach Responses,* a book based on the Rorschach response of six hundred and fifty children, aged two and one-half to ten years. This report contains a summary of the means of the Rorschach scoring categories of fifty children at each six months interval within this age range. This summarization is followed first by a section on sex differences noted in the responses of the children. A comparison of these Rorschach results with general developmental trends previously reported by Gesell concludes the presentation. *A Clinical Approach to Children's Rorschachs,* by Florence Halpern, was published in 1953. This book, which also deals with children from two-and-a-half to ten years of age, covers a variety of clinical syndromes and presents records of children manifesting various forms of mental and emotional disturbances, and is the result of years of using the Rorschach with children. One of the most recent reports on children's Rorschachs is found in Volume II of *The Developments in the Rorschach Technique,* by Klopfer et al. published in the fall of 1956. The first six chapters of this book, devoted to a discussion of children's Rorschachs, brings the reader up to date on the problems and possibilities in the use of the technique with children and in the interpretation of children's records. A few recent investigations in the children's field are discussed by the authors at some length, and the results of many other studies are integrated into a worth-while evaluation of what has been done and what needs to be done further toward realizing the potentials of the Rorschach technique as an effective tool in working with children. The authors placed considerable emphasis on the need for further Rorschach research involving the longitudinal approach--a subject of particular interest to this investigator.

Despite the great progress made in the use and understanding of children's Rorschachs during the decade and more since the initiation of this investigation, there are still gaps in the literature that seem to call for additional normative material. The nature of this study is such that the findings can be used to fill some of these obvious gaps. For example, this is the only investigation as yet reported in which the Rorschach responses of a large sample of preadolescent children have been studied at regular intervals through such an extended span of years. That this sample of one hundred and thirty-eight children, along with the two control groups, represents a great variety of socio-economic and cultural backgrounds and includes all intelligence levels is further evidence of its uniqueness and importance.

Even though many research possibilities were found later to be inherent in the Rorschach protocols and other data collected through the years from this large group of children, the primary goal of the originally outlined project was that of determining Rorschach norms for children from six through eleven years of age. It is the achievement of this initial goal that forms the basis for this report. Despite the fact that the value of norms for interpreting Rorschach records has long been a subject of controversy, it is a well known fact that every experienced Rorschacher has established for himself a set of "clinical norms" for the particular group, whether adult or child, which forms the background of his experience. The inexperienced Rorschacher, however, must depend on what the Rorschach literature has to offer him in the way of normative material. If working in the adult field, he is fortunate in having access to generally accepted norms for that group: that is, the average number of responses to be expected, the way they are most commonly distributed among the location areas of the various blots, how these responses are determined, the content most frequently used, and the concepts most often associated with each Rorschach card. These normative formulations for adults, based for the most part on the extended clinical experience of various workers in the field, are found to be fairly consistent among the various experts, despite the differences as to scoring and other minor variations. Such is not the case with children's norms. Attempts to establish Rorschach norms for children have been based on small numbers of subjects at different age levels, on selective samples that vary widely, and on different methods of administration and scoring, resulting in many discrepancies among the various studies.

The Rorschach norms for children discussed in the following pages are derived from a sample of one hundred and thirty-eight children chosen at six years of age and representative of a variety of characteristics of the large population from which they were selected. These children were given the Rorschach test annually from six through eleven years of age; and the resulting eight hundred and twenty-eight Rorschach protocols, scored according to the Klopfer method, comprise the raw data on which this study is based. The two control groups, one at seven years and the other at eleven years-- one hundred and fifty-three children in all--are used to highlight any practice effect that might have accrued from the annual repetition of the test with the longitudinal group. Various measures, such as means, standard deviations, and percentages of all Rorschach scoring categories were determined. Each category is discussed in relation to four variables: age, sex, intelligence, and the effects of repeated testing. A discussion of content used by the children from year to year culminates in the determination of children's "populars" at each age level.

A comparison of the children's Rorschach norms thus determined, with the norms generally accepted for adults, enables the Rorschacher inexperienced in the children's field to gain a better perspective of what can be expected in the Rorschach protocols of children between the ages of six and eleven years inclusive and, as a result, is helpful to him in evaluating the Rorschach responses of preadolescent children.

As the reader follows this large group of children from one year to the next, noting that general developmental trends are reflected in the various averages of their successive Rorschach protocols, it is important to keep in mind that this group is made up of one hundred and thirty-eight individuals, none of whom has given a series of Rorschach records that follow exactly the norms so far outlined. That each child expresses his individuality in his Rorschach responses is shown in the serial Rorschachs of six children, presented in the last chapter of the book.

Acknowledgments

The co-workers in this study of the Rorschach Responses of Elementary School Children are so numerous as to preclude mention of every individual who made a contribution; however, the help of certain key people and groups are herewith acknowledged.

At the very beginning in 1946, Dr. Harry M. Little, who was at that time Director of the Pittsburgh Child Guidance Center, was helpful in planning the project and has continued his interest through the years. Succeeding Directors, Dr. Doris Phillips Wheeler and Dr. William F. Finzer, have likewise been interested, encouraging, and helpful. The Boards of Directors and staff members of the Center have maintained a consistently encouraging attitude. Those Board members whose active interest is chiefly responsible for the publication of this report are: Dr. Jack Birch, Mrs. Josephine Falk, and Mrs. Kathleen Byrne.

Dr. Wayne Dennis, formerly head of the Psychology Department, University of Pittsburgh, helped in the early planning of the investigation and has followed its progress with interest and with constructive suggestions.

Dr. Henry Brosin, director of the Western Psychiatric Institute of Pennsylvania, has shown a keen interest in the project and has given valued help and counsel.

The heads of the various school systems of Pittsburgh and Allegheny County from which the children in the study were chosen, and the principals and teachers in individual schools have given invaluable aid in making possible the selection of a representative sample of children.

The children themselves and their parents deserve much credit for the success of the whole enterprise. They were, as a group, not only cooperative, but enthusiastic about the project, sustaining this positive type of response throughout the progress of the study.

There were many people who helped with the statistical treatment of the data, but special thanks is due Dr. Angela Homme, who is mainly responsible for the contents of the statistical tables. Dr. John C. Flanagan was the statistical consultant.

The skill and patience of the secretary, Mrs. Alyce Woodruff, who typed and retyped the manuscript over a period of months, made the reporting of this study a pleasant rather than a tedious task.

CONTENTS

I. Description of the Study

Purpose, Plan, and Procedure

The primary purpose of this study was to gather Rorschach norms from a representative sample of normal children in order that they might be put to immediate use in the author's work with emotionally disturbed children at the Pittsburgh Child Guidance Center. Plans for a longitudinal investigation that would result in such normative material were completed in the spring of 1946. The children chosen for the study were normally functioning in the sense that they were attending school and had not been referred to any agency because of maladjustment. The span of years during which the subjects were studied, six through eleven years of age, was determined by a number of factors, the two most outstanding being: 1) the prevalence of this age group among the children tested at the Center at that time, with the concomitant need for help in interpreting their Rorschachs, and 2) the comparative ease with which such an age range could be reached in elementary schools.

Beginning with the administration of the Rorschach test to a sample of one hundred and sixty children six years old (to be described later), the writer repeated the test with these same children yearly through eleven years of age. In this way Rorschach patterns at different age levels as well as changes in these patterns from year to year were determined. In order to test the effect of the yearly repetition of the test to the same group of children, two control groups, each approximately one-half the size of the original longitudinal group, were studied--one at the seven year level and another at the eleven year level. In such a study it has been possible to follow the personality developmental pattern of the so-called "average" child as reflected in the successive yearly Rorschach protocols of the group during the preadolescent years.

In addition to the Rorschach test, a different individual psychological test was administered each year to each child in the longitudinal group: at six years of age, the Revised Stanford-Binet Examination, Form L; at seven years, the Goodenough Draw-a-Man Test; at eight years, the Monroe Diagnostic Reading Examination; at nine years, the Grace Arthur Performance Test; at ten years, the Wechsler Intelligence Scale for Children; and at eleven years, the Human Figure Drawings. The results of these tests furnished background material from which certain characteristics of the group were determined.

The children of the two control groups, who saw the Rorschach cards only one time, took the following additional psychological tests: Stanford-Binet Examination, Form L, and Goodenough Draw-a-Man Test at the seven year level; the Binet Vocabulary and Human Figure Drawings at the eleven year level.

The Rorschach protocols and the additional psychological test data of both longitudinal and control groups--two hundred and ninety-one children in all--were analyzed with the following questions in mind:

1. How does the "average" normally functioning child respond to the Rorschach cards at each age level, six through eleven years?
2. How do the Rorschach responses change from one age to the next?
3. Does the intelligence of the child affect his responses to the cards?
4. Do the Rorschach responses of boys differ from those of girls?
5. How does the yearly repetition of the Rorschach affect the responses of the children?

Selection of Subjects

Since the original plans for the study included immediate application of the results in the psychology program at the Pittsburgh Child Guidance Center, a clinic which serves the residents of Pittsburgh and Allegheny County, that geographical location was the area from which the sample was derived. For reasons already noted, children in the elementary school grades of this area were used as the specific population from which the subjects were selected. A rough estimate of that particular population in Pittsburgh and Allegheny County, including all types of schools, was 160,000 children at the time the project was initiated in 1946. Approximately 54,000 of these children were in Catholic Parochial Schools; 45,000 in the Pittsburgh Public Schools; 32,000 in the County Schools; 25,000 in the Independent School Districts (in certain suburban localities surrounding the city); and 4,000 in private schools.

Supervising authorities in these various school systems were asked to select from the schools under their supervision those that presented a cross section of the socio-economic levels represented in their particular school districts. The thirty schools thus selected, in the opinion of all concerned with the study, presented a fair representation of all socio-economic levels in the city and county. Fused in the investigation were nine Catholic Parochial Schools, eight Pittsburgh Public Schools, six County Schools, five Independent District Schools, and two private schools--the number of schools in each system being proportionate to their respective school populations.

Between September 1946 and June 1947, the writer visited these thirty schools, examining two or more children in each school. The number of children studied in each school was determined by the size of that particular school population. A similar attempt was made to spread the sampling proportionately among the school systems. The one hundred and sixty children thus chosen--eighty boys and eighty girls--were tested during the first year of the study. The distribution of the sample was as follows: fifty-two children from Catholic Parochial Schools; forty-five from Pittsburgh Public Schools; thirty-three from County Schools; twenty-six from Independent District Schools; and four from private schools. This sample of one hundred and sixty children contained, at the time of the initial contact, approximately one child per thousand of the elementary school population of Pittsburgh and Allegheny County.

The selection of individual children was based on chronological age. Six years and eight months was arbitrarily set as the optimal age for the first contact with each child. Since the average age for entering first grade is six years, each child in the study, by the age of six years and eight months, had been in the grade for approximately one school semester, and had thus established some fairly definite pattern of school adjustment. All children in the study were born in 1940, with birthdates from January through December.

Before each school visit the writer had talked with the principal, briefly describing the project and offering an opportunity for further discussion. These talks were facilitated by the fact that each principal had been previously notified by higher school authorities to the effect that the project had official endorsement. During this first visit to each school, further explanation to teachers was sometimes necessary. If the basis for choosing the children and the consequent need for consulting the birth records were not fully explained, some teachers could not understand why their problem and/or prize children could not be arbitrarily included in the study. Often both principal and teacher were interested in further discussion of the project. In all instances there were cordiality and cooperation among the school people. The fact that the writer was so obviously accepted by these adults in authority made her an object of interest to the children and was a favorable factor in the subsequent rapport with the chosen children. When introduced to the writer, each child readily accepted the invitation to go with her. On the way to the examining room a simple explanation was given in such words as: "You were chosen as someone who might be interested in some cards and other things I brought with me today. We are going to a room where we can look at them together." Each child was given the Stanford-Binet Intelligence Examination, and this was immediately followed by the Rorschach test.

On subsequent yearly contacts, the children became even more friendly toward and accepting of the examiner. A different psychological test administered each year was followed immediately by the Rorschach test. As they grew older many of the children asked questions about the project. These questions were answered, as were those which were raised by some of the parents at various intervals through the years.

During the investigation period a few children moved out of the city or county. Several others changed neighborhoods, but were attending different schools within the city or county limits. If it were possible to trace them, the children who had not left the county were reached in their new school setting. The number of schools visited increased each year so that during the sixth and last year of the investigation there were sixty-two schools, in contrast to the original thirty. During this six year period, a small number of children was lost from the study each year, with the result that there remained at the end of the six year period one hundred and thirty-eight children--sixty-eight boys and seventy girls. These are the subjects that constitute the basis of this report. The data collected from this longitudinal group during six years of testing were analyzed and compared with those from the two control groups, one of which was tested at seven years of age and the other at eleven.

The Testing Procedure

Each child in the longitudinal group, as well as in the two control groups, was tested in a room of the school building, with only the child and examiner present. The child was always seated at a table with his back to the windows in order to get the best light on the Rorschach cards. The examiner sat across from him. This seating arrangement was found to be more satisfactory than placing the child in the traditional Rorschach testing position with his back to the examiner. Children, especially at the younger age levels, so often need the reassurance inherent in an interested and attentive adult who is visible to them. Since this arrangement of child and examiner facing each other also facilitated the transition to the Rorschach test from the other psychological tests given first at each testing session, it was adhered to through the years.

1. Administration of Tests other than the Rorschach

The Stanford-Binet Examination, administered for the purpose of determining the levels and scatter of intelligence among the subjects, proved to be a good instrument with which to transfer the first grade child from a more or less formal classroom setting to that of friendly cooperation and good rapport with the examiner. The child's first task was placing his name on the test blank. This he was proud and delighted to do, since, as a general rule, he had just learned to print his surname after having learned to print his given name during his earlier school experience. Adequate praise for this initial assignment brought added confidence. Thus, the child was off to a comfortable start.

Since frequently it is difficult for a child of this age to effect a natural adjustment in a new situation or with a strange person if questions and personal remarks are immediately directed toward him, the six year old was never directly questioned during the early stages of the examination but was first presented with the impersonal, concrete items of the Stanford-Binet Examination. The five year level of this test proved interesting to the child and effective as an "icebreaker." The first two items--completing the picture of a man and folding a triangle--promptly engaged the child in doing with his hands something he was capable of doing. Only two children were unable to complete both items successfully, and each of them was successful on one of the two. Had there been any residue of apprehension after the name-printing, it usually disappeared with the easy success at this point on the intelligence test. By the time the ceiling of the test was reached, the child was more or less at ease and, as a result, was always cooperative when asked to look at the Rorschach cards.

Other additional psychological tests listed earlier in the report were administered each succeeding year in a way similar to that described in the presentation of the Stanford-Binet material. As the study progressed through the years, many children felt free to express their opinions and often showed preferences for tests with such remarks as: "Aren't we going to do those nice puzzles like we did last year?" or "Why can't I read like I did before?" On the other hand, some remarks were expressive of dislike; for example: "I hope I don't have to draw today," or "There won't be any arithmetic problems this time, will there?" No child at any time refused to cooperate, and most of the children continued to be enthusiastic about their participation in the project. It was not uncommon, as the years went by, for the examiner to be met with such a greeting as, "I was just thinking it was the time of year for you to come."

2. Administration of the Rorschach Test

The transition from the Stanford-Binet Examination to the Rorschach test was made simply by saying to the six year old, "Now, I have some cards with pictures on them. I want you to look at these cards one at a time and tell me what they look like to you. Tell me everything you see on the card." The child was then handed the first Rorschach card. The majority of the children held the card in the same upright position in which it was presented, some immediately turned it about, and a few asked permission to do so. All the children showed interest, and some asked questions or made comments about the construction of the blots. When such interest was expressed, the method of blot construction was explained.

If the child made only one response to the first card, he was encouraged with, "Be sure to tell me everything you see on the card, and when you have done this, lay the card face down like this *demonstration*. That will be the signal for me to hand you the next card." This encouragement rarely resulted in additional responses; more often, if additional comments were made, they were elaborations of the original concept. This type of encouragement was not repeated after the first card. Sometimes, but not often, it was necessary to remind the child to lay a card down when it was obvious that he had completed his response but was uncertain what to do next. All instructions were given slowly and distinctly. Repetition was sometimes necessary, especially with a dull or overly anxious child. Each child who showed any apprehension about the correctness of his Rorschach responses was made to understand that there were no right or wrong answers, and that what he saw on the card was as acceptable as what anyone else saw.

The ten cards were shown in succession, with no further comments. The *reaction time,* or time between the presentation of the card and the beginning of the first response, and the *response time,* or time between the moment the card was handed to the child and the moment he released it, were recorded for each card. The position in which the card was held at the time of each response was noted, as well as the turning of the card at other times. An attempt was made to copy the response verbatim. A record was made of comments, questions, and such emotional expressions as giggling, sighing, frowning, and other psychomotor responses used.

The customary test inquiry, to be described later, was given to clarify the location and the determinants of any ambiguous or indefinite responses as well as to permit the child to elaborate his responses. A few of the six year olds showed impatience, and tended to object to the inquiry. Such behavior, in its extreme, has been described in a number of studies involving younger children and has led certain investigators to suggest that, with the younger child, the inquiry might follow immediately the first response and avoid presenting each card in a second sequence. This attitude of impatience or loss of interest described by other workers with preschool children was strongly expressed by one five year old in the writer's clinical experience with, "Don't show me them cards again. You were lucky I told you the first time." While modifications of this attitude could be sensed with some of the children during the first year of the study, it was never expressed in such strong terms as just described. However, such a statement as, "Only two more cards to go," or "Let's hurry up--it's time for gym," was the six year old's way of trying to camouflage his impatience. No doubt a growing conformity to school routine as well as maturation was operative in this modified behavior of the six year old over that of the preschooler. No six year old in this study actually refused to cooperate when, in the inquiry, the examiner presented the first card for the second time with the words, "I want to be sure that I see the same thing on this card that you see. Will you tell me about the (naming the concept used by the child) so that I can see it just as you see it?" If this request brought a vague, non-committal type of response, the additional questions of, "How do you see it?" or "Where do you see it?" sometimes helped the child to show determinants included but not expressed in the original concept. In a number of cases, infantile word usage was clarified in this way. For example, one child saw "dumplings" on Card III. Inquiry responses revealed she had meant "ducklings." Another child saw "a rainbow" on Card IV. This was elaborated in the inquiry to, "Here are the rainbow's horns--you know the rainbows that Santa Claus drives." Such inquiry responses as, "In the air flying," or "Red, don't you see?" were sometimes given with the obvious tonal implication that the examiner should have taken such an elaboration for granted. On the other hand, it was sometimes evident that comments or elaborations made in the inquiry had not been a part of the original concept. In a few cases the child's general insecurity caused him to change the original concept, since he thought it was being challenged. The kind or proper amount of inquiry most appropriate to the six year old was not always easy to gauge. This problem lessened, however, as the children advanced in age, and was finally no problem at all. The fact that the lessening of these inquiry problems was due not primarily to familiarity with the test or the examiner was demonstrated in the similarity between the Rorschach responses of the longitudinal group and those of the control groups who saw the cards and the examiner for the first time at seven and/or eleven years of age.

Klopfer's testing of the limits technique was tried with only a small number of the six year olds. In these few instances it was discovered that the child had sometimes failed to state a concept because of his over-critical attitude. For example, on Card I, one child said, in testing the limits, "Sure, that could look like a bat, I suppose. I thought that at first but then I didn't think a bat would have those holes." To Card III, another child said, "People don't have that kind of head. That's why I called it a bird." Because of the possible practice effect on subsequent testing, testing of the limits was not used beyond this limited application at the six year level.

The complete testing period of the six year old, including the administration of both the Stanford-Binet and the Rorschach tests, rarely exceeded an hour. Only a few children showed signs of fatigue at the end of the period. All gave evidence of a pleasurable experience, and most of them were reluctant to terminate the interview.

In succeeding years the same type of testing procedure was followed. The amount of testing time varied with the type of additional test administered as well as with the intelligence and other personality factors of the child. In general, testing time ranged between forty-five minutes and two hours, roughly averaging one and one-half hours. The children continued to enjoy the experience as they grew older. Factors like prestige attached to those chosen for the experiment as well as the opportunity to get away from school work for a brief period no doubt contributed to the enthusiasm of some of the children.

4

The analysis of the Rorschach responses of the two hundred and ninety-one children in the three groups, one longitudinal and two controls, totaling nearly a thousand protocols, began with the Klopfer method of scoring and followed the traditional Rorschach order of consideration as outlined in the subsequent discussion of data analysis.

Of the nine hundred and eighty-one Rorschach protocols analyzed in this study, eight hundred and twenty-eight of them were collected during the six yearly contacts with the one hundred and thirty-eight children in the longitudinal group; the remaining one hundred and fifty-three came from the one contact with each child in the two control groups. The data from these Rorschach records have been reviewed from many angles and subjected to the following stages of statistical analysis.

1. Scoring

Since individual differences among scorers of Rorschach responses tend to affect the quantitative results, a brief description of the author's use of certain variations from the Klopfer method will be noted here so that the reader may more accurately evaluate the report of data analysis which follows. The examples of scoring noted below are those that differ in varying degrees from the scoring developments in the Klopfer method reviewed in detail in *Development in the Rorschach Technique* by Klopfer, Ainsworth, Klopfer and Holt (Part One: Administration and Scoring).

Card I: Responses to Card I which combine the center and side D's as "two men dragging a fighting bear" or "two bears climbing up on a fat woman" are each scored as two D's combined into an additional W.

Card III: The lower black D of Card III is scored separately when designated as a specific object. For example, "two dogs pulling a skull apart" is given a W̄ and a D.

Card IV: The lower middle D of Card IV is scored separately when designated as a specific object. For example, "a giant sitting on a stump" or "a boy jumping over a fire hydrant" are each scored as a W̄ and a D.

Card VI: The lower area of Card VI excluding the upper D is scored as a W.

Card VII: The lower D of Card VII when designated as a specific object is scored separately. When combined with the rest of the blot as "two dogs balanced on a rocker," two scores, W̄ and D, are given.

Another variation in scoring on this card is a d for the small white space at the bottom center whether combined with or separate from the d just above it.

Card VIII: When the central portion of Card VIII (excluding only the "animals") was designated as one or more specific objects, one or more D scores were given depending on the number of concepts. When used with the outer D's, as "two dogs eating a dead animal," the two D's are combined in an additional W.

Scoring on the above cards other than the deviations just described followed the Klopfer method. Cards II, V, IX, and X were scored without any variations in any of the scoring categories.

2. Statistical Measures

In the normative treatment of the Rorschach data, ranges and/or standard deviations, medians, and quartiles were calculated for the frequencies and/or percentages of each scoring category at each age level in both the longitudinal and control groups and reported in the following order:

(1) Total Number of Responses - R
(2) Location - W, D, d, Dd, and S
(3) Determinants - M, FM, m, K, F, c, C', FC, CF, and C
(4) Content - Animal, Human, Object, etc.
(5) Popular Responses

To determine the effects of the three variables--age, intelligence, and sex--on the various Rorschach scoring categories, comparisons were made among the three groups of children who saw the cards only one time; i.e., the six year old longitudinal group, the seven year old control group, and the eleven year old control group. By excluding from these comparisons ages seven through eleven in the longitudinal group, any practice effect accruing from the yearly repetition of the test was eliminated. To determine the effect of repeated testing on the different Rorschach categories, comparisons were made between each control group and the corresponding age in the longitudinal group. Trends in the various categories were noted from year to year within the six ages of the longitudinal group. Attention was called to changes that seemed to be effected by repeated testing rather than maturation. In all cases, the analysis of variance, F, was used as the statistical measure.

Comparisons were made between the children's norms for the various Rorschach categories at each age level and the normal adult expectancy [derived from Klopfer, *The Rorschach Technique*] for each of these categories.

Detailed tables of the statistical treatment of the data are placed in the Appendix. Excerpts from these tables are used in the text.

II. The Children in the Study

Group Characteristics

During the six years of contact with the one hundred and thirty-eight children in the longitudinal group of the study, these boys and girls became so increasingly individualized to the author that it is with some difficulty they must now be thought of as an experimental sample from which were derived "average" Rorschach responses of children between the ages of six and eleven years inclusive. It might be noted here that the continuity and quality of the relationship between the author and each child is a variable that was not taken into account in the evaluation of the test results. In the majority of cases there seemed to be a sort of therapeutic effect, in that the child felt "set apart" in a positive way and derived much satisfaction from the research contacts. In fact, the only two exceptions to this type of relationship were: 1) a very suspicious, almost paranoid little girl who, despite repeated explanations and attempts at reassurance on the part of the examiner, never quite relinquished a feeling of stigma which she attached to the yearly testing sessions; and 2) a physically ill child who, in one of the early contacts, connected the project with his repeated trips to the hospital and was unable to accept any other explanation.

Since the quality of research results depends primarily on the sample from which the quantitative data are derived, a detailed description of some of the characteristics of the group of longitudinal subjects will help the reader to evaluate better the results reported in the chapters that follow. Such characteristics as race, national background, religion, socio-economic level, intelligence, and school achievement were evaluated for the group as a whole. The first four of these--race, national background, religion, and socio-economic level--were compared with the same factors in the larger population from which the sample was chosen. The intelligence and school achievement scores of the group were compared with national norms.

No attempt was made to analyze in like detail the characteristics of the two control groups. Since they were chosen in the same manner as the longitudinal group and were found to be similar to the larger group in such characteristics as intelligence, it was assumed that other factors were also comparable.

In order to compare the racial, cultural, and religious composition of the sample used in the study with that of the total population of Pittsburgh and Allegheny County, population figures for this area were taken from the United States population census of 1950, from the *Pittsburgh Catholic Magazine* of July 13, 1950, and from the *American Jewish Year Book,* Volume 50 (1948-1949). Statistics of 1950 were considered more appropriate for this study than those of the preceding decade.

Race, National Background, and Religion

In the 1950 census it was found that in Pittsburgh and Allegheny County, the area from which the subjects used in this study were chosen, slightly more than 92 per cent of the approximately 1,500,000 population were white, a little more than 7 per cent were Negro, and only 1/20 per cent belonged to other races. In the longitudinal sample used in this study, a little more than 93 per cent of the children are white, slightly less than 7 per cent are Negro, and other races are not represented.

Around the turn of the twentieth century, Pittsburgh and the surrounding area was a melting pot of nationality groups, mainly from continental Europe. The percentage of foreign-born has been steadily decreasing during the recent decades. For example, between 1940 and 1950, there was a drop from 13 per cent to 9 per cent among citizens born in other countries. In 1950 the countries represented among the 9 per cent foreign-born population of the area, in order of number in the groups were: Italy, Poland, Austria, Germany, U.S.S.R., England and Wales, Ireland, Hungary, Yugoslavia, Scotland, Lithuania, Greece, and Canada. Percentages ranged from 2 per cent Italian-born downward to 1/10 per cent Canadian-born. All Asiatic countries combined with a few European countries not already mentioned had less than 1/10 per cent representation. No child in the longitudinal sample was foreign-born, but all the nationalities listed above were represented in the various family backgrounds. Only a very few of the children had foreign-born parents, the old world heritage in many cases going back sometimes two or more generations and frequently including more than one nationality, thus strongly suggesting that the sample of children used in this study is a product of the melting pot of many nationality groups.

In general, religious trends are closely associated with nationality backgrounds. Although the early history of the Pittsburgh area (nineteenth century and earlier) was influenced religiously mainly by the Scotch Presbyterians, the later influx of southern European immigrants was accompanied by a great increase in Catholicism in the area. During the decade 1940 to 1950, this increase was considerably more than the increase in general population. According to the *Pittsburgh Catholic Magazine*, July 13, 1950, by that date, the percentage of Catholics in the area had reached 35 per cent of the total population. This trend is duplicated among the group of subjects in this study. Thirty-three per cent of the children chosen in 1946-47 were from Catholic schools. By 1952 at the conclusion of the investigation, after several Catholic children originally studied in public schools had been transferred to Catholic schools, 36 per cent of the children were enrolled in Catholic schools. Since case histories later revealed a number of Catholic children still in public schools at the end of the investigation, the percentage of Catholic children in the study slightly exceeds the percentage of Catholics in the general population.

According to the *American Jewish Year Book*, 1948-49, the Jewish population of Pittsburgh and Allegheny County was 4 per cent of the total population. Seven per cent of the children in this study are Jewish. While the proportion of Jewish representation in the longitudinal sample is greater than in the general population, it is interesting to note here that the proportion of Jewish children among those referred to the Child Guidance Center is even greater than in the sample. Both orthodox and reformed Jewish faiths are represented in the longitudinal sample.

No attempt was made to break down the remaining 57 per cent of the subjects so far as religion was concerned. That there were representatives of all Protestant denominations prevalent in the area was established. Church connections among this larger group varied in strength from devout churchgoers to families with weak, almost nonexistent church ties.

Socio-Economic Background

As for the socio-economic representation among the group, parents of the children in this study are scattered through all walks of life: families on relief, laborers (unskilled, semiskilled, and skilled), firemen, policemen, bus drivers, clerks, small business owners, a variety of professions (doctors, lawyers, engineers, teachers), and officers in large corporations. The Jewish families, as a whole, rate consistently highest in economic status and the Negro families, consistently lowest. The Catholic group, in contrast to the remaining white, non-Jewish group, shows less scatter in this regard. The Catholic families seem to be concentrated in the lower-middle income group and the remaining white, non-Jewish, non-Catholic members of the group run the gamut from relief to heads of corporations. This situation is also a fairly accurate representation of the socio-economic variety observed in the general population from which the subjects were drawn.

Intelligence

Since a number of previous studies have shown a direct relationship between socio-economic level and intelligence, no attempt was made to establish this type of relationship among the children in this study. Nevertheless, the distribution of intelligence within the group was determined by administering three intelligence tests, each at a different age level: the Stanford-Binet Examination, Form L, at six years; Grace Arthur Performance Scale at nine years; and Wechsler Intelligence Scale for Children at ten years. A discussion of the results of each test follows:

1. Stanford-Binet Examination, Form L

The Stanford-Binet Examination was administered to each child when he was in first grade and had been in school for approximately one semester. Since the examination was seemingly accepted as a pleasant interlude in the school routine and no child offered any resistance when confronted with the test material, it can be assumed that the results are as valid as can be expected. The means of the intelligence quotients derived from this test are shown in the table on the following page with a comparison between the scores of the boys and those of the girls.

As noted in the table, the average Binet I.Q. of the children in the longitudinal group at six years of age was 104.47 with a standard deviation of 14.0. The t-values in the table indicate that the boys and girls in this study are similar in intellectual ability as measured by the Binet. The I.Q.'s of each sex

TABLE 1

COMPARISON OF THE MEAN STANFORD-BINET I.Q. OF BOYS VS THAT OF GIRLS AT SIX YEARS OF AGE

	Total	Boys	Girls	t	p*
Number	138	68	70		
Mean I.Q.	104.47	104.32	104.61	.12	> .05
SD	14.0	13.26	14.72	1.08	> .05

as well as of the total group show a normal distribution for each grouping, ranging from 77 to 140, with boys and girls similarly represented at all intelligence levels.

The following table shows the distribution of both chronological ages and mental ages of the children tested with the Stanford-Binet Examination.

TABLE 2

DISTRIBUTION OF CHRONOLOGICAL AND BINET MENTAL AGES WITHIN THE LONGITUDINAL GROUP AT THE SIX YEAR LEVEL

	Chronological Ages (Mean 6 yrs 8 mos)			Mental Ages (Mean 6 yrs 11 mos)		
Age: 6 yrs 6 mos	6 yrs 7 mos to 6 yrs 9 mos	6 yrs 10 mos	6 yrs 0 mos and below	6 yrs 1 mo to 7 yrs 9 mos	7 yrs 10 mos and above
Boys	1	64	3	13	42	14
Girls	1	67	2	10	45	14
Total	2	131	5	23	87	28

The table above shows that at the time of the initial contact, 95 per cent of the longitudinal group--131 in number--were within one month of the average *chronological age* of six years and eight months, ranging from six years and seven months through six years and nine months in *chronological age*. Two of the seven remaining children were six years and six months, and the other five were six years and ten months of age.

Sixty-three per cent of the children--87 in number--were within a ten month range of the average *mental age* of six years and eleven months, ranging from six years and one month to seven years and nine months. Seventeen per cent--or 23 children--were below. Twenty per cent--or 28 children--were above this range *of mental ages*. The boys and girls show a distribution similar to each other so far as each of the ages, chronological and mental, is concerned.

The table that follows shows how the sample of children used in this study compares in intelligence with children from similar background areas.

TABLE 3

COMPARISON OF MEAN STANFORD-BINET I.Q. OF LEDWITH SAMPLE WITH THAT OF THE TERMAN-MERRILL REVISION SAMPLE OF "URBAN" SIX TO FOURTEEN YEAR OLD CHILDREN

	Ledwith Sample	Terman-Merrill Sample	t	p**
Number	138	864		
Mean	104.5	105.8	1.04	> .05
SD	14.0	14.7	1.3	> .05

---

*The t-values required for a .05 level of significance in this comparison is 1.979 and for an .01 level is 2.616.
**Ibid.

In comparing the Stanford-Binet I.Q.'s of the children in the longitudinal group of this study with those from a well known sample with similar characteristics--the urban industrial group of six to fourteen year olds used by Terman and Merrill in their 1937 revision of the Stanford-Binet Examination--it can be noted from the table above that the t-values on the differences between the means and between the standard deviations indicate that the very small differences between the intelligence test results of the two groups are well within expected sampling variation limits for samples of this size, and that the subjects in this study are representative so far as intelligence is concerned of urban industrial areas in general.

For purposes of later comparisons, the children in the study were divided into the following groups according to intelligence levels determined by the Stanford-Binet I.Q.'s at the six year level:

TABLE 4

INTELLIGENCE CATEGORIES OF LONGITUDINAL SUBJECTS ACCORDING TO BINET I.Q. AT THE SIX YEAR LEVEL

Intelligence Category	Binet I.Q.	Number of Subjects		
		Boys	Girls	Total
Superior	125 and above	6	7	13
Bright	110 - 124	17	15	32
Average	90 - 109	36	39	75
Dull	75 - 89	9	9	18
Inferior	Below 75	0	0	0
Total		68	70	138

More than half of the children in this study are within 10 points of 100 I.Q. which is considered a measure of average intelligence. That there is a greater number of children in the brighter groups than in the below average groups is a function of sampling. At six years of age many children of very inferior intelligence had not yet enrolled in school, the source of this sample, and none of those of superior intelligence had yet been accelerated.

2. Grace Arthur Performance Test

In order to compare the performance ability of the children in this study with their verbal ability as indicated by the Stanford-Binet test results above, the Grace Arthur Performance Test was administered when the children were nine years and eight months old. The average P.Q. (performance quotient) of these children was 104.49 with a standard deviation of 18.31. The following table indicates the difference between the P.Q.'s of the boys and those of the girls.

TABLE 5

COMPARISON OF GRACE ARTHUR P.Q.'S BOYS VS GIRLS AT NINE YEARS OF AGE FROM THE 138 CHILDREN IN THE LONGITUDINAL GROUP

	Total	Boys	Girls	t	p*
Number	138	68	70		
Mean P.Q.	104.49	106.31	102.71	1.16	> .05
SD	18.31	18.02	18.35	.15	> .05

While the average P.Q. of the boys was 3.60 higher than that of the girls, suggesting a tendency for boys to have greater performance ability than girls, this difference is not significant as noted in the t-value of 1.16. As was the case in verbal ability comparisons, there is no significant difference in performance ability between the boys and girls of this sample.

---

*Ibid.

As with the Binet I.Q.'s, the P.Q.'s of the Grace Arthur Scale were normally distributed. A comparison of these distributions is shown in the following table.

TABLE 6

COMPARISON OF STANFORD-BINET I.Q.'S AT SIX YEARS OF AGE WITH
GRACE ARTHUR P.Q.'S AT NINE YEARS OF AGE FROM
THE 138 CHILDREN IN THE LONGITUDINAL GROUP

	Stanford-Binet	G.A. Performance	t	p*
Number	138	138		
Mean	104.47	104.49	.01	>.05
SD	14.0	18.31	3.12	<.01

There was no significant difference between the means of the two tests, Binet and Grace Arthur, as can be seen from the t-value in the table above. This suggests that there is no difference between the verbal ability and the performance ability of the children in the sample as a whole. That the difference in the standard deviations is significant at the .01 level, indicates that the P.Q. scores have a much wider range than the I.Q.'s. This difference in scatter between the two tests is reflected in the many cases of disparity between these measures in individual children.

The following table points out in further detail the relationship between the Stanford-Binet and Grace Arthur scores of the children in the group as a whole as well as the relationship according to sex.

TABLE 7

RELATIONSHIP BETWEEN THE STANFORD-BINET I.Q.'S AND GRACE ARTHUR
SCALE P.Q.'S AMONG 138 CHILDREN IN THE LONGITUDINAL GROUP

Relationship	Number of Subjects			Percentage of Group
	Boys	Girls	Total	
I.Q. = P.Q.		1		1%
I.Q. > P.Q. (14 points or less)	30	31	61 ⎫	74%
I.Q. < P.Q. (14 points or less)	20	21	41 ⎭	
	50	52	102	
I.Q. > P.Q. (15 points or more)	5	9	14 ⎫	25%
I.Q. < P.Q. (15 points or more)	13	8	21 ⎭	
	18	17	35	

Only one child, a girl, had the same score on both the Stanford-Binet and Grace Arthur Scales. Seventy-four per cent of the group, the same percentage of girls and boys, had P.Q.'s that varied fourteen points or less from their Stanford-Binet I.Q.'s. This variation is within one standard deviation of both tests.

The remaining 25 per cent of the children, again the same percentage of boys as girls, had scores that varied fifteen points or more between the two tests. This variation ranged from fifteen to fifty-two points. Since a wide disparity between the functioning on the Stanford-Binet Examination and the Grace Arthur Performance Scale is considered indicative of some sort of maladjustment, further study of the extreme cases is of importance in the subsequent evaluation of the characteristics of individual children. Since it is a fairly well-accepted fact that approximately one-third of the adult population may be considered neurotic, such a proportion as one-fourth of a group of randomly selected children may be expected to present maladjustment problems.

---

*Ibid.

3. Wechsler Intelligence Scale for Children

The Wechsler Intelligence Scale for Children which had just been introduced into the psychological testing field at the time, was administered to the longitudinal group at ten years and eight months of age. The results of this testing are shown in the following table where a comparison is made between the scores of the boys and those of the girls.

TABLE 8

COMPARISON OF WISC I.Q.'S BOYS VS GIRLS IN THE LONGITUDINAL GROUP AT TEN YEARS OF AGE

Full Scale

	Total	Boys	Girls	t	p
Number	138	68	70		
Mean I.Q.	101.71	102.59	100.86	.70	> .05
SD	12.82	11.50	13.90	1.57	> .05

Verbal Scale

	Total	Boys	Girls	t	p
Number	138	68	70		
Mean I.Q.	100.33	100.93	99.76	.54	> .05
SD	12.77	11.63	13.67	1.34	> .05

Performance Scale

	Total	Boys	Girls	t	p
Number	138	68	70		
Mean I.Q.	102.83	103.96	101.73	1.26	> .05
SD	12.42	11.43	13.31	1.29	> .05

In each test category--full scale, verbal, and performance--there is a normal distribution of I.Q.'s among the longitudinal group and no significant differences between the sexes among the various means and standard deviations of the I.Q.'s of the three scales. While boys tended to make higher scores than girls in all three of these scales, the differences were not significant. All of the children, both boys and girls, tend to make higher scores on the performance scale than on the verbal. While not shown in table form, the mean of the performance I.Q.'s is not significantly higher than that of the verbal I.Q.'s.

A comparison of the full scale I.Q.'s of the Wechsler Intelligence Scale for Children with the Stanford-Binet I.Q.'s is shown in the following table.

TABLE 9

COMPARISON OF STANFORD-BINET I.Q.'S WITH THE FULL SCALE I.Q.'S OF THE WECHSLER INTELLIGENCE SCALE FOR CHILDREN OF THE 138 CHILDREN IN THE LONGITUDINAL GROUP

	Binet	WISC	t	p
Number	138	138		
Mean	104.47	101.71	1.71	> .05
SD	14.0	12.82	1.04	> .05

Inspection of Table 9 shows a tendency for the I.Q.'s of the Wechsler Intelligence Scale for Children to be less than those of the Stanford-Binet as well as a tendency for them to be grouped closer to the mean. The t-values of both the means and standard deviations, however, indicate that there is no significant difference between the two tests in regard to either measure.

School Achievement

Since the emotional development or emotional stability of the child is frequently reflected in his school achievement, this is another area of the child's functioning that was studied during this investigation. At the age of eight years and eight months, when the majority of the longitudinal group was in third grade and had been in school long enough to register a definite reaction to academic demands, the Monroe Diagnostic Reading Examination was administered. The results of this examination, which includes the three tool subjects of Reading, Spelling, and Arithmetic, are given in the following table.

TABLE 10

MEAN GRADE LEVEL WITH STANDARD DEVIATIONS OF ACHIEVEMENT
OF THE LONGITUDINAL GROUP OF 138 CHILDREN
AT THE AGE OF EIGHT YEARS AND EIGHT MONTHS

Number		Reading Grade		Spelling Grade		Arithmetic Grade	
		Mean	SD	Mean	SD	Mean	SD
Boys	68	2.9	1.1	2.6	.8	3.0	.6
Girls	70	3.5	1.5	3.1	1.0	3.0	.6
Total	138	3.2	1.4	2.9	.9	3.0	.6

Nationwide, the average grade level expected from children beginning third grade is 2.9. Since the majority of the children tested had been in third grade for two or three months at the time the test was administered, an average achievement level could be expected to fall slightly above the 3.0 grade level. The above table shows that the achievement of children in this group, as a whole, compares favorably with that of children nationally. In reading, the group as a whole, with a 3.2 grade average, approximates the expected level. The spelling grade of 2.9 average and arithmetic at 3.0 are slightly under par. Since the statistics of third grade achievement for Pittsburgh and Allegheny County as a whole were not available, comparison with those figures was not possible. However, there is every reason to believe that the children in this sample are achieving within an average range of those they represent. The girls in the group tended to surpass the boys in reading and spelling. Arithmetic scores for both sexes were the same.

Summary

The sample of one hundred and thirty-eight children in the longitudinal study was found to be representative of such characteristics of the general population of Pittsburgh and Allegheny County as race, national background, religion, and socio-economic level.

The results of the psychological and achievement tests of the group give every indication that so far as intelligence and school achievement is concerned, these children are a good representation of the school population from which they were chosen. Furthermore, there is evidence that the sample as a whole is also representative intellectually of the urban industrial areas of the nation.

Since there was found among this group of children a representative distribution of such factors as have just been enumerated, one is led to expect also a distribution of emotional adjustment typical of the general population. An evaluation of the Rorschach protocols of the individual children is the best verification of this hypothesis. Inherent in the accumulation of data regarding each child in the study are excellent possibilities for this type of investigation.

III. Rorschach Norms for Children

According to Scoring Categories

The normative findings from the approximately one thousand Rorschach protocols of two hundred and ninety-one children of elementary school age are reported in the pages that follow, with due recognition of the fact that no child at any age will duplicate in every detail the age norms herein outlined--in other words, there is no "average" child at any age level so far as Rorschach responses are concerned. Likewise, no two children, even though identical in age, intelligence, and sex will have identical reactions to the Rorschach cards. In no other situation is the individuality of the child more clearly expressed than in his Rorschach responses. One of the most effective aids in the interpretation of these individual records, however, is the knowledge wherein and how much each child's protocol differs from the Rorschach norms applicable to his age, sex, and intelligence. It is at such a point that a study of this kind assumes primary importance, especially to those having a minimum of experience with children's Rorschachs. Many experienced clinicians, in the repeated use of the Rorschach technique with children, have arrived at valid clinical impressions corresponding closely to the kind of quantitative results reported herein. Since few of them have had the time or inclination to objectify and publish their impressions, such a report as this helps to fill the need for objective norms felt by Rorschachers inexperienced in the children's field.

The following presentation of Rorschach norms for children from six to twelve years of age is made, therefore, with the hope that it will be helpful to all clinicians who work with children, but especially to those having limited experience with children's Rorschachs. It is well to be reminded at this point that, despite the detailed way in which these normative results are reported, the actual interpretation of the individual record must be approached from a global or over-all point of view, with one child in mind, rather than in an atomistic or category-by-category normative manner, as reported here.

The discussion of the normative findings follow the traditional Rorschach scoring approach: 1) total number of responses, R; 2) location areas, W, D, d, Dd, and S; 3) determinants, form, movement, shading, color; 4) content; and 5) popular responses.

Since there is a working hypothesis among Rorschachers that the various scoring categories are influenced by certain variables, a careful analysis of the responses of the children in this study has taken into account four such variables: age, intelligence, sex, and repeated testing. The statistical tables used in the text are abbreviations in rounded figures from the master tables, but the discussion often takes into account the complete statistical picture in these tables as they appear in the appendix.

TOTAL NUMBER OF RESPONSES, R

The feature of the Rorschach protocol usually appraised first is the total number of responses, R, which the individual gives to the ten cards. The table on the following page shows the average or mean R, with standard deviation, for each age level in both the longitudinal and control groups.

It can be noted from the abbreviated table that age effects an increase in the number of responses given by children to the Rorschach cards. Beginning with sixteen responses at six years of age, the number gradually increases through the years, reaching twenty-six among the eleven year old control group. Just as the mean R increases as the children grow older, so does the scatter about this R tend to increase with age. Although the range of R was excessive among the children in the study--from five responses given by a six year old girl to one hundred sixty-seven responses given by an eleven year old boy--the R of the majority of the children, as can be seen from the standard deviation figures in the table below, tended to cluster fairly closely about the average R for their age groups.

Not shown in the table below, but pictured in the master table in the appendix, is the fact that brighter children gave a greater number of responses than the less bright. Thus, there is a positive relationship between R and both age and intelligence. No such relationship was found between R and the sex of the child or the repetition of the test. While there was a trend for boys at each age level to give more

TABLE 11*

MEAN R WITH STANDARD DEVIATION FOR EACH AGE LEVEL IN BOTH LONGITUDINAL AND CONTROL GROUPS OF ELEMENTARY SCHOOL CHILDREN

Age Level Longitudinal	Control	Number	Mean R	Standard Deviation
6 yrs		138	16	7
7 yrs		138	16	6
	7 yrs	73	17	8
8 yrs		138	20	8
9 yrs		138	24	10
10 yrs		138	28	17
11 yrs		138	30	22
	11 yrs	80	26	16

responses than girls, this trend was found to lack statistical significance. Likewise, the slight increase in R which seems from the table to be related positively to repeated testing, especially at the eleven year level, is only a tendency and not significant.

That variables other than age, intelligence, sex, and repeated testing can affect the number of responses is a premise upon which certain Rorschach interpretations are made. Case studies of individual children in the study have substantiated this premise. Further analysis of the Rorschach data and other historical and anecdotal material about the children would no doubt point to other specific variables related to number of responses given by children.

"CARD PULL" FOR R

Even though the unstructured nature of the Rorschach inkblots leaves the response entirely up to the individual, the qualitative aspects of each card tends to limit or stimulate the number as well as the kind of responses which the individual gives. This property of the cards is called "card pull"** by certain investigators and is determined for each card by dividing the number of responses to a particular card by the total number of responses to the ten cards. The following table shows how the responses of the children in this study were divided on the average among the ten cards.

TABLE 12

"CARD PULL" FOR R

MEAN PERCENTAGE OF RESPONSES GIVEN TO EACH CARD AT EACH AGE LEVEL IN BOTH LONGITUDINAL AND CONTROL GROUPS OF ELEMENTARY SCHOOL CHILDREN

Age Level	N	Card I	Card II	Card III	Card IV	Card V	Card VI	Card VII	Card VIII	Card IX	Card X
6 yrs (Long)	138	9%	10%	13%	8%	7%	8%	9%	11%	9%	15%
7 yrs (Long)	138	9%	9%	13%	8%	7%	7%	9%	11%	9%	17%
7 yrs (Cont)	73	9%	10%	13%	9%	7%	7%	9%	11%	9%	16%
8 yrs (Long)	138	8%	9%	13%	8%	7%	8%	9%	11%	10%	18%
9 yrs (Long)	138	10%	9%	13%	8%	7%	7%	9%	11%	9%	17%
10 yrs (Long)	138	9%	9%	12%	8%	7%	8%	9%	10%	9%	19%
11 yrs (Long)	138	9%	10%	12%	9%	7%	7%	8%	10%	9%	18%
11 yrs (Cont)	80	10%	9%	11%	8%	7%	8%	8%	10%	10%	18%

---

*From Table A, Appendix
**"Through Adolescence with the Rorschach," McFate and Orr, *Journal of Projective Techniques,* 1949, 13, pp. 302-319.

It can be noted from the table above that the largest mean percentage of responses at each age level in both the longitudinal and control groups was given to Card X, these percentages varying through the years from 15 per cent to 19 per cent. Card III ranked second, with a mean percentage of 13 per cent. That these two percentages are highest among the cards may be partly a function of the fact that Cards X and III contain color and that both lend themselves more easily to detail responses than to whole responses. Card V stimulates consistently the lowest mean percentage, 7 per cent, at each age level, and Card VI was second in this respect varying through the years from 7 per cent to 8 per cent. In contrast to the two cards eliciting the highest percentages, neither of these Cards, V and VI, contain color, and each can be easily responded to as a whole. The tendency in general throughout the study is that color cards account for higher mean percentages of responses than do the achromatic cards. While the ten cards vary considerably among themselves as to percentage of responses elicited, each card percentage remains fairly stable through the years, with agreement between longitudinal and control groups. Neither the sex nor the intelligence level of the child seemed to affect these percentages. The mean percentage of responses given to the last three cards, VIII, IX, and X combined, shows only a slight variation from year to year with a low of 35 per cent and a high of 38 per cent.

CARD REJECTIONS

Closely related to "Card Pull" is the matter of card rejection. A rejection is scored in adult records when the subject has made a definite effort at giving a response to a card and is unable to do so after three to five minutes. Because of the tendency for younger children to build up resistance when required to hold a card beyond their desire to lay it down, this adult time limit was not adhered to in this study. If, after mild and/or intermittent encouragement from the examiner for a maximum of two minutes, the child persisted in laying the card down, refusing to respond or saying he could see nothing, he was handed the next card. Sometimes a response was given in the inquiry to a card rejected in the performance proper or a response was denied in the inquiry. These were scored as additional responses.

The following table shows the percentage of children who rejected each card at each age level, and the percentage of children who rejected one or more cards at each age level.

TABLE 13

PERCENTAGE OF CHILDREN REJECTING RORSCHACH CARDS AT EACH AGE LEVEL IN BOTH LONGITUDINAL AND CONTROL GROUPS OF ELEMENTARY SCHOOL CHILDREN

A. Percentage of Each Group Rejecting One or More Cards

Age Level	6 yrs (L)	7 yrs (L)	7 yrs (C)	8 yrs (L)	9 yrs (L)	10 yrs (L)	11 yrs (L)	11 yrs (C)
Number	138	138	73	138	138	138	138	80
Percentage	13%	10%	20%	2%	1%	1%	0	1%

B. Percentage According to Sex and Individual Cards

Age Level	Sex	N	Card I	Card II	Card III	Card IV	Card V	Card VI	Card VII	Card VIII	Card IX	Card X
6 yrs (Long)	Boys	68	0	0	0	1%	0	1%	0	1%	0	1%
	Girls	70	1%	2%	0	1%	0	4%	1%	1%	4%	1%
7 yrs (Long)	Boys	68	0	0	0	1%	0	3%	0	0	1%	0
	Girls	70	0	1%	0	3%	0	3%	1%	0	2%	1%
7 yrs (Cont)	Boys	38	0	0	1%	1%	0	7%	1%	0	3%	0
	Girls	35	0	3%	0	1%	0	4%	1%	1%	5%	1%
8 yrs (Long)	Boys	68	0	0	0	1%	0	0	0	0	1%	0
	Girls	70	0	0	0	1%	0	1%	0	0	1%	0
9 yrs (Long)	Boys	68	0	0	0	0	1%	1%	0	0	0	0
	Girls	70	0	0	1%	0	0	0	0	0	0	0
10 yrs (Long)	Boys	68	0	0	0	0	0	0	0	0	1%	0
	Girls	70	0	0	0	0	0	0	0	0	0	0
11 yrs (Long)	Boys	68	0	0	0	0	0	0	0	0	0	0
	Girls	70	0	0	0	0	0	0	0	0	0	0
11 yrs (Cont)	Boys	40	0	0	0	0	0	0	0	0	0	0
	Girls	40	0	0	0	2%	0	0	0	0	0	0

Table 13 shows that the rejection of one or more cards can be expected from a few children at the ages of six and seven, but that after seven years of age rejections are rare. More girls than boys tend, on the average, to reject cards, and more of the cards are rejected by the girls than by the boys.

It may be noted also that certain Rorschach cards are rejected by a greater percentage of children than other cards. The cards are rejected in the following order of frequency: VI, IX, IV, II, VII, VIII, X, I, III, and V.

REACTION TIME

Another factor related in part to the qualitative aspects of the blot is the time taken by an individual between his first view of the blot and his first response to it: i.e., the reaction time. It is important to measure this time on each of the cards in order to determine whether or not some cards effect a reaction time more prolonged than that of others. Further comparison is made between the average reaction time to the five achromatic cards with that to the color cards in order to determine whether one type of cards more than the other affects the individual's reaction time.

In the following table is found the average reaction time to each card at each age level with the averages for both achromatic and color cards.

TABLE 14

MEAN REACTION TIME TO RORSCHACH CARDS AT EACH AGE LEVEL IN BOTH LONGITUDINAL AND CONTROL GROUPS OF ELEMENTARY SCHOOL CHILDREN

Age Level	N	Card I	Card II	Card III	Card IV	Card V	Card VI	Card VII	Card VIII	Card IX	Card X	Achr Cards	Color Cards
6 yrs (Long)	138	11"	13"	8"	13"	5"	15"	9"	13"	15"	12"	11"	12"
7 yrs (Long)	138	10"	13"	6"	11"	6"	14"	9"	9"	12"	9"	10"	10"
7 yrs (Cont)	73	13"	19"	10"	17"	9"	20"	13"	12"	20"	11"	14"	14"
8 yrs (Long)	138	11"	12"	8"	13"	7"	14"	9"	9"	18"	11"	11"	12"
9 yrs (Long)	138	11"	10"	7"	11"	7"	14"	8"	7"	15"	7"	10"	9"
10 yrs (Long)	138	8"	6"	5"	7"	5"	9"	5"	6"	11"	6"	7"	7"
11 yrs (Long)	138	9"	7"	5"	8"	5"	9"	5"	7"	10"	6"	7"	7"
11 yrs (Cont)	80	15"	15"	10"	13"	7"	17"	14"	13"	17"	14"	13"	14"

Table 14 shows a fluctuation of average reaction times among the different cards with two cards, III and V, consistently lowest, and two cards, VI and IX, consistently highest at all ages. The average reaction time to each card remains fairly consistent through the years, showing little relation to age, intelligence, or sex. The decrease noted appears to be related only to repeated testing and could be the function of familiarity with the cards, the examiner, and/or the testing situation.

Further indicated in the above table is the fact that at each age level the difference between the average reaction time to the achromatic cards and that to the color cards is negligible.

LOCATION OF RORSCHACH RESPONSES

For each response given to a Rorschach card the individual chooses one of the following *locations,* or areas of the blot: the whole blot, W; a large usual detail, D; a small usual detail, d; an unusual detail, Dd; or a white space, S. Since there is considerable variation among the total number of responses given by the children in this study, percentages of the location areas appear to be more meaningful than frequencies, and are therefore used in the following discussion of the location of responses.

The Whole Response, W%

Responses scored W in this study include: 1) a response where the whole blot is used, like "a bird," "an emblem," or "clouds" for Card I; and 2) a response which integrates the parts of the blot into a whole response, like "two clowns pat-a-caking" to Card II. When all except a small area of the blot is used, like "this looks like a bat if you leave this (outer d) off" to Card V, the score is W, (cut off W).

WS is scored when the entire blot including the white space is used, like "a face" to Card I. These whole responses were combined in the statistical treatment of W, with no distinction made among them. It was observed, however, that the older and/or brighter the child, the greater the tendency to give integrated wholes; WS responses tended to decrease with age; and W showed little change with age or intelligence.

Whole responses appeared in all but three records--those of two boys and one girl at the lower age levels. There were four children--three girls and one boy--who gave 100 per cent whole responses at one or more age levels.

The following table shows the average percentages of W, with standard deviations, given by children at each age level.

TABLE 15*

MEAN W% WITH STANDARD DEVIATION AT EACH AGE LEVEL IN BOTH LONGITUDINAL AND CONTROL GROUPS OF ELEMENTARY SCHOOL CHILDREN

Age Level	Number	Mean W%	Standard Deviation
6 years (Long)	138	44%	18
7 years (Long)	138	40%	18
7 years (Cont)	73	43%	21
8 years (Long)	138	34%	15
9 years (Long)	138	28%	14
10 years (Long)	138	27%	13
11 years (Long)	138	26%	14
11 years (Cont)	80	35%	19

The highest percentage of W, 44 per cent, is found at the six year level, with the proportion decreasing through the years. While this decrease in W% is related to age, it also seems accentuated by repeated testing as noted in a significant difference at the eleven year level between the W% of the longitudinal group and that of the control group, 26 per cent vs 35 per cent. This finding suggests that the mean W%, from seven years through eleven years in the longitudinal group, is higher than would be expected if the children had seen the cards for the first time at each age level. No relationship was found between W% and sex or intelligence. The standard deviation, or variation from the average, while unaffected by age, intelligence, or sex, tended to decrease with repeated testing. The scores of the three groups independently tested--six year old longitudinals, seven year controls, and eleven year controls-- suggest that the majority of the children use W% within approximately 20 points of the average for their age groups.

The Large Usual Detail Response, D%

Responses located in the large usual details of the blot commonly fall into two classifications: (1) D's of good form, like the animal, people, or objects frequently seen in these areas, and (2) those of vague, indefinite, and sometimes inaccurate form, like "blood," "water," or concepts that do not fit the form of the blot area. Younger and/or less intelligent children tend to give more responses of the latter type than do the older and/or brighter children.

D responses were given by 97 per cent of the six and seven year olds and 99 per cent of the eleven year olds. Of the few who did not respond to a D area, the girls outnumbered the boys. No child gave more than 90 per cent D responses. The average D%, with standard deviations, for each age level is found in the table on the following page.

The lowest mean percentage of D responses, 50 per cent, is found at the six year level. The increase noted through the years seems to be a function of repeated testing rather than increasing age since the control groups showed no significant increase. Mean D% likewise seemed to be unrelated to the sex or intelligence of the children.

---

*Excerpts from Table B in the appendix.

TABLE 16*

MEAN D% WITH STANDARD DEVIATION FOR EACH AGE LEVEL IN BOTH LONGITUDINAL
AND CONTROL GROUPS OF ELEMENTARY SCHOOL CHILDREN

Age Level	Number	Mean D%	Standard Deviation
6 years (Long)	138	50%	17
7 years (Long)	138	54%	16
7 years (Cont)	73	52%	20
8 years (Long)	138	60%	12
9 years (Long)	138	62%	12
10 years (Long)	138	61%	11
11 years (Long)	138	60%	13
11 years (Cont)	80	52%	16

The Small Usual Detail, d%

A third of the six year old children used one or more of the small, usual detail locations on the blot. The proportion of children giving such responses increased with age with no difference found as to sex or intelligence in this regard.

The following table shows the mean d%, with standard deviation, given by the children at each age level in both the longitudinal and control groups.

TABLE 17**

MEAN d% WITH STANDARD DEVIATION AT EACH AGE LEVEL IN BOTH LONGITUDINAL
AND CONTROL GROUPS OF ELEMENTARY SCHOOL CHILDREN

Age Level	Number	Mean d%	Standard Deviation
6 years (Long)	138	3%	5
7 years (Long)	138	3%	6
7 years (Cont)	73	3%	6
8 years (Long)	138	4%	6
9 years (Long)	138	6%	8
10 years (Long)	138	7%	8
11 years (Long)	138	8%	8
11 years (Cont)	80	6%	8

The lowest mean percentage of d responses is found at the six and seven year levels, with the proportion of such responses increasing with age. There was also a positive relationship between mean d% and intelligence. Repeated testing and sex differences, however, appeared to have little effect on the children's choice of this area.

The Unusual Detail Response, Dd%

Only a small number of six year old children used unusual detail. The number of children using this location, gradually increasing with years, was less than 25 per cent at the eight year level; at nine and ten years of age between 25 per cent and 50 per cent of the children gave at least one Dd response; and by eleven years of age the proportion had reached approximately half of the children in each group, longitudinal and control.

The following table shows the mean Dd%, with standard deviation, for each age level of children in both longitudinal and control groups.

---

*Excerpt from Table C in the appendix.
**Excerpt from Table D in the appendix.

TABLE 18*

MEAN Dd% WITH STANDARD DEVIATION FOR EACH AGE LEVEL IN BOTH LONGITUDINAL
AND CONTROL GROUPS OF ELEMENTARY SCHOOL CHILDREN

Age Level	Number	Mean Dd%	Standard Deviation
6 years (Long)	138	1%	3
7 years (Long)	138	2%	5
7 years (Cont)	73	1%	3
8 years (Long)	138	2%	4
9 years (Long)	138	3%	5
10 years (Long)	138	4%	7
11 years (Long)	138	6%	9
11 years (Cont)	80	5%	6

The lowest mean Dd percentage, 1 per cent, was found at the six year level, and the proportion increased with age. No relationship was found between the Dd percentage and the other variables, sex, intelligence, and repeated testing.

The White Space Responses, S%

Only a small number of six year old children used S location for responses. The proportion of children giving such responses tended to increase slightly with age, but the highest proportion reached was 24 per cent of the eleven year olds in the control group.

The mean S%, with standard deviation, for each age level in both longitudinal and control groups are shown in the following table.

TABLE 19**

MEAN S% WITH STANDARD DEVIATION FOR EACH AGE LEVEL IN BOTH LONGITUDINAL
AND CONTROL GROUPS OF ELEMENTARY SCHOOL CHILDREN

Age Level	Number	Mean S%	Standard Deviation
6 years (Long)	138	1%	2
7 years (Long)	138	1%	2
7 years (Cont)	73	1%	3
8 years (Long)	138	1%	2
9 years (Long)	138	1%	2
10 years (Long)	138	1%	2
11 years (Long)	138	1%	3
11 years (Cont)	80	1%	3

The mean S percentage remained consistently low through the years and there seemed to be no relationship with sex or intelligence.

Summary of Location Responses

A summarization of the mean percentages of the five location areas, W, D, d, Dd, and S, are presented in the table on the following page.

As noted in the table, the percentage of whole responses given by the children decreases through the years, with six year olds giving an average of 44 per cent W, and the eleven year old control group giving 35 per cent. Since repeated testing seems to accelerate this decrease, the percentages at ages eight through eleven years in the longitudinal group appear to be spuriously deflated and should be so evaluated.

---

*Excerpt from Table E in the appendix.
**Excerpt from Table F in the appendix.

TABLE 20

SUMMARIZATION OF THE PERCENTAGES OF THE LOCATIONS OF RESPONSES GIVEN
TO THE RORSCHACH CARDS BY CHILDREN FROM SIX THROUGH ELEVEN
YEARS OF AGE IN BOTH LONGITUDINAL AND CONTROL GROUPS

Age Levels	Number	Location Percentage				
		W%	D%	d%	Dd%	S%
6 years (Long)	138	44%	50%	3%	1%	1%
7 years (Long)	138	40%	54%	3%	2%	1%
7 years (Cont)	73	43%	52%	3%	1%	1%
8 years (Long)	138	34%	60%	4%	2%	1%
9 years (Long)	138	28%	62%	6%	3%	1%
10 years (Long)	138	27%	61%	7%	4%	1%
11 years (Long)	138	26%	60%	8%	6%	1%
11 years (Cont)	80	35%	52%	6%	5%	1%

D% remains fairly constant through the years. It should be noted that repeated testing seems to effect an increase from six to eight years, with little change thereafter. These spuriously inflated percentages should be so evaluated.

The two areas, d and Dd, each show a significant increase in percentage with age. Mean d% increases from 3 per cent at age six to 6 per cent at age eleven; mean Dd% shows a similar increase with age, from 1 per cent at age six to 5 per cent at age eleven.

S% remains fairly stable, approximately 1 per cent at each age level.

Since D% and S% remain fairly constant, it would appear that the compensation for the decrease of W% is found in the rise in the percentage of d and Dd responses.

While an increase in age tended to effect significant changes in the percentages of certain location areas, neither the sex nor the intelligence of the child showed any such effect.

Repeated testing appeared to exert some influence upon the percentage of certain location areas used. While no difference in this regard was noted between the children in the two seven year old groups, longitudinal and control, the effects of repeated testing were evidenced on certain locations at the eleven year level. The following significant differences in location areas were noted between the eleven year old longitudinal group and the eleven year old control group. The W% of the eleven year olds, seeing the cards for the sixth time, was lower than that of the eleven year old group, seeing the cards for the first time. D% was higher; and no demonstrable effect was shown on d%, Dd% or S%. Additional effects attributable to repeated testing are: the brighter the child, the greater the percentage of d and Dd responses through the years of testing. It was noted in addition that the older and/or brighter children tended to integrate parts of the blot and to make elaboration of concepts more than did the younger and/or less bright children.

Since there are no control groups with which to compare the percentage of location areas used by the eight, nine, and ten year olds in this study, these averages should be evaluated in light of the over-all change in each location percentage between the six year old longitudinal group and the eleven year old control group.

DETERMINANTS OF RESPONSES

In making a response to a Rorschach card, the individual is influenced in his choice of a blot area by specific characteristics which he sees or projects in the area. These specific factors, called determinants, consist of form, movement, shading, and color.

Form Responses, F

The form responses, those determined solely by the outlines of the interpreted areas, constitute the greatest percentage among the various determinants used by the children at each age level. Only two children, a six year old girl and a seven year old boy, failed to include at least one $\overline{F}$ among their responses. The record of one child, a seven year old girl, contained only form determined responses.

As in the case of location responses, it is both expedient and customary to discuss form responses in terms of $\underline{F\%}$. The following table shows the mean $\underline{F\%}$, with standard deviation, at each age level in both the longitudinal and control groups.

TABLE 21*

MEAN $\underline{F\%}$ WITH STANDARD DEVIATION FOR EACH AGE LEVEL IN BOTH LONGITUDINAL
AND CONTROL GROUPS OF ELEMENTARY SCHOOL CHILDREN

Age Level	Number	Mean F%	Standard Deviation
6 years (Long)	138	45%	20
7 years (Long)	138	51%	19
7 years (Cont)	73	49%	22
8 years (Long)	138	49%	16
9 years (Long)	138	49%	16
10 years (Long)	138	44%	15
11 years (Long)	138	42%	16
11 years (Cont)	80	47%	14

While $\underline{F\%}$ seemed to decrease with age among the independently tested groups, no definite trend was established. Furthermore, no definite relationship was found between $\underline{F\%}$ and the other variables of sex and intelligence. When the $\underline{F\%}$ of each of the control groups at seven and eleven years was compared to that of the longitudinal group at the same age, no significant difference was noted at seven years of age, but the 47 per cent $\overline{F}$ of the eleven year old control group was significantly higher than the 42 per cent $\overline{F}$ of the longitudinal group of the same age indicating a decrease in $\underline{F\%}$ with repeated testing. However, comparisons among the three independently tested groups suggest that the mean $\underline{F\%}$ remains fairly stable at slightly less than 50 per cent, regardless of age, intelligence, and sex. The majority of children at each age level stay within fifteen to twenty points of the mean $\underline{F\%}$ for their particular age group.

While $\underline{F+\%}$ was not treated statistically in this study, it was noted that the younger and less bright children tended to give more poor form responses than did the older and brighter children.

Movement Responses, $\underline{M}$, $\underline{FM}$, and $\underline{m}$

Since form is the determinant responsible for an average of nearly 50 per cent of the total number of responses given at each age level, the remainder or slightly more than 50 per cent is divided among the three other determinants--movement, shading, and color--with the percentage of movement responses greater than that of each of the other two.

Few of the children at any age level failed to give at least one type of movement response. Animal movement was the most commonly used, then human movement, with inanimate movement being given by the lowest percentage of children.

Following is a table showing the mean percentage of each type of movement responses at each age level in both the longitudinal and control groups. Since the usual interpretation procedure takes into account the actual number of these responses, frequencies are also included.

a. Human Movement Responses, $\underline{M}$. More than half of the children at ages six, seven, and eight gave at least one human movement, $\underline{M}$, responses, and at least one-fourth of these children gave two $\underline{M}$. These proportions gradually increased through the years so that from nine through eleven years of age, more than three-fourths of the children gave one or more $\underline{M}$; at least one-half gave two or more; and at least one-fourth gave three or more.

As shown in the following table, the percentage as well as the number of human movement responses was related to the age of the child. Beginning with an average of one $\underline{M}$ at six years, the average number has increased from 7 per cent $\underline{M}$ to 10 per cent during this period. Just as older children can be

---

*Excerpt from Table G in the appendix.

TABLE 22*

MEAN PERCENTAGE WITH MEAN FREQUENCY OF EACH TYPE OF MOVEMENT RESPONSE, M, FM, AND m, AT EACH AGE LEVEL IN BOTH LONGITUDINAL AND CONTROL GROUPS OF ELEMENTARY SCHOOL CHILDREN

Age Level	Number	Mean M %	Freq.	Mean FM %	Freq.	Mean m** %	Freq.	Mean % M + FM + m
6 years (Long)	138	7%	1.1	19%	3.0	2%	.3	27%
7 years (Long)	138	7%	1.1	23%	3.8	1%	.2	31%
7 years (Cont)	73	8%	1.4	19%	3.3	2%	.3	29%
8 years (Long)	138	9%	1.8	24%	4.8	1%	.3	35%
9 years (Long)	138	10%	2.3	24%	5.7	1%	.3	35%
10 years (Long)	138	9%	2.6	28%	7.8	2%	.5	39%
11 years (Long)	138	11%	3.3	29%	8.6	2%	.5	40%
11 years (Cont)	80	10%	2.7	23%	6.0	3%	.8	36%

expected to use more $\underline{M}$ than the younger, so it is with the bright vs the less bright. Another relationship not shown in the table is that of mean $\underline{M}$ to the sex of the child--i.e., girls give on the average more human movement responses than the boys.

At every age level the range of $\underline{M}$ responses begins at zero and the upper score shows an increase with age. The $\underline{M}$ range of 0-6 at six years of age increases gradually through the years until at eleven years of age the control group shows a 0-9 range. There were only three children in the longitudinal group who exceeded this 9M upper limit of the eleven year old control group: an eleven year old of average intelligence who gave 10 $\underline{M}$; an eleven year old boy of superior intelligence who gave 14 $\underline{M}$; and a boy in the bright group who gave 25 $\underline{M}$ at ten years of age and 24 $\underline{M}$ at the eleven year level. However, since each of the three children had an unusually large $\underline{R}$, their $\underline{M}\%$ was no higher than that of many other children of their age groups.

b. Animal Movement Responses, $\underline{FM}$. Three-fourths of the children at six and seven years of age gave one or more $\underline{FM}$ responses, and from eight years on three-fourths of them gave three or more $\underline{FM}$. At ten and eleven years of age, every child, with the exception of one boy in the eleven year old control group, gave at least one $\underline{FM}$ response.

No significant relationship was found between the mean $\underline{FM}$ of the children and their age, intelligence, or sex, but it was found that repeated testing increased this $\underline{FM}$ average through the years. These findings, together with the $\underline{FM}$ figures in the table above, indicate that children from six years through eleven years of age can be expected to give approximately 20 per cent $\underline{FM}$ responses regardless of age, intelligence, or sex, and that the mean $\underline{FM}$ of the children from seven through eleven years of age in the longitudinal group are spuriously high and should be so evaluated.

The range of $\underline{FM}$ responses, beginning with 0-12 at six years of age, showed a slight increase through the years with 0-18 as the eleven year level range.

c. Less than a fourth of the six year old children gave inanimate movement responses. The proportion of children giving such responses increased gradually with age until at eleven years of age nearly half of them--a greater number in the control group than in the longitudinal group at this age--gave at least one $\underline{m}$. Due to the extremely low mean frequency of each type of $\underline{m}$ response, the three, $\underline{m}$, $\underline{mF}$, and $\underline{Fm}$, were viewed in combination.

Figures in the mean $\underline{m}$ column of Table 22 suggest a trend for older children to use more inanimate movement than younger children. Such a trend was also noted in relation to intelligence. Neither trend was substantiated statistically, suggesting that $\underline{m}$ responses are not affected by age or intelligence. No sex differences were noted for this determinant. Therefore, children regardless of age, intelligence, or sex can be expected to give on the average from .3 to .8 $\underline{m}$. The slight tendency noted in regard to an increase of $\underline{m}$ with age and intelligence was further minimized by repeated testing where no trend was suggested in regard to either of these variables.

The range of $\underline{m}$ responses showed a slight increase through the years from 0-3 at six years of age to 0-8 at the eleven year level in the control group.

*Excerpt from Tables H, I, and J in the appendix.
**$\underline{mF}$ and $\underline{Fm}$ responses are included under $\underline{m}$.

d. Summary of Movement Responses, $\underline{M}$ + $\underline{FM}$ and $\underline{m}$. The increase of mean $\underline{M}$ with age was found to be significant, the means of $\underline{FM}$ and $\underline{m}$ showing slight but not significant trends in the same direction. Repeated testing appeared to have little effect on mean $\underline{M}$ but tended to inflate the mean $\underline{FM}$ and to deflate the mean $\underline{m}$ through the six years of testing. Such relationships should be considered when evaluating the average $\underline{FM}$ and $\underline{m}$ from the age of seven through eleven years in the longitudinal group.

An increase in the percentage of the movement responses combined can be noted through the years beginning with 27 per cent at six years and reaching 36 per cent among the eleven year old control group. A slight tendency for repeated testing to inflate this percentage should be noted so that the scores of the longitudinal group from seven through eleven years can be so evaluated.

Shading Responses, $\underline{k}$, $\underline{K}$, $\underline{c}$, $\underline{C}'$

The shading in the Rorschach blots creates for some individuals a three dimensional impression. If this three dimensional expanse is projected on a two dimensional plane, like an "X-ray" or a "topographical map," the score is $\underline{k}$ ($\underline{k}$, $\underline{kF}$ or $\underline{Fk}$); if it is diffusion, like "clouds" or "smoke," the score is $\underline{K}$ or $\underline{KF}$; and if depth or vista, like "mountain peaks in the distance," $\underline{FK}$ is scored. Shading sometimes suggests surface or texture impressions like "highly polished wood" or "fur" in which case the score is $\underline{c}$ ($\underline{c}$, $\underline{cF}$, or $\underline{Fc}$). Still another use of shading is as achromatic color; black, white, or gray, with the score of $\underline{C}'$ ($\overline{C'}$, $\underline{C'F}$, or $\underline{FC'}$).

Following is a table showing the mean percentages with frequencies of the various shading responses given at each age level by the children in both the longitudinal and control groups.

TABLE 23*

MEAN PERCENTAGE WITH MEAN FREQUENCY OF EACH TYPE OF SHADING RESPONSE,
$\underline{K}$, $\underline{FK}$, $\underline{c}$, AND $\underline{C}'$, AT EACH AGE LEVEL IN BOTH LONGITUDINAL
AND CONTROL GROUPS OF ELEMENTARY SCHOOL CHILDREN

| Age Level | Mean K+KF | | Mean FK | | Mean c** | | Mean C'** | | Mean % of |
	%	Freq.	%	Freq.	%	Freq.	%	Freq.	$\underline{K + FK + c + C'}$
6 years (Long)	4%	.6	.5%	.1	1.8%	.3	4%	.7	10%
7 years (Long)	2%	.3	.4%	.1	1.6%	.3	2%	.4	6%
7 years (Cont)	2%	.4	.7%	.1	1.6%	.3	3%	.5	7%
8 years (Long)	1%	.2	.5%	.1	2.0%	.4	1%	.2	5%
9 years (Long)	1%	.3	.4%	.1	2.7%	.6	1%	.2	5%
10 years (Long)	1%	.3	.7%	.2	3.4%	.9	1%	.2	6%
11 years (Long)	1%	.3	1.2%	.4	4.6%	1.4	1%	.2	8%
11 years (Cont)	1%	.2	1.1%	.3	3.4%	.9	1%	.3	6%

a. Shading as Three Dimensional, $\underline{k}$, $\underline{K}$, $\underline{FK}$. Only six children, two in the longitudinal group and four in the eleven year old control group, gave $\underline{k}$ responses or those in which there was an impression of a three dimensional expanse projected on a two dimensional plan. These were an intellectually superior six year old girl and a bright eleven year old boy, both in the longitudinal group; and two boys and two girls in the eleven year old control group. Since each child gave only one such response, the small amount of $\underline{k}$ was not sufficient for any kind of statistical evaluation. Suffice it to say that the use of the $\underline{k}$ type of response is extremely rare among children of elementary school age.

More than a fourth of the six year old children and a like proportion among the seven year old controls gave diffusion responses. This proportion decreased through the years until at eleven years of age only 12 per cent of the children used $\underline{K}$ or $\underline{KF}$. Because of the low frequency of these scores, they were combined in the above table. This type of response showed a decrease with age, with no trend noted for intelligence and a slight tendency to be used more by boys than by girls. Repeated testing does not show any significant effect. According to the figures in the above table six year olds can be expected to give on the average .6 $\underline{K}$, and this mean $\underline{K}$ decreases to .2 by eleven years of age.

---

*Excerpt from Tables $\underline{K}$, L, $\underline{M}$ and $\underline{N}$ in the appendix.
**Both form combinations are included.

Vista or depth responses, FK, were given only by 7 per cent of the six year olds, but this proportion increased gradually through this year until at eleven years of age nearly one-fourth of the children used the FK determinant.

While there appeared to be an increase in mean FK with age and/or intelligence, this was not statistically substantiated in this study. No difference was noted between boys and girls in regard to FK, but there was some indication that repeated testing effected an increase in this type of response. According to the figures in the table above, FK is rare among children at the elementary school level, with a mean of .1 FK at six years which showed a gradual increase through the years, reaching only .3 at the eleven year level.

b. Shading as Surface Impression or Texture, c. When the shading of the Rorschach blot gives the effect of surface impressions or texture, the response is scored c, cF, or Fc, depending on the influence of form on the concept. All such responses are reported under c in the above table. Less than a fourth of the children at the six and seven year levels gave c responses. There was a gradual increase in this proportion until at eleven years of age approximately half of the children used this determinant. There was a significant trend for mean c to increase with age, but no particular relationship with sex or intelligence was noted. At six years of age there was a mean c of .3 which increased with age to reach a mean of .9 at the eleven year level.

c. Shading as Achromatic Color, C'. All achromatic color responses, C', C'F, and FC' are reported as C'. More than a fourth of the six and seven year old children gave one or more of these C' responses. This proportion decreased with the years until only 17 per cent of the eleven year old control group gave such responses. There was a tendency for C' responses to decrease with age, but no relationship was noted with intelligence, sex, or repeated testing. The six year olds had a mean C' of .7, which decreased with age until at the eleven year level there was a mean of .3.

d. Summary of Shading Responses. The mean percentage of all shading responses combined tended to decrease with age, from 10 per cent at six years to 6 per cent at eleven years. The diffusion and achromatic responses, K and C', showed a significant decrease with age, while vista responses as well as texture and surface impressions, FK and c showed a significant increase. None of these seemed to be related to intelligence or sex, and repeated testing apparently had little effect on these changes.

Color Responses, FC, CF, and C

Responses involving the color of the blots are sometimes thought of as including the achromatic color. This is especially the case when the individual giving achromatic responses uses the chromatic color freely. In such instances, the hypothesis is that the individual's receptivity to color is extended to include the achromatic as well as the chromatic aspects of the blots. In this study no attempt was made to relate the two types of color responses.

Following is a table showing the mean percentages with frequencies of the three types of color responses given at each age level by the children in both longitudinal and control groups.

TABLE 24*

MEAN PERCENTAGE WITH MEAN FREQUENCY OF EACH TYPE OF COLOR RESPONSE,
FC, CF, AND C, AT EACH AGE LEVEL IN BOTH LONGITUDINAL
AND CONTROL GROUPS OF ELEMENTARY SCHOOL CHILDREN

| Age Level | Number | Mean FC | | Mean CF | | Mean C | | Mean % of |
		%	Freq.	%	Freq.	%	Freq.	FC + CF + C
6 years (Long)	138	6%	1.1	6%	1.1	4%	.7	17%
7 years (Long)	138	6%	.9	5%	.8	1%	.2	12%
7 years (Cont)	73	6%	1.1	6%	1.1	2%	.3	14%
8 years (Long)	138	6%	1.3	5%	.9	1%	.2	12%
9 years (Long)	138	6%	1.4	4%	.9	1%	.2	11%
10 years (Long)	138	6%	1.9	3%	.9	1%	.2	11%
11 years (Long)	138	7%	2.0	3%	1.0	0%	.0	10%
11 years (Cont)	80	4%	1.0	5%	1.4	1%	.3	10%

*Excerpt from Tables O, P, and Q, in the appendix.

26

a. Form-Color Response, FC. When a color response has a definite form with color an integrated part of the concept as "tomato worms" for the lower green section of Card X, the score is FC. If the color is a less integral part of the concept, with the subject feeling compelled to include it, like "blue spiders" on Card X, this is considered "forced" or "loose" use of color with form and is scored F ←→ C. Another type of form-color response, scored F/C, is the arbitrary use of color to mark off areas as on a map, which Klopfer calls a "colorless" use of color. If the form of the form-color response is poor, the response is scored FC-. These various types of FC were used by the children in this study and treated statistically under FC.

More than half of the children at the six year level gave at least one FC response. While this proportion of children increased with repeated testing in the longitudinal group, little change was noted in the percentage of children in the control groups who gave such responses. The kind of FC used, however, tended to vary, with more "forced" or "loose" form-color responses being given at the lower age levels.

From the FC column in the table above, it can be seen that while there was a tendency for the mean frequency as well as the mean percentage of FC to increase among the children in the longitudinal group, the opposite was true so far as the control groups were concerned. This suggests that repeated testing increased the production of FC responses, while on the other hand tended to decrease when only the age variable was considered. No significant differences were found for either intelligence or sex variables. The findings suggest that the average record of a child of elementary school age is one FC response.

b. Color-Form Response, CF. Color-form responses are distinguished from form-color in that the color plays the major role in the concept, as a "spots of blood" to the red areas on Card II. The same classification of natured, forced, arbitrary or minus that were applied to FC responses were also applied to CF responses and treated statistically under CF.

More than half of the six year old children gave CF responses. In fact, the percentage was only slightly higher than those who gave FC responses at this age. This proportion remained approximately the same among the two control groups but tended to decrease with repeated testing.

Inspection of the above table shows that the mean percentage of CF tends to decrease with repeated testing but not with age. While not indicated in full in the table, it was found that regardless of age, intelligence, or sex, children of elementary school age tend to give on the average one CF response.

c. Pure Color, C. When color responses are given without implication of form in the concept as "shy" to bluish areas of the cards, the score is C. Another variation of this pure color response is the naming of the color. Such responses are included in the C category for statistical treatment.

At least one-fourth of the six year old children gave pure color responses and the proportion was approximately the same for the seven year old control group. Among all other age levels including the eleven year old group, fewer than one-fourth of them used this determinant. There was a tendency for the younger and/or less intelligent children to give more C responses than the older and/or brighter. The mean frequency of this response decreased from .7 at the six year level to .3 among the eleven year old control group with this trend of decrease with age a significant one. No difference was noted for either intelligence or sex variables. According to these results it would appear that while we can expect pure color responses fairly frequently among the younger children, these tend to become less common with age.

Summary of Color Responses

Reference to the total mean percentage of color responses in the table above indicates a definite decrease with age from 17 per cent at six years to 10 per cent at the eleven year level. While there was a significant decrease with age in C responses, CF remained fairly stable through the years. Although FC responses showed a tendency to increase through the years among the longitudinal group, this could have been the result of repeated testing since the eleven year old control group showed a significantly smaller proportion of such responses than that given by the eleven year olds in the longitudinal group. It is possible that this significant difference between the two eleven year old groups may be in part a result of the perseveration of the forced arbitrary FC responses which were fairly common among the younger children. While there was a tendency for the children in the longitudinal group to cling to such responses through the years, the records of the children in the eleven year old control group were relatively free of this less acceptable type of FC.

The relationship among the four general classifications of determinants--form, movement, shading, and color--changed with age from six through eleven years. The mean percentage of each determinant used at each age level is shown in the following table.

TABLE 25

MEAN PERCENTAGE OF EACH DETERMINANT USED AT EACH AGE LEVEL SIX THROUGH
ELEVEN YEARS IN BOTH THE LONGITUDINAL AND CONTROL GROUPS

Age Levels	Number	Form %	Movement %	Shading %	Color %
6 years (Long)	138	45%	27%	10%	17%
7 years (Long)	138	51%	31%	6%	12%
7 years (Cont)	73	49%	29%	7%	14%
8 years (Long)	138	49%	35%	5%	12%
9 years (Long)	138	49%	35%	5%	11%
10 years (Long)	138	44%	39%	6%	11%
11 years (Long)	138	42%	40%	8%	10%
11 years (Cont)	80	47%	36%	6%	10%

The above table indicates the shifts with age among the mean percentages of the four determinants. Form, with a mean percentage approximately 50 per cent through the years is lowest at the six year level and highest at the seven year level. The mean percentages of movement responses increase with age while shading and color percentages decrease. At six years of age the mean percentages of shading and color together equal that of movement. By eleven years of age, the gradual decrease of shading and color percentages and the gradual increase of movement percentages are such that movement is more than twice shading and color combined. Reference to percentages among longitudinal groups suggests that repeated testing tends to deflate the form percentage and increase the total movement percentage without undue effect on the total shading or total color percentages.

CONTENT

Another aspect of the response to be considered is *content;* that is, the essential picture stimulated by the blot or parts of the blot. Each response is classified according to the kind of content used, such as animal, A; human, H; object, Obj.; nature, N; blood, Bl.

Because of the wide variety of content given at each age level as well as through the years, it is impossible to analyze each content group. Only the two categories most frequently used by children at all ages--*animal* and *human* content--are treated statistically in this report.

The mean percentages with standard deviations of each of the two content categories--*animal* and *human*--are presented in the following table.

TABLE 26*

MEAN PERCENTAGE WITH STANDARD DEVIATION OF THE TWO CONTENT CATEGORIES,
ANIMAL AND HUMAN, FOR EACH AGE LEVEL IN BOTH LONGITUDINAL
AND CONTROL GROUPS OF ELEMENTARY SCHOOL CHILDREN

Age Level	A%		H%	
	Mean	SD	Mean	SD
6 years (Long)	47	19	13	10
7 years (Long)	57	19	12	9
7 years (Cont)	51	21	14	10
8 years (Long)	56	18	14	9
9 years (Long)	55	16	16	9
10 years (Long)	56	14	15	9
11 years (Long)	54	14	16	10
11 years (Cont)	48	17	14	9

*Excerpt from Tables R and S in the appendix.

28

Animal Content <u>A</u> and <u>Ad</u>

All except two children, both girls, gave at least one animal content response, <u>A</u>. A few children at the six year level used *only* animal content, or 100 per cent <u>A</u>. This number gradually decreased through the years so that no child at eleven years of age gave 100 per cent <u>A</u>. Reference to the table above shows that the average animal content given at each age level approximates 50 per cent, with the majority of the children within 21 points or less of the average percentage for their particular age level. Few children in the study had less than 30 per cent or more than 70 per cent animal content among their responses. There was a trend for duller children to give more animal content than the more intelligent but no relationship was found between <u>A</u>% and sex. There was a significant trend for <u>A</u>% to increase with repeated testing as indicated by the significantly higher mean <u>A</u>% in the eleven year old longitudinal group as compared with that of the control group at the same age level.

Human Content, <u>H</u> and <u>Hd</u>

More than three-fourths of the children at each age level gave human content responses. A few of the older and brighter children had as high as 50 per cent <u>H</u> in their records. The average percentage, however, was around 14 per cent to 16 per cent, with the majority of all the children within ten points of the average percentage for their particular age group. The increase of <u>H</u>% was found to be related not only to age but to the intelligence and sex variables as well. The older and/or brighter the child the greater tendency there was toward a higher percentage of human content responses, and there was a trend for girls to have a higher <u>H</u>% than boys.

Content other than *Animal* or *Human*

While *animal* and *human* content account for nearly two-thirds of the responses given by the children in this study, the approximately 35 per cent remainder of responses is spread among a wide variety of other content categories. *Object* and *nature* concepts tend to vie for third place depending on the age group considered. Pathognomic responses, like "blood," "fire," "water," "clouds," were also given by all age groups, but in all cases with less frequency than *object* and *nature*.

Because of the great variety and wide scatter of the content other than *animal* and *human*, none of them was treated statistically. Instead a card by card descriptive summary of content will be given in the following chapter.

POPULAR RESPONSES

Scoring of the popular responses in the protocols of the children in this study was in accordance with the Klopfer scoring. The following table indicates the mean number of such responses given by the children at each age level in both the longitudinal and control groups.

TABLE 27*

MEAN NUMBER OF KLOPFER POPULARS WITH RANGE AT EACH AGE LEVEL IN BOTH
LONGITUDINAL AND CONTROL GROUPS OF ELEMENTARY SCHOOL CHILDREN

Age Level	Number	Number of Populars	Range
6 yrs (Long)	138	3.2	0-8
7 yrs (Long)	138	3.8	0-8
7 yrs (Cont)	73	3.4	1-7
8 yrs (Long)	138	4.8	1-10
9 yrs (Long)	138	5.2	2-9
10 yrs (Long)	138	5.7	0-10
11 yrs (Long)	138	6.1	1-10
11 yrs (Cont)	80	4.5	1-9

*Excerpt from Table T in appendix.

All of the children except a few at the younger age levels gave one or more popular responses. At least 75 per cent of the six year olds gave two $\underline{P}$ or more, and by eleven years of age at least 75 per cent gave three $\underline{P}$ or more. As noted in the above table, six year old children gave on the average three popular responses with a range of 0-8. The average $\underline{P}$ as well as the upper limit of the range tended to increase with years, so that by eleven years of age, the control group gave on the average 4.5 popular responses with a range of 1-9. There was also a positive relationship between mean $\underline{P}$ and intelligence, since there was an increase in $\underline{P}$ with intelligence level as well as with age. There seemed to be little difference between boys and girls in regard to average number of popular responses. Repeated testing tended to effect a slight increase as evidenced by the 6.0 $\underline{P}$ vs 4.5 $\underline{P}$ between the longitudinal and control groups at eleven years of age.

In addition to the adult popular responses which showed an increase from one year to the next in the records of the children, it was noted that there was a number of responses, especially among the younger children, that were given frequently enough to be considered popular at different age levels. These will be discussed in the following chapter.

General Summary

In bringing to a conclusion this discussion of Rorschach norms for children, Table 28 is presented as a bird's eye view of the results of this normative study. In this over-all picture is seen at a glance the trends of the various Rorschach categories, percentages and ratios found in the serial records of the children as they pass through the preadolescent years. The reader should again be reminded that the averages which comprise this table are to be used as points of departure and not as absolute measures in evaluating the Rorschach records of children. It must be remembered, also, that these "average" responses may be affected by many variables, some of which have been discussed in this chapter; and that no child can be expected to adhere strictly to these "average" age profiles. As with all such norms, they are offered as crude measuring sticks by which the Rorschach records of children of different ages can be compared. It is hoped that they will serve as guide posts to help the Rorschacher, inexperienced in the children's field, find his way with greater confidence.

The obvious tendency of the normative results presented in this table to make through the years a gradual approach toward the Rorschach norms of adults has probably already been observed in the discussion of individual Rorschach categories during the progress of the chapters. This reflection in the Rorschach or developmental trends is the theme of a later chapter in which a comparison is made between the Rorschach norms of children and those of adults.

Without further elaboration at this time, the following table is presented as a brief recapitulation of the Rorschach norms of preadolescent children. In Chapter V these normative results will be compared with adult expectancies for the same categories.

TABLE 28

MEANS OF RORSCHACH CATEGORIES, PERCENTAGES AND RATIOS IN RECORDS AT EACH AGE LEVEL OF BOTH LONGITUDINAL AND CONTROL GROUPS

Categories and Percentages	6 Years (L) N-138	7 Years (L) N-138	7 Years (C) N-73	Age Groups 8 Years N-138	9 Years N-138	10 Years N-138	11 Years (L) N-138	11 Years (C) N-80
R	16.5	16.3	17.0	20.1	23.7	27.7	30.1	26.5
Rejections (% of children)	13%	10%	20%	2%	1%	1%	0%	1%
Reaction Time (Ach. Cards)	11"	14"	10"	11"	10"	7"	7"	13"
Time (Col. Cards)	12"	14"	10"	12"	9"	7"	7"	14"
Content %								
A%	47.3	57.0	50.6	56.0	55.0	56.4	53.6	47.5
H%	12.9	12.5	14.3	15.5	15.6	15.1	15.6	14.1
P	3.2	3.8	4.8	5.2	5.2	5.7	6.1	4.5
Location %								
W%	44.0	39.7	42.8	33.1	28.1	27.3	25.9	35.4
D%	50.4	54.3	51.8	59.9	61.6	60.5	59.7	52.2
d%	3.2	3.3	3.0	4.3	6.5	7.4	7.6	6.4
Dd + S%	2.4	2.8	2.2	2.4	3.6	5.3	6.7	6.1
Determinant %								
F%	45.2%	50.8	48.8	48.6	49.2	44.1	41.5	47.3
Movement %	27.2	31.4	29.3	34.6	35.2	39.3	40.3	35.0
Shading (K + FK%	4.0	2.1	3.1	1.6	1.7	1.7	2.2	1.8
(c + C'%	6.0	4.1	4.3	3.2	3.5	4.2	5.4	4.3
Color %	17.1	11.0	14.5	11.9	10.9	10.8	10.1	10.1
Determinants								
M	1.1	1.1	1.4	2.0	2.3	2.5	3.0	2.7
FM	3.0	3.8	3.3	4.8	5.7	7.8	8.6	6.0
m	0.3	0.2	0.3	0.4	0.3	0.5	0.5	0.8
K	0.6	0.3	0.4	0.2	0.3	0.3	0.3	0.2
FK	0.1	0.1	0.1	0.1	0.1	0.2	0.4	0.3
c	0.3	0.3	0.3	0.4	0.6	0.9	1.4	0.9
C'	0.7	0.4	0.5	0.2	0.2	0.2	0.2	0.3
FC	1.0	0.9	1.1	1.3	1.4	1.9	2.0	1.0
CF	1.1	0.8	1.1	0.9	0.9	0.9	1.0	1.4
C	0.7	0.2	0.3	0.2	0.2	0.2	0.0	0.3
Sum C	2.6	1.6	2.1	1.9	1.9	2.2	2.0	2.4
Ratios								
W:M	7:1	6:1	6:1	7:2	7:2	8:3	8:3	9:3
M:FM	1:3	1:4	1:3	2:5	2:6	3:8	3:9	3:6
(FM + m):(c + C')	3:1	4:1	4:1	5:1	6:1	8:1	9:2	7:1
M:Sum C	1:3	1:2	1:2	2:2	2:2	3:2	3:2	3:2
(c + C'):(FC + CF + C)	1:3	1:2	1:2	1:3	1:2	1:3	2:3	1:3
FC:(CF + C)	1:2	1:1	1:1	1:1	1:1	2:1	2:1	1:2
% of R to last 3 Cards	35%	37%	36%	38%	37%	38%	37%	38%

IV. Popular Responses in Children's Rorschachs

A Card-by Card Summary of Content

In addition to the universally popular responses to the Rorschach cards common to all ages and groups, as discussed in the preceding chapter, there are other responses which occur at certain age levels or in certain groups with sufficient frequency to warrant designation as group populars. As the author set about the task of determining such populars among the responses of the children in this study, it was found that experts differ on the statistical criterion for determining popular responses. Rorschach originally suggested that a response be classified as "popular," if it occurred with a frequency of at least one in three records. Other authorities have suggested a frequency of one in six records. It is generally agreed, however, that regardless of the criterion used, popular responses differ among different groups of subjects and that there is value in establishing such populars in as many group situations as possible.

In order to establish what concepts were common enough in the children's Rorschach responses to be called "popular," a card-by-card study was made of the content used by the children in this study. The following descriptive summary suggests that children's populars, although varying with the age of the child, tend as the child grows older toward generally accepted universally popular responses.

Descriptive Summary of Content

The following card-by-card summarization of content categories used by the children in this study include not only the types of content elicited by each blot, but the changes in content that are related to age, intelligence, and sex. Note is also made of the instances in which the repetition of the test seems to effect some change in the trend of content responses. In this way can be seen the gradual year by year development of concepts that are considered universally popular.

CARD I

On Card I *animal* figures were seen more frequently than all other types of concepts combined. The other content categories of any appreciable frequency were *human, nature,* and *object,* in that order.

W Responses to Card I.

Of the animal figures seen in the whole blot, W, of Card I, a *winged creature* was the most common, being given by one-third to one-half of the children, depending on the age level. The three concepts of "butterfly," "bird," and "bat," shifted in frequency with age, intelligence, and sex. For example, the proportion of children seeing a "butterfly" tended to increase with age and intelligence, with more girls than boys giving this response; on the other hand, the "bird" response decreased with age and intelligence and was seen by more boys than girls; the "bat" response, far less common than the other two, tended to increase with age, with the highest percentage of children, 13 per cent, giving this response at eleven years of age and no noticeable difference as to intelligence or sex.

Animal figures other than winged creatures, seen infrequently in the whole blot area, were as a rule poor in form. The number of such responses tended to have a negative relation to age and intelligence. The older and/or brighter the child, the less the tendency to give such responses.

Another whole response to Card I was that of "face," WS, usually *animal* in content, but often *object,* such as "pumpkin" or "mask," and sometimes *human.* Given by 20 per cent of the six year olds, a "face" was seen with equal frequency by boys and girls. This ratio between boys and girls shifted with age to the extent that among the eleven year old control group, in which 24 per cent of the children saw this "face," there were twice as many boys as girls who gave this response.

The *human* responses other than "face" seen in the whole blot of Card I were poor in form and tended, as did similar *animal* responses, to decrease in frequency with age and/or intelligence.

D Responses to Card I.

Approximately 10 per cent of the children, regardless of age, intelligence, or sex, saw an animal in one or more of the three major D areas in the blot on Card I. "Elephant," "bear," and "dog," were given in that order of frequency. There was a trend for the older and/or brighter children to combine the three areas into a whole response, as "two dogs climbing on a bear."

These same areas also stimulated *human* content responses, with the center D leading in frequency. From 10 per cent to 20 per cent of the children, the proportion increasing with frequency, saw a *human* figure in the center D. At six years of age, boys and girls gave such a response with equal frequency, with all girls seeing a female figure and only half of the boys seeing a female. As the children grew older, the proportion of boys seeing a *human* figure decreased, with a concomitant increase among the girls. All such figures were female after the six year level. The side D areas, whether interpreted as *animal* or *human,* were frequently combined with the center D by the older and/or brighter children, resulting in whole responses like "two bears killing a woman" or "two witches dragging a little girl away."

d, Dd, and S Areas.

The small proportion of children responding to areas of Card I, other than the W and D areas, used a wide variety of content, the majority of which, however, was *animal* and *human.* There was a slight increase with age in the percentage of children using the d, Dd, and S areas as well as the less common D areas, with a concomitant increase in the variety of content given.

Concepts other than *animal* or *human* stimulated by Card I were varied in content as well as location, and were usually poor or vague in form, such as "house with windows," "broken tree," "dark sky," "airplane." Such responses were given by only a small proportion of six year olds and tended to decrease with age and/or intelligence.

CARD II

Animal concepts were seen in Card II more frequently than that of any other content. Other content categories used on this card were *human, object, nature,* and *pathognomic* responses like "blood" and "fire."

Whole Blot Areas.

The infrequent *animal* and *human* content responses given to the whole blot were usually poor in form, like "a cat's face" or "a lady turning somersault." Such responses tended to decrease with age. Such responses as "bombs bursting" or "volcano" were given by approximately 10 per cent of the children at each age level. At six years of age this "explosion" type of response was given with equal frequency by the sexes, but with increasing age there was a tendency for more boys than girls to use this type of whole response. A wide variety of other responses to the whole blot includes infrequent concepts, like "fallen down house," "mountain," "clouds."

Black D Areas.

The side black areas were seen as *animals* by 30 per cent of the six year old children. The proportion of children giving such a response increased with age until at the eleven year level, 70 per cent of the longitudinal group, and 50 per cent of the control group saw some kind of *animal* in this area. "Bears," "elephants," "dogs," "gorillas," "rabbits," were given in that order of frequency, regardless of age. The bright and/or older children tended to see them in relation to one another as "bears fighting" or "elephants shaking hands with their trunks," but little difference was noted as to sex.

Another *animal* response given fairly frequently to Card II combined the side black and upper red areas into a "chicken" or other fowl.

Human figures were seen in a combination of the side black and upper red areas by 10 per cent of the six year old children, with only a slight increase as the children increased in age. Male figures were most frequently seen, with interaction between the two designated more often by the brighter and/or older children than by the duller and/or younger, such as "clowns pat-a-caking" or "witches dancing."

Red Areas.

The red D areas of Card II stimulated animal responses from a small proportion of the six year olds, and this proportion increased with age and intelligence. For example, the "butterfly" in the lower red

34

area was seen by only 3 per cent of the six year olds, but this proportion increased to 15 per cent among the eleven year olds. The upper red areas were seen as a variety of *animal* figures by a similarly small percentage of six year olds, the proportion increasing slightly with age. These animals were frequently seen in relation to one another by the older children.

The red areas were seen as "fire" and "blood" by 19 per cent of the six year olds, with little difference between the sexes. The percentage of children giving such responses tended to decrease through the years, with a change in ratio between boys and girls. Among the 14 per cent of eleven year old control group giving these responses, the boys predominated.

d, Dd, and S Areas

Responses to d and Dd areas consisted mainly of "heads," both *animal* and *human,* and though infrequent at the six year level, showed a slight increase through the years. The center white space area stimulated a variety of responses with little change as to age, intelligence, or sex. These consisted of such concepts as "top," "tree," "cave," "ballet dancer," "white rat."

CARD III

Human concepts were seen more frequently on Card III than any other content category. *Animal* figures were also seen by a large proportion of the children. *Object* content was third in order of frequency with *pathognomic* responses of "fire" and "blood" fourth.

Whole Responses.

Human and *animal* and other content responses, each more or less of poor form quality, were seen in the whole blot by approximately 10 per cent of the six year olds. These responses, such as "frog," "animal," "monster," "tree," tended to decrease with age and intelligence.

Black D Areas.

The side black areas of Card III were seen as *human* figures, usually in an activity involving the lower black D area such as "two men picking up a skeleton" by 27 per cent of the six year old children, with a steady increase with age in the proportion of children giving such responses. For example, by eleven years of age, 70 per cent of the longitudinal group and 44 per cent of the control group saw these *human* figures. The majority of them were male; a few were undesignated as to sex, like "people," "elves," "fairies"; a few were female figures; and even fewer were one of each sex, as "a mama and a papa."

The *animal* figures seen in the side black areas were, like the *human* figures, usually seen in action involving the lower black D, as "two lambs playing in a little pond." This type of response was given by 10 per cent of the six year olds, with a slight increase in the proportion of children through the years, as evidenced at eleven years of age by 25 per cent of the longitudinal and 15 per cent of the control groups who gave such *animal* responses. At all ages, the most common animal response in this area was "monkeys in human-like action."

The lower black D area, among other content too varied to list here, stimulated one type of *object* response which was given by 7 per cent of the six year old children--that of container, such as "pan," "bucket," "basket." The proportion of children giving such a response increased through the years until at eleven years of age, 15 per cent of the longitudinal group and 25 per cent of the control group saw some sort of container in this area. Other responses to this lower black area including "rocks," "skeleton," "fire," "face," "water," are too varied and infrequent to warrant comparisons.

Red Areas of Card III.

The *animal* response most frequently given to either of the red areas was "butterfly," which the center area stimulated among 6 per cent of the six year olds. This proportion fluctuated upward through the years with 20 per cent of the eleven year control group using this concept. The outer red areas on this card elicited *animal* responses among a small proportion of children at each age level, but the variety of such concepts as well as the small percentage of children using them make comparisons meaningless.

Pathognomic responses to the red areas, such as "blood" and/or "fire" were given by 16 per cent of the six year old children. This percentage decreased through the years to such an extent that no child in the eleven year longitudinal group and only 5 per cent of the eleven year old control group gave such a response.

Among the *object* responses given to the red areas, the "bow," including "ribbon," "hairbow," "bow-tie," was seen in the central red area by 26 per cent of the six year old children. This percentage increased through the years to 67 per cent among the eleven year old longitudinal group. Since the percentage of eleven year olds in the control group was significantly lower, it is evident that repeated testing was a factor in the age increase of the "bow" response. At all ages in both control and longitudinal groups, more girls than boys gave this response.

d, Dd, S, and other D Areas.

Such D areas as the lower side black and the upper side black as well as the d, Dd, and S areas of Card III were too infrequently used by the children in this study and the content given too varied for meaningful comparisons.

CARD IV

Animal responses to Card IV were given by more children than any other content. *Human* figures were seen with less frequency. *Object* responses were next in order, with *animal object* the most commonly given by the older children.

Whole Blot Area.

The *animal* responses most frequently stimulated by the whole blot on Card IV among the children was "winged creature," "bear," "gorilla," given in that order by 42 per cent of the six year olds. The proportion of children giving such responses fluctuated downward among the longitudinal group. There was a concomitant trend for the concepts to reverse order through the years. For example, by seven years of age, the "bear" responses had taken precedence over the "winged creature"; by nine years of age the "gorilla" was seen more frequently than the "bear"; and by eleven years of age, the "winged creature" response had almost disappeared. Since at eleven years of age, 41 per cent of the control in contrast to 29 per cent of the longitudinal group gave at least one of these *animal* responses, it appears that the decrease in frequency of these responses was related to repeated testing. The older and/or more intelligent the child, the more often these animals were seen in motion, with human movement given increasing preference through the years.

The *human* figure was seen in the whole blot of Card IV by 31 per cent of the six year old children, with twice as many girls as boys using this concept. By eleven years of age, the proportion of children giving this response had decreased slightly, with boys and girls approximately equal. A masculine figure was by far the most common, with "giant" the most frequent choice of the boys, and "man" most often seen by the girls. A few children failed to designate the sex, and no female figure was seen on this card.

The *animal object* response to this card, while given by very few of the six year olds, was given by 7 per cent of the eight year olds; and by eleven years of age, 27 per cent of the longitudinal group gave this response. Since only 10 per cent of the eleven year old control group saw the "animal skin," it appears that much of the increase can be attributable to repeated testing. Boys and girls gave this response with similar frequency.

A variety of other content was used in response to the whole blot by a small proportion of children, but these were usually vague or poor in form, like "dark cloud" or "tree." Such responses tended to be related negatively to age and intelligence.

Content of Responses to D Areas of Card IV.

The control of the responses stimulated by the side D areas of Card IV was predominantly "feet" with or without shoes, usually *human* but sometimes *animal*. The proportion of children giving this response increased from 5 per cent at the six year level to 18 per cent among the control group at the eleven year level, with the longitudinal and control groups in similar proportions.

In the lower D area of Card IV, *object* responses of the "seat" variety, including such content as "tree," "stump," and "stool," were given by 10 per cent of the six year old children with boys and girls approximately equated. This proportion increased through the years until at eleven years of age, 35 per cent of the longitudinal group gave such a response. Since only 13 per cent of the eleven year old controls used this specific content, it is apparent that repeated testing rather than age was the primary factor in the increase of this response.

Animal responses were also elicited by the lower D̲ area of Card IV. Animal heads such as "alligator," "bull," "caterpillar," were seen by 3 per cent of the six year olds, the proportion increasing through the years to 15 per cent of the longitudinal group and 10 per cent of the control group at eleven years of age.

d, Dd, and S Areas of Card IV.

The content of the responses to areas other than discussed above was varied, with "heads," both human and animal, the most frequently given to the various d̲, D̲d, and S̲ areas.

CARD V

Animal content responses were stimulated by Card V among a larger proportion of children than any other type of response. A small percentage of the children saw *human* figures, and even fewer used a variety of content, the most common of which was *object* and *nature*.

The Whole Blot on Card V.

A "winged creature," of varying kinds, a response given by 70 per cent of the six year old children, increased in frequency through the years, until at eleven years of age, more than 90 per cent of the children in both the longitudinal and control group gave such a response. "Butterfly," the most commonly designated of the winged creatures, was given by 40 per cent to 50 per cent of the children at each age level, in both the longitudinal and control groups. This response seemed to be affected very little by intelligence or sex.

The other winged creatures, "bat," "bird," and "insect," were each seen by 10 per cent of the six year olds. Of these three, the "bird" and "insect" responses decreased through the years, while the "bat" response increased. By eleven years of age, approximately 30 per cent of the children in both longitudinal and control groups saw the "bat," with more boys than girls giving this response at this older age level.

Responses other than winged creatures to the whole blot, which were few in number, were vague in concept, and/or poor of form, included such content as "smoke," "mountain," "monster."

Center D Area of Card V.

The center D̲ area of Card V stimulated *animal* responses, most common of which was a "rabbit," from approximately 10 per cent of the children at each age level, with the exception of the eleven year old control group in which 15 per cent of the children gave such a response.

Dd, and S and other D Areas.

The content of the few responses given to areas other than center D̲ and the whole blot of Card V included several varieties, with "heads," both *animal* and *human,* the most frequently seen. The proportion of children giving responses to these less used areas tended to increase with age, but the content of the responses was too varied to justify classification and comparison.

CARD VI

The content of the responses to Card VI showed considerable change through the years. To the various locations in this blot, *animal* responses were given by a large proportion of children, especially in the early years, and *animal object,* which was used by only a few of the younger children, became increasingly more frequent with age. *Human* figures were seen fairly frequently by the older and/or brighter children. Other content was so varied and so uncommon on this card that meaningful comparisons are not possible.

Whole Blot Area of Card VI.

Among the responses to the whole blot on Card VI, *animal* concepts were seen by a large proportion of the younger children. A variety of animals, "cat" and "turtle" being the most common, was seen by 30 per cent of the six year olds, with the proportion remaining fairly constant through nine years of age.

By eleven years of age, only 15 per cent of the children in both longitudinal and control groups gave such responses, with an increase in the variety of animals seen.

Concurrent with the age decrease in proportion of children seeing an animal in the whole blot of Card VI was an increase in the percentage of children giving an *animal object* response. While only 2 per cent of the six year olds saw the "animal skin rug," 11 per cent of the seven year old control group and 16 per cent of the eight year olds used this concept. The proportion continued to increase to such an extent that approximately 53 per cent of the eleven year old children in the longitudinal group and 43 per cent of the control group at the same age gave such a response. With Card VI in a reversed position, the whole blot was seen as two *human* beings usually in contact with each other, by 20 per cent of the eleven year old children in the longitudinal group. While none of the six year olds gave the response, the concept appeared with an increased image and seemed to be related also to intelligence and sex with more boys than girls seeing the figures. *Animal* figures usually in human action or position were seen in the same area by small proportion of the old groups.

A variety of content other than *animal, animal object,* and *human* was seen in the whole blot of Card VI. Vague in outline and/or poor in form, such responses as "black clouds" "explosion" and "mountain" were given by a small percentage of children at all age levels, in both longitudinal and control groups.

Upper D Area of Card VI.

The upper D area in Card VI was seen as a "winged creature" by 20 per cent of the six year old children. This percentage tended to fluctuate downward among the various age levels of the longitudinal groups. Control groups, however, maintained a higher percentage: 19 per cent at the seven year level, and 23 per cent at the eleven year level, gave this type of *animal* response.

d, Dd, and S and other D areas on Card VI.

Only a small percentage of children used D areas other than the upper D. For example, "feathers" for the "wing" part of the upper D and a variety of concepts for the central D of the same area. Likewise a small percentage of children, the proportion increasing slightly with age, gave responses of great content variety to the d, Dd, and S areas of this blot. Classification of the content categories among these areas is meaningless because of the low frequency as well as wide variety of such responses.

CARD VII

Responses of animal content on Card VII were given by a larger proportion of children at each age level than any other type of response. *Human* figures were next in order of frequency at all age levels. "Clouds" and/or "smoke" responses, common at the six year level, decreased through the years. *Architecture* responses in this area were also fairly common among the younger children.

Whole Area of Card VII.

"Clouds" and/or "smoke" responses to the whole blot were given by one in four or 26 per cent of the six year old children, but this percentage decreased through the years to such an extent that at eleven years of age, only 4 per cent of the children or one in twenty-five used this concept. There was little difference noted as to intelligence, but there was tendency for more boys than girls to give such a response on this card.

Side D Areas.

A large proportion of the children at each age level saw in the side D areas *animals* which were usually related to each other or engaged in some activity. The lower D area was sometimes included in the *animal* concept, and at other times involved in the activity. In addition to the three most commonly used concepts, "animals," "dogs," and "rabbits," there was a wide variety of others, such as "lambs" and "monkeys." At least one-third of the children, regardless of age or intelligence, saw either "dogs" or "rabbits' in this area. Repeated testing tended to increase the proportion of children giving such responses, and more girls than boys saw either "dogs" or "rabbits" rather than some other type of animal.

Human figures were also seen in these areas. At six years of age 11 per cent of the children, with girls in excess of boys, gave such a *human* content response. The proportion increased with age to the extent that among the eleven year old control group, 30 per cent of the children, with boys and girls fairly equated, saw people in the side areas. An overwhelming majority of the figures were female; a few undesignated as to sex; and a very small number, male.

Lower D Area of Card VII.

The most frequent response to the lower D area of Card VII was that of "butterfly" given by 5 per cent of the six year old children. While the proportion of children giving this response had increased to 20 per cent at eleven years of age in the longitudinal group, only 5 per cent of the control group at that age saw the "butterfly" in this area--suggesting that the increase was a function of repeated testing rather than age. Boys and girls at all ages gave this response with equal frequency.

A variety of other content was used by a small proportion of children in their response to this lower D area. These included "rocks," "trees," "animals," "crushed ice," "smoke," and were frequently used in connection with the activity of the side D figures.

d, Dd, S, and other D areas on Card VII.

Responses to the various location areas on Card VII not already discussed include a variety of content and were each given by only a small proportion of children. The one exception is the *architecture* concept seen in the small S area at the lower center of the blot, sometimes combined with the d area just above, as "building," "church," "jail," "gate," by 15 per cent of the six year old children. This response tends to decrease with age as evidenced by only 7 per cent of the eleven year old control group using such a concept.

CARD VIII

Animal responses to Card VIII were given by a larger proportion of children than any other content on this or any other card. Responses other than animal in content were so varied and given by such a small percentage of children that comparisons among them were not warranted.

Whole Blot Area of Card VIII.

Responses to Card VIII involving the blot as a whole rather than a combination of parts were usually indefinite or poor in form, such as "design," "flower garden," "insides," and were given by a very small percentage of children. Combined wholes were usually scored as D's with an additional W, and will be discussed in the following paragraph.

Side D Areas of Card VIII.

The side red D areas on Card VIII stimulated animal responses from a larger proportion of children than any other area on this or any other Rorschach Card. The responses most frequently given were *animal* in content, such as "bears," animals of the cat or rodent families, and undesignated "animals." Among the age levels of the longitudinal group, the percentage of children giving such responses began at 50 per cent among the six year olds, with this proportion increasing through the years. That repeated testing tended to inflate this increase in percentage is shown by the 62 per cent of the eleven year old control group in contrast to the 79 per cent of the longitudinal group at the same age. About 25 per cent of the six year olds saw animals not included in those listed above, such as "frogs," "butterflies," "crabs," which were poorly suited to the form of the blot, but this type of response tended to decrease with age as well as intelligence.

Younger and/or less bright children frequently saw the animals without relationship to the rest of the blot. As a rule, however, a climbing position was described with some convenient concept such as "rocks," or "trees," often ascribed to the center area. Such a combinatory whole was positively related to intelligence and age.

Center D Areas on Card VIII.

The D areas on Card VIII other than the side red already discussed elicited a variety of content. While 50 per cent of the children, the proportion changing little with age, responded to one or more of these areas, the content used seemed little related to any variable. The "mountain," "tree," or "rocks," response given to the combination of center D's seemed to be given primarily because these were the sorts of things that animals climbed. However, attempts were sometimes made to fit the concept to the color or form of one or more of these areas. For example: the responses which were fairly adequate in form for the area used were "tree" to the upper gray area; "butterfly" or "flower" to the lower red and/or orange area and "skeleton" or "skull" to the central D area.

d, Dd, and S Areas on Card VIII.

Among the small number of responses to the d, Dd, and S areas on Card VIII, there was a variety of content but no one category was used frequently enough to justify comparisons.

CARD IX

The blot on Card IX elicited a variety of content, of which *animal, human,* and *nature,* in that order, were the most frequent, and together make up the bulk of the responses to this card. Each of these categories, while given by a fairly large proportion of children, was so varied in types and so scattered among the different blot areas that statistical comparisons were not attempted. *Pathognomic* responses, including "explosion" and "waterfall," were given by a small proportion of the children at each age level. Other content was too infrequently used to warrant classification.

Whole Blot Area of Card IX.

Responses to the whole blot on Card IX were usually vague in form and often influenced by the color of the blot as: "sunset," "rainbow," "bomb bursting," "design." Such responses were given by approximately one in ten or 10 per cent of the six year olds, with a gradual decrease through the years. The decrease in this type of whole response resulted in some cases in a transfer of such content to D areas.

D Areas of Card IX.

Each of the three brightly colored areas on Card IX stimulated *animal* responses from differing proportions of children, with each proportion increasing with age. Boys and girls differed little as to types of animals seen.

Animals in the orange D area were seen by 18 per cent of the six year olds, with the percentage fluctuating upward through the years until at eleven years of age, 29 per cent of the longitudinal group and 24 per cent of the control group gave animal responses to this area. The most commonly seen animals were "deer," "lobster," "crab," but there was a wide variety of others. In the green D area, animals were seen by only 3 per cent of the six year olds, but the proportion increased through the years. This increase was probably inflated with repeated testing since at eleven years of age, 20 per cent of the seven year old longitudinal group, in contrast to 9 per cent of the control group, gave animal responses to the green area. The animals seen were of a wide variety, with "bears" and "dogs" being most frequently designated. In the red D area at the bottom of Card IX, usually held sidewise, 9 per cent of the six year olds saw animals. The proportion increased with the years until at eleven years of age, 20 per cent of both the longitudinal and control groups gave such responses to this area. The variety of animals was again scattered with "bears," "buffaloes," and "bulls," the most frequently named.

The same D areas of orange, green, and red were each seen as *human* figures by approximately the same proportion of children as gave animal responses, beginning with a small percentage of six years of age and increasing through the years. The most common human content seen in the orange D area was "clowns" and "witches"; in the green D area, "women" and "men"; and in the red area, "heads" (usually of men).

Content other than *animal* and *human* was given to the same brightly colored areas by a small percentage of children in each age group. The variety of content categories includes *object,* such as "red umbrella" to the red area inverted; *food,* "carrots" to the orange area and "four red apples" to the red; *clothing,* such as a "red fluffy sweater" to red area; and *plant,* as "tree" to green area.

d, Dd, S, and other D Areas on Card IX.

Responses to the d, Dd, S, and D areas of Card IX not already discussed were given by very few of the children at any age level. The variety in content, too wide to warrant classification, includes *nature* as "waterfall" in the center gray D area; *human,* as "Kilroy" in the center D portion between green areas; and *object,* as "violin" to the area which combines the two central D areas just mentioned.

40

CARD X

Card X elicited animal responses from at least 75 per cent of the children in the study, regardless of age, intelligence, or sex. By contrast, other content categories are inconsequential in frequency and in the proportion of children using them.

Whole Blot of Card X.

Card X as a whole stimulated various types of *animal* responses from 15 per cent of the six year old children. This proportion appeared to decrease with age, but the drop was probably influenced by repeated testing since the percentage in each control group--18 per cent at seven years and 16 per cent at eleven years--was greater than the percentage in the longitudinal groups at the same age levels.

Content of responses to the whole blot other than *animal* were given by approximately 25 per cent of the six year olds. A decrease in this percentage seemed likewise to be affected by repeated testing since at eleven years of age, only 5 per cent of the children in the longitudinal group gave such responses, while 25 per cent of each of the control groups used a variety of content other than *animal* in their responses to the whole blot. "Bones," "fireworks," "colors," "design," were the most common of such responses among all groups.

D areas on Card X.

Each D area on Card X stimulated *animal* responses of varying types. The proportion of children giving such responses varied with the D areas as well as with the age of the child.

The upper gray D area, with or without the elongation, was seen as *animals* by a larger percentage of children at each age than those who saw animals in any other area. While the kinds of animals designated are too varied to list, "spiders" was the most common. At six years of age, 32 per cent of the children gave animal responses to this area, and the proportion increased through the years until at eleven years of age 50 per cent of both longitudinal and control groups saw some type of animal in this area.

The "rabbit" in the lower green area was so designated by 25 per cent of the six year olds. The percentage of children giving this response fluctuated with the years until at eleven years of age, 45 per cent of the longitudinal and 20 per cent of the control group saw the "rabbit" in this area.

Another D area responded to with consistently high frequency is the side blue. A "spider" or "crab" was seen in this area by 25 per cent of the six year old children. This percentage increased with age until at eleven years of age, 54 per cent of the longitudinal group and 50 per cent of the control group saw a "spider" or "crab" in this area.

In the lower green elongated areas, 13 per cent of the six year old children saw a "snake," "worm," or "caterpillar." These concepts were used with increasing frequency among the longitudinal group so that at eleven years of age, 43 per cent of these children gave such responses. Since 15 per cent of the control group gave the same responses, this increase appeared to be related to repeated testing rather than age.

The "dog" or "lion" figure seen in the inner yellow D area, while given by only 10 per cent of the six year olds, increased with age as well as repeated testing, as evidenced by the fact that at eleven years of age 37 per cent of the children in the longitudinal group and 23 per cent of the control group saw one of the animals in this area.

Other D areas which were seen as animals by a very small percentage of six year olds and which showed a percentage increase through the years are the upper green D, seen often as an "animal jumping;" the outer orange with card turned sidewise as "dog sleeping"; outer brown seen as "deer" or "horse leaping"; and the outer yellow seen as a "bird." While each of these *animal* figures were seen by 10 per cent or less of the six year olds, there was a slight increase with age in each. By eleven years of age each of these figures were seen by 10 per cent or more of the children in both longitudinal and control groups.

Human content was stimulated by only two D areas: the inner blue D and the red D area. "Men" were seen in the inner blue area by 10 per cent or less of the children, the proportion varying with the age, the greatest percentage being at the eight year level. The red area, sometimes including the upper gray D, stimulated a minimum of *human* figure responses, like "babies," "cooks with caps on," and "elves." The same red area, however, elicited a great many other responses with a wide variety of content, like "fire," "cliffs," "animals," "logs."

An *object* response on Card X, given frequently enough to be noted here, is that of the "stick" or

TABLE 29

RESPONSES MOST FREQUENTLY GIVEN TO EACH OF THE RORSCHACH CARDS WITH PERCENTAGE OF CHILDREN GIVING EACH RESPONSE AT EACH AGE LEVEL IN BOTH LONGITUDINAL AND CONTROL GROUPS OF ELEMENTARY SCHOOL CHILDREN

Card	Response	Percentage of Children							
		6 yrs N=138	7 yrs (L) N=138	7 yrs (C) N=73	8 yrs N=138	9 yrs N=138	10 yrs N=138	11 yrs (L) N=138	11 yrs (C) N=80
I	Winged Creature	45%	38%	36%	51%	39%	39%	36%	56%
	Face	20%	16%	19%	19%	10%	13%	14%	24%
II	Bear, Dog, Elephant	24%	30%	27%	32%	44%	43%	41%	23%
	Blood or Fire	19%	12%	19%	15%	12%	12%	12%	14%
III	People	27%	43%	51%	55%	62%	65%	66%	44%
	Bow	26%	38%	28%	46%	54%	62%	67%	38%
	Butterfly	6%	9%	8%	11%	17%	15%	13%	20%
IV	Man	31%	22%	28%	24%	26%	23%	27%	24%
	Bear, Gorilla, Winged Creature	42%	39%	36%	35%	42%	32%	29%	41%
	Feet	4%	11%	15%	13%	15%	20%	16%	18%
V	Butterfly	50%	49%	52%	59%	52%	49%	52%	40%
	Bat	9%	12%	7%	17%	24%	28%	27%	30%
VI	Animal Skin	2%	4%	11%	16%	28%	42%	53%	43%
	Winged Creature (D)	20%	10%	19%	16%	18%	19%	17%	23%
VII	Clouds or Smoke	26%	16%	4%	12%	12%	8%	4%	4%
	Dogs, Rabbits	31%	39%	33%	54%	58%	54%	62%	33%
	People	11%	12%	10%	18%	16%	11%	16%	30%
VIII	Bears	15%	20%	19%	25%	29%	26%	25%	10%
	Cat Family	14%	7%	16%	17%	28%	18%	16%	11%
	Mice	9%	8%	8%	6%	7%	10%	10%	10%
	Undesignated Animals	12%	12%	21%	16%	14%	19%	28%	31%
	Total of Above Animals	50%	47%	64%	64%	78%	73%	79%	62%
X	Spiders (blue)	25%	28%	35%	41%	46%	50%	54%	50%
	Rabbit	22%	22%	20%	24%	28%	49%	45%	20%
	Worms, Snakes, Caterpillars, or Seahorse	13%	24%	18%	36%	47%	49%	43%	19%
	Dogs (Inner yellow)	10%	14%	8%	25%	17%	28%	37%	23%

"candle" or "tree trunk" variety seen in the top most $\underline{D}$ area. From 15 per cent of the six year olds who gave responses of this type to this area, the percentage increased through the years so that at the eleven year level, 26 per cent of the longitudinal group and 38 per cent of the control group saw similar objects in that area. More boys than girls gave such responses. The phallic nature of the area, as well as the type of responses, were positively related to age as well as sex.

Dd and S Areas of Card X.

While the responses to the $\underline{Dd}$ and $\underline{S}$ areas on Card X were infrequent, their content was so varied that no attempt will be made to classify or compare them. Suffice it to say that the proportion of children responding to these areas increased from 5 per cent of the six year olds to approximately 10 per cent of the eleven year olds on both the longitudinal and control groups.

It may be added here that response to the $\underline{D}$ areas other than those described above were given by such a small percentage of children and included such a variety of content that here, also, any attempt at comparisons seemed unwarranted.

POPULAR RESPONSES ACCORDING TO AGE LEVELS

The preceding descriptive summary of the content used by the children in this study suggests that children's "populars" tend to vary with the age of the child. In determining which concepts met the criteria for "popular" at the different age levels, it was noted that some of these concepts tended to be influenced by repeated testing. For example, the "animal skin" response to the whole blot of Card IV, given by less than 10 per cent of the children through nine years of age, showed an increase among the longitudinal group at the ten and eleven year level, with 26 per cent of the eleven year olds giving such a response. Since less than 10 per cent of the eleven year old control group used this concept, it was evident that the increase noted in the longitudinal group at the same age level was the result of repeated testing. Likewise, there was a tendency for the percentage of children giving certain other responses to decrease through the years. In order to rule out such effects of test repetition, the criteria for children's "populars" were applied only to the responses of the three groups of children who saw the cards for the first time: the six year old longitudinal, the seven year old control, and the eleven year old control. A survey of the Rorschach responses at all age levels in both longitudinal and control groups is reported in Table 29. Included in this table are responses that were given by 17 per cent (one in six) or more of the children in at least *one* of the three independently tested groups listed above. Such percentages are underlined.

As can be noted in Table 29, the percentage of children giving certain responses tended to increase through the years, without a concomitant increase in one or both of the control groups. When the criterion of a response being given one or more times in three records--that is, 33 per cent or more of the children giving such a response--was met, the response was rated popular, and given a $\underline{P}$ score. For the one-in-six criterion--17 per cent to 33 per cent of the children--a tendency to popular, $\rightarrow\underline{P}$ was indicated. These concepts are presented in the table on the following page.

Inspection of Table 30 indicates that at six years of age popular responses that meet the one-in-three criterion are four in number as follows:

Card	I	Winged Creature	W
Card	IV	Bear, Gorilla or Winged Creature	W
Card	V	Butterfly	W
Card	VIII	Animals, Bears, Mice or Cat Family	D

These populars are predominantly whole responses and animal in content, with $\underline{F}$ or $\underline{FM}$ as the only determinants. With the exception of the response to Card IV, all are Klopfer populars.

Within the protocols of the six year olds there are eleven other responses which meet the one-in-six criterion for populars, as follows:

Card	I	Face	WS
Card	II	Blood or Fire	D
Card	III	People	D or W
		Bow	D
Card	IV	Man	W

TABLE 30

POPULAR RESPONSES GIVEN TO THE RORSCHACH CARDS BY CHILDREN IN THE INDEPENDENTLY TESTED GROUPS WITH KLOPFER POPULARS INCLUDED

Card	Response	6 yrs	Age Group 7 yrs	11 yrs	Klopfer Populars
I	Winged Creature W	P	P	P	P
	Face WS	→P	→P	→P	-
II	Bear, Dog, Elephant D or W	→P	→P	→P	P
	Blood or Fire D	→P	→P	-	-
III	People D or W	→P	→P	P	P
	Bow D	→P	→P	P	P
	Butterfly D	-	-	→P	P
IV	Man W	→P	→P	→P	-
	Bear, Gorilla, Winged Creature W	P	P	P	-
	Feet D	-	-	→P	-
V	Butterfly W	P	P	P	P
	Bat W	-	-	P	P
VI	Animal Skin W	-	-	P	P
	Winged Creature D	→P	→P	→P	-
VII	Clouds or Smoke W	→P	-	-	-
	Dogs, Rabbits E	→P	P	P	-
	People D	-	-	→P	-
VIII	Animals, Bears, Mice, Cat Family D	P	P	P	P
X	Crabs, Spiders (blue D)	→P	P	P	P
	Rabbit D	→P	→P	→P	P
	Worms, Snakes D } Caterpillars, Seahorse	-	→P	→P	P
	Dogs, Lions (inner yellow D)	-	-	→P	-

(Continued from p. 43):

    Card VII   Clouds or Smoke   W
               Dogs or Rabbits   D or W

    Card   X   Crabs or Spiders   (blue D)
              Rabbit   D

    The majority of these responses are D in location and animal in content. Other content categories represented are *human, object,* and *nature.* Responses to Cards III and X are Klopfer populars.

    Within the fifteen popular responses, both P and →P, at the six year level, the following determinants are found: human movement, animal movement, form, color, and shading seen as diffusion.

    At seven years of age, three of the →P responses used by the six year olds have now met the one-in-three criterion.

    Card III   People   D or W

    Card VII   Dogs or Rabbits   D or W

    Card   X   Crabs or Spiders   (blue D)

    With these three additions, there are at the seven year level seven responses that fulfill the more rigid requirements of a P response. With the exception of the responses to Card VII, all are Klopfer populars. Other changes in popular responses between six and seven years of age were the disappearance of the clouds and smoke responses for Card VII, and the appearance of another response which fulfilled the one-in-six criterion or →P, as follows:

Card   X   Worms, Snakes, Seahorse, or Caterpillar   (green D)

With the exception of shading, the same determinants appear in the fifteen popular responses of the seven year olds as were found in the six year old group.

Although several of the ➔ P responses fulfilled the one-in-three criterion required for the score of P among the longitudinal group at ages eight through eleven years, some of these changes were evidently the effect of repeated testing. However, by eleven years of age, as evidenced by the results from the control group, the P responses of the one-in-three variety had been augmented by former ➔ P response at the seven year level, and the appearance full blown of a second one-in-three response. These are respectively:

Card   III   Bow   D

Card   VI   Animal Skin   'W

Between the seven and eleven year level, the blood and fire ➔ P response disappeared and the five following popular responses appeared as additions:

Card   III   Butterfly   D

Card   IV   Feet   D

Card   V   Bat   W

Card   VII   People   D or W

Card   X   Dogs or Lions   (inner yellow D)

These changes result in twenty popular responses that meet the one-in-six requirement at the eleven year level. Nine of these responses fulfill the more rigid requirement of one-in-three records. The Klopfer populars not reached by this higher standard, although they appear in the one in six group of the eleven year old children, are:

Card   II   Animals of the bear, dog, or elephant type

Card   III   Butterfly

Card   V   Bat

Card   X   Rabbit, Worms, Snake

The P responses that reach the one in six requirements among the eleven year olds but not considered adult populars by Klopfer are:

Card   I   Face

Card   IV   Animals, W; man, W; and feet, D

Card   VI   Winged Creature   D

Card   VII   People and Dog or Rabbit

Card   X   Dogs or Lions   (inner yellow D)

Just as the "populars" or more stereotyped responses of the children in this study change from year to year in a gradual approach with each passing year to the stereotypes of the adult world in which he lives, so do other aspects of the Rorschach records of these children change with increasing age in the direction of what is expected in the Rorschach protocols of the normal adult. This gradual development as reflected in the changes of the Rorschach responses of children from one year to the next is further highlighted in the following chapter where the Rorschach norms of children are compared with those of adults.

V. Rorschach Norms of Children versus Adult Norms

Developmental Trends as Reflected in the Rorschach

Attempts to make interstudy comparisons of Rorschach quantitive findings are fraught with difficulties, due in part to the sampling and scoring differences among the various investigations. Children's studies are no exception in this regard. For example, the fact that the sample of children used in this study includes a broader range of intelligence and socio-economic levels than other samples described in the literature tends to make comparisons with other children's Rorschach studies less meaningful than would otherwise be the case. Scoring differences also present problems. For such reasons, no serious attempt was made to compare the findings of this study with similar studies. It was observed, however, that there is general agreement among the investigators in the children's field as to the year-by-year trends of the various Rorschach categories and ratios, and that any interstudy differences of these trends appear to be related, for the most part, to the differences in the sampling and scoring used in the various investigations.

A comparison that seems to have more meaning, on the other hand, is that between the results of this study and the normal expectancies of an adult Rorschach record. To the reader familiar with normal adult Rorschachs, it was obvious in the discussion of children's Rorschach norms in Chapter III that as the children grew older their Rorschach patterns tended to approach that found in adult records. As basis for further investigation of this developmental trend, the following table presents both the Rorschach norms of the children arrived at in this study and the generally accepted expectations for the same measures in the record of a normal adult.

Table 29 gives a brief summarization of the averages of the different Rorschach categories, including certain percentages and ratios found in the protocols of the three groups of children seeing the Rorschach cards for the first time--the six-year-olds in the longitudinal group and the children in each of the control groups at seven years and eleven years of age respectively. Since there were indications that repeated testing of the longitudinal group tended to have a slight effect on certain categories at different age levels, the Rorschach norms of the children in the three independently tested groups seemed to offer the simplest and surest way of showing the changes in the Rorschach responses of the children through the years. In the last column of the table are the generally accepted expectancies for each of the same scoring categories in the protocol of a normal adult, as derived from *The Rorschach Technique* by Klopfer, World Book Company, 1942.

Although the table contains only the means of the various categories as used by each age group, the discussion which follows includes other information implicit in the master tables in the appendix, such results from the longitudinal group at ages other than the six year level, or the way in which the sex or intelligence of a child may affect his Rorschach responses. In comparing the norms of the children in this study with those of adults, we will proceed from one scoring category to the next as they are presented in the following table.

Inspection of Table 31 shows the trends in the use of each Rorschach scoring category in the records of children between ages of six and eleven years inclusive, and points up the differences between the Rorschach norms for children and those of adults. In the following discussion of these trends, references are frequently made to statistical measures found only in the more detailed tabular data of the complete normative results of the study, comprising the appendix.

Rejection of Cards

Rejection of one or more cards was not uncommon among the six and seven year old children, but from eight years on, this seemed to be a rare occurrence, and was as uncommon among the eleven year olds as among adults. A greater number of girls than boys rejected cards and more cards per girl were rejected. The cards most commonly rejected by children were VI, IX, IV and II, in that order of frequency. These same cards, according to Klopfer, are most often rejected by adults, but in a different frequency order: IX, II and VI vying for second place, and then Card IV.

TABLE 31

MEANS OF RORSCHACH CATEGORIES, PERCENTAGES AND RATIOS IN RECORDS OF CHILDREN, AND ADULT EXPECTANCIES FOR THE SAME MEASURES

Rorschach Measures	6 years	7 years	11 years	Adult*
Rejection (% of Children)	13%	20%	1%	Rare
	M	M	M	
R, Total Number of Responses	16.5	17.0	26.5	30
Reaction Time (Achr. Cards)	11''	10''	13''	{ = or < 10''
(Color Cards)	12''	10''	14''	{ difference
Location Percentage	M	M	M	
W%	44.0%	42.8%	35.4%	20% to 30%
D%	50.4%	51.8%	52.2%	45% to 55%
d%	3.2%	3.0%	6.4%	5% to 15%
Dd + S%	2.4%	2.2%	6.1%	< 10%
Determinant Percentage	M	M	M	
F%	45.2%	48.8%	47.3%	20% to 50%
Movement (M + FM + m)%	27.2%	29.3%	35.0%	
Shading (K + FK)%	4.0%	3.1%	1.8%	
(c + C')%	6.0%	4.3%	4.3%	
Color (FC + CF + C)%	17.1%	14.5%	10.1%	
Determinant Frequency	M	M	M	
M	1.1	1.4	2.7	3 or more
FM	3.0	3.3	6.0	< M
m	0.3	0.3	0.8	< 3
K	0.6 }	0.4 }	0.2 }	
FK	0.1 }	0.1 }	0.3 }	< 3
c	{ 0.3	{ 0.3	{ 0.9	
C'	{ 0.7	{ 0.5	{ 0.3	< 2(FC + CF + C)
FC	1.0	1.1	1.0	> CF + C
CF	1.1 }	1.1 }	1.4 }	
C	0.7 }	0.3 }	0.3 }	< FC
Sum C	2.6	2.1	2.4	
Ratios				
W:M	7:1	6:1	9:3	2:1
M:FM	1:3	1:3	3:6	M > FM
(FM + m):(c + C')	3:1	4:1	7:1	1:1
M:Sum C	1:3	1:2	3:2	1:1
(c + C'):(FC + CF + C)	1:3	1:2	1:3	< 2:1
FC:(CF + C)	1:2	1:1	1:2	FC > CF + C
R% for Cards VIII, IX, X	35%	36%	38%	Between 30% and 40%
Content	M	M	M	
A%	47.3%	50.6%	47.5%	50% or less
H%	12.9%	14.3%	14.1%	75% - A%
P	3.2	3.4	4.5	5 or more

---

*Derived from Klopfer's *The Rorschach Technique*, World Book Company, 1942.

Number of Responses

The six year old children gave on the average 16 or 17 responses to the ten Rorschach cards and the average number of responses increased gradually with age. By eleven years of age, the average of 26 or 27 responses approximated the 30 responses normally expected from adults. While the majority of children at six years of age varied no more than six or seven responses from the average giving from 10 to 24 responses, this variation increased with age, so that at eleven years of age, the responses from the majority of the children ranged from 10 to 44. It was found that not only did older children give more responses than the younger, but that brighter children at all ages gave more responses than the less bright. Despite the tendency for boys to give more responses than girls, and for repeated testing to increase the number of responses, neither of these two factors had a significant effect. Tests of significance showed that age and intelligence were the two variables that effected a significant increase in the number of responses.

Reaction Time

The average reaction time of children at all ages from 10″ at seven years to 14″ at eleven years tended to approximate the lower limit of an adult expectancy of 10″. There was little difference, only one second in fact, between the average reaction time to color cards and that to the achromatic cards on the part of the children at any age level. This trend is also consistent with the adult expectancy of no difference or less than 10″ difference between the averages of these two sets of reaction times.

Location of Responses

The percentage of whole responses, W%, given by the children decreased through the years, with six-year-olds giving an average of 44 per cent and the eleven-year-olds, 35 per cent. Repeated testing seemed to accelerate the decrease, but no relation was found between W% and sex or intelligence. It was noted, however, that the quality of the W's was better among the brighter, as well as older children. Whole responses were included in practically all records.

The percentage of large detail, D%, remained fairly constant, approximately 50 per cent through the years, and was little affected by sex, age, or intelligence. Repeated testing seemed to effect a slight increase during the early years. Only a few children failed to give at least one D response.

While the percentage of responses to the small detail areas, d%, was only 3 per cent among the six-year-olds, this proportion increased significantly with age. There was a similar relationship between intelligence and d%. While only a third of the six-year-olds used this location, this proportion showed an increase through the years so that at the eleven year level, more than a half of the children gave d responses.

Unusual detail responses Dd% accounts for only 1 per cent of the total responses at six years of age, but this percentage steadily increased through the years to 5 per cent at the eleven year level. Only a few six-year-olds used this area, but by eleven years of age approximately half of the children gave at least one Dd response. No relationship was found between Dd% and sex, intelligence, or repeated testing.

Responses to white space, S%, accounted for only 1 per cent of the responses at each age level. Less than a fourth of the children at any age level used this area, and the greatest proportion, 24 per cent, was among the eleven-year-olds.

The relationship among the average percentages of the various location areas shows a shift with the age of the child. At six years of age, the children, in comparison with adults, tend to over-emphasize W% and under-emphasize d + Dd + S%, with D% fairly consistent with adult expectancy. The changes in these percentages through the years indicates a trend toward the percentages expected from adults: W = 20% - 30%; D = 45% - 55%; d = 5% - 15%; and Dd and/or S = <10%. The eleven-year-olds showed on the average location percentages within the range of those given by normal adults, with the exception of W% which was only slightly emphasized.

Determinants

Of all the determinants, *Form* is used most frequently by children at each age level. The average F% remains fairly stable at slightly less than 50 per cent, regardless of age, intelligence, and sex; but repeated testing tended to effect a decrease in F%. Only two children, a six-year-old girl and seven-year-old boy failed to include at least one F among their responses. The record of only one child, a seven-year-old girl, contained *only* form determined responses. While F + % was not treated statistically in this study, it was noted that the younger and/or less intelligent the child, the poorer the quality of form used.

Among the determinants other than form, *movement* accounted for the largest percentages of responses among the children at all ages, with animal movement, human movement, and inanimate movement in that proportional order. Human movement responses increased from an average of one $\underline{M}$, or 7 per cent, at six years of age, to three $\underline{M}$, or 10 per cent, at eleven years of age. The proportion of human responses was also affected by intelligence and sex. Girls gave on the average more $\underline{M}$ than boys; and the more intelligent the child the greater the proportion of $\underline{M}$. Slightly more than half of the six-year-olds gave at least one $\underline{M}$ response, and this proportion of children increased until at eleven years of age more than three-fourths of them gave at least one $\underline{M}$.

Animal movement responses account for the majority of the movement responses and the percentage remains fairly stable, between 19 per cent and 23 per cent, regardless of age, sex, or intelligence of the children. Repeated testing tends to increase the proportion of $\underline{FM}$. More than 75 per cent of the six-year-olds gave at least one $\underline{FM}$. This proportion increased through the years to the point that only one eleven-year-old, a boy, failed to use this determinant.

Inanimate movement accounts for a very small percentage of the children's responses, less than 1 per cent at any age level. Less than 25 per cent of the six-year-olds used this determinant. While this proportion increased with age, less than 50 per cent of the eleven-year-olds gave such a response. No relationships were noted between $\underline{m\%}$ and age, intelligence, sex, or repeated testing.

An increase in the combined percentages of movement responses takes place through the years beginning with 27 per cent at six years and reaching 36 per cent among the eleven-year-olds.

The third group of determinants of children's responses in order of size is that of *color,* with color-form and pure color responses combined, $(\underline{CF + C})$ always greater than the controlled or $\underline{FC}$ responses.

The average of $\underline{FC}$ as well as the percentage of $\underline{FC}$ responses remained fairly stable through the years and was not affected by either age or intelligence. Repeated testing, however, tended to increase this average. More than half of the six-year-old children gave at least one $\underline{FC}$, and this proportion had increased only slightly at the eleven year level. It was noted, however, that the quality of the response improved through the years, with "forced" or "loose" form-color being given by the younger children.

The color-form, $\underline{CF}$, responses approximated that of $\underline{FC}$ among the children. Regardless of age, sex or intelligence, they tended to give on the average one $\underline{CF}$ response. More than half of the six-year-olds used this determinant, and this proportion remained approximately the same through the eleven-year level.

Pure color $\underline{C}$ accounted on the average for less than 1 per cent of the responses at the six-year level and showed a steady decrease through the years. No difference was noted as to sex or intelligence. Slightly more than 25 per cent of the six and seven-year-olds used this determinant, but this proportion of children decreased through the years so that by eleven years of age very few of the children gave pure color responses.

The combined percentages of the color responses show a decrease with age, from 17 per cent at six years to 10 per cent at the eleven-year level. The $\underline{FC\%}$ and $\underline{CF\%}$ cropped only slightly during this period, with the main decrease accounted for by the $\underline{C\%}$.

Shading accounted for the smallest percentage of determinants used by the children at any age level. Each of the three dimensional shading responses, $\underline{k}$, $\underline{KF}$, and $\underline{FK}$, accounts for so small a percentage of responses as to be statistically negligible. The only exception is that of diffusion responses, $\underline{K + KF}$, like "clouds" and "smoke," which make up 5 per cent of the responses at six years of age and 2 per cent of those at the seven-year level, with the other ages ranging from 1 per cent downward. There was a tendency for diffusion responses to decrease with age and for vista responses, $\underline{FK}$, to increase, but this was not found to be statistically significant. Only 7 per cent of the six-year-olds gave $\underline{FK}$ responses, but the proportion of children increased with age so that at eleven years of age nearly a fourth, or 22 per cent, of the children used this determinant.

The two types of shading--surface impression and texture, and shading as achromatic color--$\underline{c}$ and $\underline{C'}$, are, like the $\underline{k + KF + FK}$ group, found in only a small percentage of the responses of children. The percentage of $\underline{c}$ increases through the years from 1.8 per cent at six years of age to 3.4 per cent at eleven years. On the other hand, $\underline{C'\%}$ decreases from 4 per cent at six years to 1 per cent at eleven years. Less than 25 per cent of the six-year-olds gave $\underline{c}$ responses, and this proportion increased to approximately 50 per cent of the eleven-year-olds, who gave responses of either surface impressions or texture. Shading as achromatic color, $\underline{C'}$ was the reverse of $\underline{c}$, in that more than 25 per cent of the six-year-olds used this determinant, and this proportion decreased with the years until only 17 per cent of the eleven-year-olds gave such responses.

When the average percentages of all shading responses were combined, it was noted that there was a decrease with age from 10 per cent at six years of age to 6 per cent at eleven years. The diffusion and achromatic responses K and C' showed a significant decrease with age, while vista and texture responses FK and c showed a significant increase through the years. None of these changes seemed to be related to sex, intelligence, or repeated testing.

The relationship among the four general classifications of determinants--form, movement, color and shading--changed through the years, as noted in the following table.

TABLE 32

CHANGES IN AVERAGE PERCENTAGE OF DETERMINANTS
FROM AGES SIX THROUGH ELEVEN YEARS

Percentages of Determinants	Age Level		
	6 yrs.	7 yrs.	11 yrs.
Form %	45%	49%	47%
Movement %	27%	29%	36%
Color %	17%	14%	10%
Shading %	10%	7%	6%

The above table indicates the shift with age among the four groups of determinants. With form remaining slightly below 50 per cent, movement increases with age and both color and shading decrease. At six years of age the percentage of movement responses is equal to a combined percentage of color and shading, but by eleven years of age, movement percentage is more than twice that of color and shading combined. It was noted that repeated testing tended to deflate the F% and increase the total movement percentage but had little effect on either color percentage of shading percentage.

In comparing the relationships found among the determinants used by children with those expected from normal adults the following comments can be made:

The average F% of children at all ages falls below the upper limit of 50 per cent expected from adults.

In the area of movement, the percentages of animal movement exceeds that of human movement, the reverse of what is expected from adults. Only a few of the children used inanimate movement, as is the case with adults.

Color responses show a proportion of more CF + C than FC, which is the reverse of adult expectation, of FC > (CF + C).

Shading responses, as a rule, are given by only a few six and seven-year-old children, but beginning at eight years of age there was a gradual increase through the years until more than 50 per cent of the eleven-year-olds gave responses with texture or surface impression. This finding is fairly consistent with what is expected in adult records.

Rorschach Ratios

The Rorschach ratios between various scoring categories used in the interpretation of adult records were found to be quite different in the records of children. For example, the W:M ratio, which is considered optimal at 2:1 in an adult record, started at 7:1 among the six-year-olds and decreased with age. By eleven years of age, however, it had not quite reached a 3:1 ratio, much less the 2:1 expectancy in an adult record. As has already been noted, the M:FM relationship which in normal adult records is expected to be M > FM, is completely reversed among children of all ages. With a M:FM ratio 1:3 at six years of age, there was only a gradual decrease through the years so that at eleven years of age the FM responses were still slightly more than double the M responses. The two ratios (FM + m):(c + C') and M:Sum C, which show, each in a different way, the relationship between the influences of internal and external stimuli upon Rorschach responses, and both of which are optimal in an adult record in a 1:1 relationship, not only differ in children's records from the optimal adult expectancy, but differ from each other among the children at different age levels. At six years of age, there was an (FM + m):(c + C') relationship of 3:1, which increased through the years until at eleven years of age, the ratio approximated 6:1. The M:Sum C ratio, on the other hand, began at a 1:2.6 relationship at six years of age and shifted gradually through the years, with the M increasing and the Sum C decreasing, until at eleven years the ratio was 2.7:2.4, and approximated the optimal 1:1 ratio expected in a normal adult record.

Of the two other ratios involving color $(c + C'):(FC + CF + C)$ and $(FC:(CF + C)$ the expectancy of the first in an adult record is a relationship of $< 2:1$. Among the children in this study the $(c + C')$ was less than $(FC + CF + C)$ at all age levels; but, since such a small number of children at any age level used either c or C', any comparison of this ratio with that in the adult record seems meaningless. For the second ratio of $FC:(FC + C)$, in which the normal adult record shows $FC > (CF + C)$, this relationship is the reverse among children, with $FC < (CF + C)$ at all ages.

The average percentage of responses given by children to the last three cards, VIII, IX and X, ranged from 35 per cent at six years of age to 38 per cent at eleven years and was consistent with the adult expectancy that at least 30 per cent but less than 40 per cent of the total number of responses be given to these cards.

Content Categories

Among normal adults, *animal* plus *human* content, $A\% + H\%$, accounts for about 75 per cent of the responses, with *animal* never exceeding 50 per cent. Among the children in this study $A\%$ approximated 50 per cent or the upper limit of adult expectancy at each age level, but at no age level did $H\%$ make up the remaining 25 per cent or more which would be expected in a normal adult record. With *human* content at 12.9 per cent among the six year old children, there was only a very slight change through the years with eleven-year-olds giving 14.1 per cent. Among the children in this study, where at all ages the $A\% + H\%$ was on the average less than 65 per cent, the other content categories most commonly used were *object* and *nature,* with *blood, fire* and *clouds* or *smoke* fairly common among the six and seven years.

Popular Responses

Of the ten popular responses which Klopfer lists, a normal adult is expected to give five or more. The six year old children gave on the average 3.2. A gradual increase through the years resulted in a 4.5 average at eleven years of age, approximating the lower limit of five populars in a normal adult record.

Children's Populars

According to suggestions frequently encountered in the literature in regard to establishing group populars, the popular responses were determined for each age group included in this study. By the criterion of one response in three records being considered a popular response, six year old children gave three such responses: "winged creature" (of various kinds) to W of Card I; "butterfly" to W of Card V; and "animals" (mainly bear, mice, and animals of cat family) to side D in Card VIII. All of these are adult populars, which are rarely omitted in an adult record.

With age, other adult populars were included in the records of children. At seven years of age, "people" on Card III and "crabs" or "spiders" on the outer blue areas of Card X were added. At this age, "dogs" or "rabbits" to Card VII met the one in three criterion--a children's popular not included in the ten Klopfer adult populars. By eleven years of age, the following adult populars were found in the records of children: "Bear," "dog," "elephant" to Card II; "bow" to the red area of Card III; and "animal skin" to Card VIII. The only adult populars not yet given were the "rabbit" and "green worms" in the lower green area of Card X. These, however, had reached the one in six criterion at this time.

In comparing the Rorschach norms of children to those of adults, the outstanding revelation is the way in which the Rorschach responses reflected from year to year the child's maturation and development--his encompassing gradually the attitudes and reactions of the adult world about him. The knowledge that the Rorschach pattern of an eleven-year-old is much nearer that of an adult than can be expected from a six-year-old is helpful in interpreting children's records. The more exact knowledge of how the records of each age group differs not only from those of adults but from other age groups, gives further confidence in determining the stage of maturation which the child of a given age has reached.

The interpretation of records of individual children is a subject that requires more space and time than can be allotted to this report. The author is at present preparing an extended report of case studies of individual children in which the developmental aspects of each child's personality is reflected in his year-to-year Rorschach responses. To acquaint the reader with some of the types of Rorschach records which he can expect from children, serial Rorschachs from six children with a variety of backgrounds are presented in the following chapter.

VI. Serial Rorschachs of Individual Children

Reflections of Individual Developmental Patterns

Equal in importance to the knowledge that children at different age levels tend to follow a recognized Rorschach pattern in their development is the realization that no two children, even though alike in age, intelligence, and sex give identical Rorschach protocols. This deviation from the Rorschach norms of a particular age group need not necessarily label a child as deviant, but rather emphasizes his individuality, revealing combinations of personality traits peculiar to that particular child.

This difference in personality development among children identical in age is immediately apparent when the serial Rorschach records of the children in this study are compared one series with another. By way of demonstrating this fact, the series of six yearly records given by each of six children between the ages of six and eleven years inclusive are presented in this chapter. In order to acquaint the reader with the children, each set of Rorschachs is preceded by certain historical information and psychological data accumulated through the years of contact with each of the children. In the selection of the children with whom the reader will thus become acquainted, an attempt was made to include as many varieties of backgrounds and personal assets as possible.

The first child to appear in the pages of this chapter is *Bobby*, a boy of average intelligence, who at six years of age was the youngest of six children in a Negro family of very low income. Maternal grandfather, who had migrated from the deep South to Pittsburgh following World War I, lived with the family at that time. Differing from Bobby in every detail except age is *Marcene*, a white girl of superior intelligence, the middle of three sisters in a well-to-do, academically ambitious family. Following Marcene is *Johnny*, a white boy of average intelligence, the middle of seven children in a devout Catholic family in the high income bracket. The fourth child, *Gertie*, a white girl of high average intelligence, one of two children in a middle income Protestant family. *Bernard*, the next child to be introduced is a Jewish boy, slightly superior in intelligence, the only child in a low middle income family, with parents whose academic ambitions for their son are great. *Nora* is a little Irish girl of average intelligence, who, at the age of six years, was the oldest of three sisters in a low income family of mixed religious backgrounds, father being Protestant and mother, Catholic.

BOBBY

At the time of the first Rorschach, when Bobby was a little over six and a half years of age, he was in the first grade of a city public school where he was one of a fairly large percentage of Negro children in a class of fifty boys and girls. The teacher thought he was doing as well as could be expected, because he was cooperative and usually attentive. In the test situation he seemed apprehensive and had difficulty in verbalizing his replies to the Binet test questions and his responses to the Rorschach cards. There developed a kind of passive resistance as the testing session proceeded, even though he remained superficially cooperative. He was a pathetic looking little fellow, breathing through his mouth because of a heavy cold, a sad expression on his face, and a most unkempt appearance. He achieved an I.Q. of 94 on the Stanford Binet and gave the following Rorschach responses at this time:

Bobby's Rorschach Responses at the Six-Year Level

Performance		Inquiry
Card I	6'' 1. Looks like a bird.	1. Bird looks like it's flying.
	2. Looks like hands--looks like feet.	2. Of a boy. Q. Here's a little of his
	50''	body.
Card II	4'' 1. Looks like blood.	1. Cause it's red.
	2. Looks like a point going up.	2. Sword. (d)
	3. Looks like somebody is gonna kill	3. Men (here).
	25'' somebody.	

		Performance	Inquiry

Card III	3''	1. Two persons cooking.	
	35''	2. Looks like blood around the picture.	2. Cause it's red.
Card IV	6''	1. Looks like a giant.	1. His face. Here's his feet, hands, body.
	35''		
Card V	9''	1. Looks like an airplane.	1. W
	23''	2. Looks like a rabbit.	2. Q. Face, ears, buttons and his legs.
Card VI	7''	1. Looks like a cat.	1. Legs, face, tail. Is there one on this side? (turns card over)
	20''	2. Looks like an elevator going up.	2. (d in center)
Card VII	3''	1. Looks like a house (pointing).	1. (d)
		2. Smoke coming out of the house and	2. (W)
	20''	chimney.	
Card VIII	4''	1. Looks like teeth.	1. (White) Teeth belong to boy. (Boy not there.)
		2. Some pink, some orange, blue, and	2. (Points to colors)
	30''	some white.	
Card IX	8''	1. Some orange--some green around	1. (Points to colors)
	20''	orange--some pink.	
Card X	9''	1. Some is gray--some looks like blue, green, and some pink, some yellow	1. (Points)
	25''	and some orange.	

A year after the above Rorschach was obtained, Bobby was again reached in the school setting. He had changed little in appearance, but appeared less apprehensive in the test situation than on the previous occasion. The second grade teacher saw him as outgoing and active in the classroom but easily distracted and slightly retarded in achievement. When asked to draw a man he produced the accompanying figure, which, according to the Goodenough scoring, suggests much better than average ability.

Following are Bobby's Rorschach responses at this time when he was a little more than seven and a half years of age.

Bobby's Rorschach Responses at the Seven Year Level

		Performance	Inquiry

Card I	8''	1. Looks like a statute of something. Got lines across and hands up in the	1. (D) Q. Of a person's. The person's hands. Q. Has four hands. What you
	50''	air and one hand moving across wall.	have the statue on?
Card II	7''	1. Yard and a house at the end of it-- with	1. (WS yard and sidewalk--house--upper d) Can't see much of it.
	30''	2. A flag on the other side.	2. Red flag.
Card III	2''	1. Two people cooking trying to make	1. (What kind?) Mexicans. Q. Have
	17''	some oats.	shoes.
Card IV	3''	1. A giant--with his legs real long.	1. A statue. (Alive or dead?) Alive. Q. He looks like he's moving.
	18''		
Card V	3''	1. Looks like a bird flying.	1. What kind? Robin.
	11''		
Card VI	6''	1. Looks like a hatchet with a nail on top of it.	1. dr
	13''	2. With some fire across it.	2. di

Bobby – 4-16-47 – 7 yrs. 7 mos.

Performance			Inquiry
Card VII	4"	1. Here's a house straight down here.	1. What kind? Brick (lower d).
		2. Then there's mountains. W	2. Got crashes all in them (runs fingers around the edge).
	21"		
Card VIII	10"	1. Looks like the body of a person.	1. On the inside.
	24"	2. And bears.	2. (How?) They are climbing on the body.
Card IX	4"	1. Looks like the streak of a hand-- somebody's.	1. Somebody's hand. (dd)
	17"		
Card X	4"	1. Bones.	1. (Of what?) (Upper D) Person's body.
		2. Little pigs.	2. Legs and face (right blue).
	25"	3. Some shepherds.	3. Sheep (left blue).

When seen a year later, at eight and a half years of age, Bobby was unkempt, but smiling. He gave superficial cooperation in the test situation. On the Monroe Diagnostic Reading Examination, he showed little progress in reading or spelling, both of which were beginning first grade level. Arithmetic, on the other hand was only slightly below his third grade placement. The teacher confirmed these findings, but because of many other poor readers in the class, did not show undue concern.

Bobby gave the following Rorschach responses on this occasion.

Bobby's Rorschach Responses at the Eight Year Level

Performance			Inquiry
Card I	6"	1. Two people. (inner D)	1. Standing with hands up.
	30"	2. Wing over here and wings here.	2. Just the wings of a bird. (outer D)
Card II	3"	1. Lots of blood.	1. Here and here.
		2. House way back here and pair of steps.	2. (upper d)
	18"	3. Grass with blood on it.	3. (Lower red)
Card III	4"	1. Two people cooking. Two little men	1. Two men.
	10"	cooking together.	
Card IV	2"	1. A giant.	1. He's walking with hands down going home. Q. That's the road he walks on.
	10"		
Card V	3"	1. This looks like a hawk--a butterfly	1. Wings and six legs. Q. Here.
	15"	with his legs--six legs.	
Card VI	3"	1. This looks like a cliff with open space.	1. d.
		2. Feathers at top.	2. dr
	20"	1. (Cont.) and whole gang of grass.	
Card VII	9"	1. This looks like a house.	1. (lower d) Down here.
	14"	2. With smoke coming out the top.	2. W No, that's clouds.
Card VIII	3"	1. This looks like teeth (inner S)	1. Real white like people's teeth.
		2. Green water and	2. Almost light blue like waters.
		3. Two bears.	3. Climbing up to the top. I can see its face.
	18"		
Card IX	5"	1. This looks like two orange animals.	1. Bull. Q. This here top looks almost like horns.
		2. Two green animals.	2. Elephants with trunk hanging down climbing up a hill.
	29"	3. Long thing with bumps on it like rocks.	3. Red rocks.
Card X	4"	1. This looks like bones.	1. Whole thing. Pieces. Some pieces look like they came out of a person's body.
	12"		a. These look like bones of a crab, (outer blue)

When seen the next year, Bobby was in fourth grade, despite continued poor achievement and frequent absences from school. His examination was delayed because he was out of school, having stepped on a nail. When finally met he again presented a smiling appearance, but in contrast to most of the children in this fourth contact, Bobby did not recognize the examiner. He was persistent in the test situation, but achieved only 84 P.Q. on the Grace Arthur Performance test. He continued to do poorly in school, and the teacher believed that his mother frequently kept him at home to help with the housework. There were many absences.

At this time, when he was nine years and eight months of age, Bobby gave the following Rorschach responses:

Bobby's Rorschach Responses at the Nine Year Level

		Performance	Inquiry
Card I	5'' 15''	1. Looks like two people.	1. Have their hands up in air. (inner D)
Card II	10'' 20''	1. Building with steps. (upper d) 2. Some blood and grass. (W)	1. Building with steps. 2. Looks like green grass with blood on it.
Card III	7'' 17''	1. Two funny people cooking something.	1. Two men.
Card IV	6'' 13''	1. Looks like giant.	1. Walking. Q. That is something in back of him. Q. I don't know what it is.
Card V	7'' 10''	1. Looks like bat flying through the air.	1. Two things like a bat and legs like it.
Card VI	8'' 19''	1. Looks like some feathers. 2. And mountains. Feathers on a mountain.	1. Painted like Indian feathers. Black on feathers. 2. Space between the mountain is hole with water in it.
Card VII	9'' 14''	1. Looks like a house. (lower d)	1. Smoke from the house--dark part of it. W
Card VIII	10'' 16''	1. Looks like two bears climbing a hill.	1. Here and here.
Card IX	10'' 18''	1. Looks like buffalo (red). 2. Some green grass.	1. Half of buffalo. 2. Green like grass.
Card X	6'' 16''	1. Looks like whole gang of bones.	1. From some fishes and crabs.

When seen a year later, at ten and a half years of age, Bobby wore a serious expression on his face and presented a dull unkempt expression. He was still doing poorly in school and had frequent absences. A baby brother had been born a short time before, and mother depended on Bobby to help her with the baby and the housework. Though lacking in spontaniety on this occasion, he was docilely cooperative in the testing situation, achieving on the WISC a full scale I.Q. of 90, with a Verbal I.Q. of 86 and Performance I.Q. of 96. These two latter scores are the reverse of what would have been expected from his Binet I.Q. of 94 and Grace Arthur P.Q. of 84. Regardless of his poor school achievement, he was in fifth grade and hopelessly lost academically.

The following Rorschach responses were given on this occasion:

Bobby's Rorschach Responses at the Ten Year Level

		Performance	Inquiry
Card I	7'' 12''	1. Two men.	1. (Inner D) Standing together. Must be singing. Q. Hands, heads, body, feet.

		Performance	Inquiry
Card II	4″	1. Like a house and	1. Here's steps and there's the house.
		2. Two animals and	2. Looks like two bears. Q. They're walking around by the house.
	15″	3. Some blood.	3. Red and all this.
Card III	2″	1. Looks like two people are cooking and	1. Looks like two men.
	8″	2. Here's a butterfly. It is flying around.	2. Looks kinda reddish and orange.
Card IV	3″	1. Looks like a giant.	1. Walking along the
	7″		a. road (lower D) going straight.
Card V	4″	1. This looks like a bat flying in the air.	1. Has two things that a bat got and the way they are in back and got wings.
	9″		
Card VI	9″	1. Looks like a mountain. Got	1. All this.
	17″	2. feathers along side of it.	2. The way they are.
Card VII	10″	1. This looks like a little house. (lower d)	1. Here is the house and
	18″	2. With smoke coming out the chimney.	2. Here is smoke coming out.
Card VIII	4″	1. This looks like two bears climbing up	1. Polar bears. Q. They look so much like I've seen them in a. . .
	10″	2. a mountain	2. The way they are climbing it.
Card IX	10″	1. This looks like two bears	1. (Green) Climbing
			a. a ridge (orange).
	20″	2. A bull.	2. On the bottom of the ridge.
Card X	4″	1. This looks like crabs. (blue)	1. They're here. Q. Out of the sea.
		2. Bone, skins.	2. That's the way some bones look. Q. Veins in them (dd).
	14″		

When seen at eleven and a half years of age, Bobby was still preadolescent in appearance, slight in stature, soft spoken, and seemingly shy, but pleasant and cooperative in the test situation. He produced the accompanying human figure drawings. He was able to talk with more spontaniety than on any previous occasion. With little prodding he complained about having to assume responsibility for the care of the baby and of being mistreated by the brother just older than he. He described his concern about his eighteen year old brother who had been stabbed in a fight, of a teenage sister who was sick, and because his mother would not tell him what was wrong with her. His description suggested that she was pregnant. He told how he frequently has to resort to tears to get what he wanted from his mother--like money for a show. Father was not mentioned, and grandfather had died some time before.

Bobby gave the following Rorschach responses on this occasion:

Bobby's Rorschach Responses at the Eleven Year Level

		Performance	Inquiry
Card I	10″	1. Here's two people.	1. Their hands are up in the air--and here are their feet. Q. They are standing close together. Q. Looks like two ladies.
	21″	2. And a pair of wings.	2. Bird's probably (doesn't see bird).
Card II	5″	1. Here is a house. (upper d)	1. Got like steps running up to it and comes to a point at the top. Q. Brick house. Q. You live in.
		2. Here's some blood and there's a walk. That's all.	2. It's red blood and it could have come from an animal walking around that had been shot (doesn't see animal).
	30″		

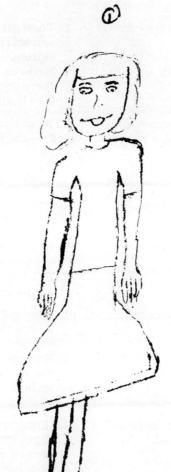

about 12 years old

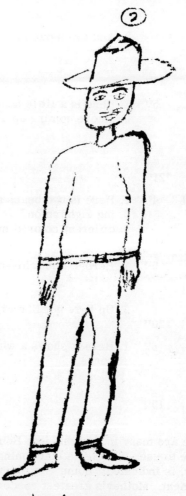

about 14 years old

Bobby — 9-11-51 — 11 yrs. 7 mos.

		Performance	Inquiry

		Performance	**Inquiry**
Card III	5''	1. Well, here is two men and they got tea kettles.	1. They got man's arms, legs, got pants and shirts. Q. They are holding the kettles.
		2. And there's a butterfly flying around.	2. Between them there's like a butterfly there flying around. Q. Monarch. Q. All different colors.
	20''		
Card IV	4''	1. Here it seems there's a picture of a giant and he's got like a tree in back of him.	1. He got great big feet and you can hardly--and his head is like you see his back. Q. Out in the woods. Q. Where there's hardly any trees. Q. As he is walking there's a tree in front of him.
	17''		
Card V	10''	1. Here looks like two mountains. W	1. These two mountains are close together and a split in between them to divide them. Q. Large and wide.
		2. With an Indian between them.	2. (Can't find the Indian--said it was on another card.)
		3. And a butterfly.	3. Has legs like a butterfly, butterfly's wings are not so long. Q. Right here.
	27''		
Card VI	9''	1. Here's a whole gang of feathers.	1. They got at the tip a different color. Q. See them on an Indian's head (doesn't see head).
		2. And two mountains.	2. Right here. Q. In between is like a river. Q. It's white. Mountains are up high and water is down at the bottom of the mountains.
	23''		
Card VII	5''	1. Here is a little house down here and	1. (lower d)
		2. smoke coming up all around.	2. It got smoke coming out--so thick it's coming out around the house. Q. Smoke is going up--not staying down.
			a. In the smoke is like a person--making the face of a man. Q. He's not too big.
	21''		
Card VIII	4''	1. Here is two bears and they are climbing right up on	1. Here two bears climbing up like mountains of different colors. Q. See it in
		2. different colored mountains	2. the zoo. Q. Brown bears. Q. The way they look (not color).
	16''		
Card IX	5''	1. Here's a buffalo--a buffalo (red) and	1. Big round head. Q. Head and body. Q. Probably on the ground (sees them upside down).
		2. Up here got like crabs (orange).	2. Probably alive. Q. Looks like it's moving--here's his arms sticking out.
	20''		
Card X	6''	1. Here it shows a whole gang of animals bones.	a. Right here looks like crabs (blue).
			b. This here looks like a grasshopper bones. Q. Got big eyes. Q. They are just plain--got no skin or no shade to make them look as if they got skin on.
	19''		

There are many indications that Bobby had, and probably still has, greater potentials than he has been able to use. That he is functioning at an immature, dependent level, with much obviously neurotic behavior, is indicated. Home environment no doubt plays an important part in his retarded emotional development. Mother's greatest concern at this time was that Bobby commit some aggressive act that would cause censure from the community.

It is with pleasure and some relief from the depressing picture that Bobby presents that Marcene is now introduced. At the age of six years and nine months of age she was a very neat, attractive, self-assured, pleasant little girl of whom the first grade teacher said rather effusively: "Marcene is a dear little schoolgirl. She does excellent work, follows directions perfectly, and has wonderful initiative. She is a happy child with very good manners. She plays very well with other children and they enjoy her. She has a good background with wonderful home training." During the testing period, she lived up to her teacher's praises, based at year VII on the Binet with a ceiling at year XIV, and achieved an I.Q. of 140. There were indications that this was a minimal score. She gave the following responses to the Rorschach cards on this occasion:

Marcene's Rorschach Responses at the Six Year Level

		Performance	Inquiry
Card I	7'' 20''	1. Looks like a butterfly.	1. It has a couple of holes--has funny wings on it. Q. Flying in the air.
Card II	59'' 80''	(Needs encouragement) 1. Looks like some kind of a thing but I can't -- oh, a thing with blood on it.	1. Animal--looks like bears. Q. On the ground.
Card III	10'' 25''	1. Looks like skulls (skeletons). 2. Some spots of blood.	1. Of people. 2. Here and here and here.
Card IV	3'' 5''	1. Part of a scarecrow.	1. Neck, arms, post, he stands on, legs, feet.
Card V	24'' 26''	1. Looks like a fly or something.	1. Flying.
Card VI	22'' 24''	1. Bee or something.	1. Head, wings.
Card VII	6'' 10''	1. Looks like a rabbit cut in half.	1. Cut and spread out.
Card VIII	12'' 25''	1. Looks like a Christmas tree, with some squirrels or something climbing up.	1. The way it's shaped.
Card IX	6'' 8''	1. Part of a door.	1. The dividing line. Q. Going into some kind of fancy hall. Q. Color and shape.
Card X	15'' 25''	1. Looks like a forest with animals and spiders around.	1. At the side of the tree (red) in the forest.

When seen the next year, at seven years and eight months of age, Marcene again stood out from her classmates as an alert, attractive, physically well-developed child. While the second grade teacher was not as high in her praises as the previous teacher, she was positive in her appraisal, seeing her as an active little girl, slightly advanced in school achievement and little distracted by outside stimuli. Marcene was pleasant and cooperative in the test situation, producing the accompanying figure of a man when asked to draw. By the Goodenough scoring, the drawing confirms the superior intellectual rating found on the Binet. To the Rorschach cards, she gave the following responses on this occasion:

Marcene's Rorschach Responses at the Seven Year Level

		Performance	Inquiry
Card I	6''	1. Looks like a butterfly.	1. It has big wings and has a couple of holes on its back. Q. Where it's flying, from the top.

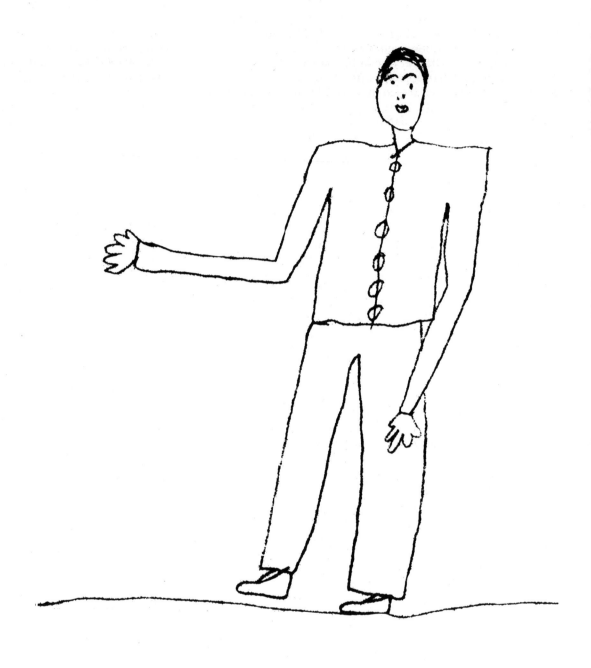

Marlene — 5-11-48 — 7 yrs. 8 months

Performance	Inquiry
2. It might be a woman's dress.	2. It comes down here and this is part of her legs. The dress is around up here. (Can't see woman.)
30'' Shakes her head.	
Card II 4'' 1. This might be two hands with gloves on.	1. Wrists are stuck up. There's skin and there's a big red thing.
2. This is something. It could be a cat all curled up. S	
3. This could be a monkey face.	3. Nose, ears. (Edge)
1'02'' 4. This could be a hippopotamus.	4. Two of them. (Popular figures)
Card III 6'' 1. This is a ribbon.	1. Has two big ruffles on each side just like ordinary ribbon in the middle.
24'' 2. This looks like two skeletons	2. Of people.
Card IV 8'' 1. This could be a giant	
16'' 2. sitting on a tree.	
Card V 3'' 1. A bee maybe.	1. Head, backend. (Middle d)
2. Could be a dragon.	2. Mouth open and he's all hunched up. W
40'' Looks at examiner.	
Card VI 18'' 1. This could be a torn leaf.	
2. That up there maybe could be a firefly.	2. It's wings. It looks like it's lighting up back here. The little white part here.
32''	
Card VII 11'' 1. Could be a wall.	
2. With a door through it.	
3. This could be two rabbits.	3. Ears, face, and little tail. Q. Seeing them from the side.
Card VIII 18'' 1. This could be squirrels, two squirrels.	1. Face, body, legs. a. Climbing up a tree.
2. This could be a butterfly.	2. Has pretty big wings. Very skinny head. Fairly large.
48''	
Card IX 1. This could be a dog. (orange)	1. Nose, looks like it has it's nose up.
2. This could be ladies. (points to upper S)	2. (Orange projections) Looks like falling off of something. Legs out, no feet out. Little bit of head.
60''	
Card X (Looks at examiner and smiles.)	
8'' 1. This could be face of sheep, looking from the top.	1. dd
16'' (inner part of inner blue)	

At eight years and eight months of age, Marcene was mature in her actions, with a somewhat sophisticated air, but she was pleasant and cooperative at all times in the testing period. She approached the Monroe Diagnostic Reading Examination with confidence, and well she might since her achievement in reading and spelling was above the sixth grade level and her arithmetic around the fifth grade level. Her teacher was proud of her and had only praise for her as a pupil.

On this occasion, Marcene gave the following Rorschach responses.

Marcene's Rorschach Responses at the Eight Year Level

Performance	Inquiry
Card I 3'' 1. Butterfly.	1. Up in the air. Q. Flying.
2. Looks something like a person	2. Standing on the floor or something.
35'' without a head.	

		Performance		Inquiry

		Performance		Inquiry

Card II   8''   1. Two hands.

1. Human being's hands. Wrists and have gloves on.

2. Mouse.

2. Fat mouse. (S)

32''   3. Two people fighting.

3. Here and here.

Card III   6''   1. Monkeys.

1. (upper black D) In a cave building
a. a fire (lower D)

26''   2. Two arms. (lower side D)

2. Man or woman's arms.

Card IV   4''   1. Giant.
2. Limbs of trees.

1. Sitting on a tree.

20''   3. Tree stump.

3. Stump.

Card V   4''   1. Some sort of a bug.
2. Dragon.

1. (inner D) Up in the air.
2. Just the head. (outer d)

19''   3. Rabbit head.

3. Up here.

Card VI   6''   1. Fly.
2. Torn off piece of paper.

1. Flying up in the air.

19''   3. A leaf.

Card VII   3''   1. Two rabbits.

1. Ears sticking up this way.
Q. Standing on

2. Stones.

2. Stones.

22''   3. Human being's face.

3. Man's face. (upper D)

Card VIII   4''   1. Two bears climbing up
2. a Christmas tree.

17''   3. Butterfly.

Card IX   7''   1. Limbs of tree.

1. (Projections on orange)

16''   2. Cat faces (in green)

2. Shape

Card X   5''   1. Spiders.
2. Goat's head. (inner part of inner blue)
3. Deer.

3. It has antlers on this side.

27''   4. Rabbit.

4. Face

At nine years and eight months of age Marcene looked like a teenager in her skirt, blouse, and bobby socks. She talked in a self-assured and spontaneous manner. In talking about her lefthandedness, she said that she had taught herself to use her right hand and could do everything equally well with each hand. On the Grace Arthur Performance Test she achieved a P.Q. of 142, confirming previous ratings of superior ability.

She gave the following Rorschach responses at this age:

Marcene's Rorschach Responses at the Nine Year Level

		Performance		Inquiry

Card I   9''   1. Looks like a butterfly and

1. Whole thing is the butterfly.
Q. Ragged, dead.

2. a woman's dress.
3. Open mouth there. (lower right S)
4. This could be a cliff. (head)
5. Fishes mouth or a turtle's mouth. (same as)

2. Just the dress part of the dress.
3. Outline of open mouth. (animal)
4. Extends out.
5. More like a turtle.

2'15''   That's all I see.

Card II   12''   1. That could be two hands with gloves on.

1. Hands with red gloves.

		Performance	Inquiry

		2. And a monkey's face there.	
		3. Icicles hanging down there. (v v or red).	3. The way it's shaped.
		4. Could be a little mouse there with a little collar on. (S)	4. Fat one.
	1'32''	5. Could be two animals fighting. (P)	5. Bears
Card III	4''	1. Arm and that's an arm.	1. People's arms.
		2. Could be two people.	2. They're bending over.
		3. That might be a skull of something. (lower D)	3. Lighter black.
	50''	4. That could be a girl falling.	4. (outer red)
Card IV	10''	1. Looks like a big giant sitting on a	
		2. stump. (laughs)	
		3. Looks like some kind of a weird face	(lower half of D)
	6''	from here down (D).	3. Animal's face.
Card V	5''	1. Looks like an alligator's head.	1. Looks like it may be in water and dipping head for a drink.
		2. Looks like some kind of a bug with big wings.	2. In the air. Q. Flying.
		3. That could be some kind of an ani-	(lower d)
	38''	mal's mouth.	3. Another alligator.
Card VI	12''	1. Some kind of an insect.	1. Resting on the ground.
	23''	2. Could be a torn leaf there. (W)	
Card VII	10''	1. Two faces there.	1. Could be babies. Q. Could be fighting.
		2. Rabbit's ears.	
		3. Cat's body around there. (2/3)	3. Tail
		4. Some kind of an insect down there	
	36''	(D).	
Card VIII	6''	1. Looks like two bears could be climbing up	
		2. a pine tree.	2. Shaped like a pine tree.
		3. Maybe that's a torn piece of material there.	3. Edges are frayed.
		4. That could be some kind of an insect.	4. Flying. Little like a butterfly. Wings are thin.
	45''		
Card IX	11''	1. Two funny kind of bodies. (orange)	1. People. Q. Laughing.
	73''	2. Could be a lake in a map. (green)	2. Shaped sort of like a lake.
Card X	9''	1. Could be a (P) rabbit's face. (points)	
		2. That could be the side of a mountain.	2. It just looks like that. Runs in like. (red)
		3. That looks like an octopus.	3. Have too many legs to be an octopus. Q. On land. Fighting to get back into water.
	71''	4. Maybe a dog or cat there. (inner yellow)	4. Sitting there in front of a nice hot fireside. (doesn't see fire)

At the age of ten years and seven months Marcene had the appearance of a pubescent girl and said that she was now as tall as her sister who was in the twelfth grade. While she talked and looked mature, some of her actions were less stable than in previous years. She was distractible and lacked persistence in the testing situation. This attitude was reflected in her WISC scores: Full scale, 126 I.Q.; Verbal, 131 I.Q.; and Performance, 115 I.Q. While these suggest superior ability, they also indicate some lapse in functioning as compared with previous test results.

On this occasion she gave the following Rorschach responses:

Marcene's Rorschach Responses at the Ten Year Level

		Performance	Inquiry
Card I	9''	I can almost remember these.	
		1. A woman without a head (D)	1. There's the woman there. This is her dress. Her arms. Q. Her arms are curled up.
		2. A butterfly. (Tilts the cards and head sideways.)	2. Head. Two little feelers. Q. Flying.
		3. Umm. Two bears. (D)	3. On the sides. Q. Walking along the road. Q. Front legs. (wings) Hind legs with knees bent.
	36''	That's all on there.	
Card II	4''	1. A mouse (S).	1. White part in here is the mouse. Q. A fat mouse. Q. Creeping along the ground.
		2. Monkey's head.	2. Mouth (Indian profile) and head goes back. Front part of head then all the face.
		3. Pair of hands with gloves on.	3. (upper red) Looks like they could be a woman's. Q. The way the arms are shaped. Man's are a little wider. Q. Mittens--just have the thumb.
	29''		
Card III	7''	1. Two people. Two arms.	1. They look like they are stooping over to pick something up. Their feet are down here and arms are here.
		2. Butterfly.	2. I don't know much of anything about butterflies. Just a plain butterfly.
		3. And a sea horse.	3. Hanging by its tail. Way its head is shaped.
	29''		
Card IV	2''	1. Big giant sitting on	1. Up here. Q. Its feet are big and it looks fierce.
		2. a log and	
		3. tattered leaf.	3. This part is shaped like a leaf and these are some holes in it.
	19''		
Card V	4''	1. Crocodile's head.	1. (outer d) He could be crawling along behind some bushes.
		2. Rabbit.	2. Legs, head, body. Q. Hopping, through the air.
		3. Some kind of an insect.	3. Flying. Q. Has legs, wings, and head with two little feelers.
	19''		
Card VI	7''	Umm.	
		1. Another leaf.	1. It looks like it could be a maple leaf with a lot of places torn out.
	15''	2. Fly.	2. Flying. Q. Plain ordinary house fly.
Card VII	3''	1. Two little people.	1. Head, neck and little of body. (upper 2/3) Q. Looks like they are mad at each other. Q. Their expression on their faces.
		2. Cat's tail.	2. Just the tail. (vertical projections)
		3. Rabbit's ears. Umm.	3. (Upper projection) Just the ears.

Performance	Inquiry
4. A moth. (lower D)	4. Because of its big wings. Q. Flying up to eat something. Q. After these things up here.
23''	
Card VIII 5'' 1. An evergreen tree.	1. Shape. Q. There's the bottom. It's uneven and comes out diagonally.
2. Two big bears.	2. Climbing on something.
3. Butterfly.	3. Take part of tree. Q. Big wings and small head. Q. Crawling along the ground.
27''	
Card IX 19'' 1. There is a scotty dog.	1. Just his head. (outer upper green edge)
2. Something that resembles a person's head.	2. Mouth, eyes, and big nose. (upper part of orange) Q. Boy.
42'' Humph.	
Card X 4'' 1. A rabbit.	1. Rabbit's head.
2. Two worms.	2. Grub worms. Q. Long and thin.
3. A lion.	3. Looks like a female lion. Q. Have a lot of hair on neck. Usually a male lion doesn't have much hair very high. Q. On the ground looks like they might be looking up at something.
4. Octopus.	4. Looks like he's under water going after a fish.
5. Two cliffs.	5. (red) Come out and have ragged like edges of mountain.
6. Lobsters.	6. (upper gray) Alive. Q. Seem to have claws open.
50''	

At eleven years and seven months of age Marcene had a tall, adolescent figure and acned face. She was spontaneous in an awkward teenage way. She had been menstruating for nearly a year, having started shortly after she saw the examiner the year before. Her worries at the time concerned making good marks in school and keeping up her friendships. She was also concerned about her looks. Her pimples bothered her. She liked to look nice and "today, I don't look so nice." She complained about her sisters: for example, when the older one monopolizes the phone at the time Marcene wants to use it; and when the younger one won't do what Marcene wants her to do. She thinks mother "babies" this sister and Marcene resents that.

On this occasion, Marcene gave the following Rorschach responses.

Marcene's Rorschach Responses at the Eleven Year Level

Performance	Inquiry
Card I 5'' 1. Well, the middle looks like a woman without a head.	1. Looks like if she had a head she would be fixing her hair.
2. The side things look like some kind of an animal--I don't know just what.	2. Jumping in the air. Q. Profile of two animals.
25'' That's about all.	
Card II 3'' 1. The middle white part looks like a rat.	1. From the back--tail back here. Q. Creeping along the floor.
2. Two things at the top look like gloves.	2. Plain ordinary red mittens.
3. Looks like the profile of a monkey's face.	3. Looks like he could be opening his mouth for something to eat.
I saw these same pictures in my psychology book. P.C.W.	

abrut 20 or 21

abrut 30

Marcene — 4-1-52 — 11 yrs 7 mos.

68

	Performance	Inquiry

Card III	7''	1. Looks like a couple of men with maybe	1. Looks like they are just bending over picking the balls up.
		2. bowling balls in their hands.	
		3. And upside down sea horses on sides there.	3. Looks like they are hanging by their tails.
	22''	4. Moth of some kind in the middle.	4. No particular kind.
Card IV		That's hard to figure out.	
		1. Looks like a monster of some kind	1. Like a hideous giant. Q. For one thing his feet are much much bigger than his head and the position in which he is sitting looks like he's ready to attack something.
	72''	2. sitting on a stump.	
Card V	7''	1. They look like two heads of alligators.	1. Not any particular way--two heads of alligators--that's the way I see them.
		2. And insect of some kind. Sort with antennae.	2. Right here in the middle and here are antennae. Q. Could be up in the air or could be falling. Q. Falling.
	21''		
Card VI	5''	1. Some kind of fly or something at the top.	1. Like he's trapped--something is holding him back or he could fly.
		2. At the bottom looks like a torn leaf.	2. Looks wet like it's been raining. Q. Seems to have a gloss on it.
	15''		
Card VII	10''	1. Well, it could be two little rabbits with a human face--none of these look quite human.	1. By the expression on their faces they look mad at each other and look like they are angry.
		2. Insect or something with very large wings.	2. It's hard to tell about insects--I'm not that much of an authority on them--it could be flying.
	30''		
Card VIII	6''	1. Looks like a couple of polar bears.	1. On the sides. Q. Might be standing on their hind legs.
		2. Pine tree.	2. The way it comes to a point at the top-- at the bottom it isn't perfectly shaped but there's ragged edges.
		3. Butterfly or mother or something that looks about like that.	3. For one thing it has a few different colors in it and it's shaped like a butterfly wing.
	30''		
Card IX	15''	1. Looks like maybe part of a skeleton of a human being.	1. This part here looks like armpits. Q. It seems to be standing upright like a human being.
		2. Couple of animals of some sort--maybe prehistoric animals.	2. Queer looking things--just seem to be standing and I'm looking at their profile.
	50''	That's all I think I can make out of that.	
Card X	7''	1. There's an octopus.	1. Up here. Q. Like they are fighting-- not with one another but with something.
		2. A rabbit's face.	2. Down here.
		3. Two green worms.	3. Seem to be chewing at the eyelid, of the rabbit.
		4. Two lions--looks like they are howling--or braking.	
	47''	Of course lions.	

Marcene is not without her problems, what with early pubescence and concomitant adjustment problems. Interpersonal relationships also present difficulties for her. However, there is a feeling that her intelligence and basic ego strength will stand her in good stead as she continues to develop through her adolescent years.

JOHNNY

At the age of six years and ten months Johnny was a tall, thin, shy boy attending a Catholic parochial school. He was most conforming and cooperative in the test situation, pleasant but completely lacking in spontaneity. His teacher saw him as a quiet child who never gave any trouble and was always attentive in class. He was doing average work in first grade at the time. He achieved an I.Q. of 102 on the Binet Intelligence Scale.

Johnny gave the following Rorschach responses on this occasion:

Johnny's Rorschach Responses at the Six Year Level

		Performance	Inquiry
Card I	10''	1. Two men pulling a	1. Elbows out, pulling away. Lady have her hands up (demonstrates).
	30''	2. lady away.	
Card II	4''	1. Skies (W)	1. Clouds
		2. Boat getting on fire.	2. Here (lower red).
	30''	3. Plane's getting on fire too.	3. Here (upper red).
Card III	4''	1. Two morons pulling	1. Long nose--people when they are real dumb.
		2. This ball.	2. Here, red.
	30''	3. In the back of them is fire and in front.	
Card IV	5''	1. Looks like an animal--the kind that goes on the water--an alligator. That's what I'm going to get--a baby one--'cause I'm going to keep it in	1. Foot, another foot, head (Q) He is sleeping. They look like they are dead --they don't move an inch.
	20''	a tub.	
Card V	2''	1. A bat or a butterfly.	1. A butterfly--wings--Q. He's up in the air.
	13''		
Card VI	5''	1. A bird trying to get out of the skies. (clouds)	
		2. Looks like fire coming out of the water.	2. Water shooting up here.
Card VII	4''	1. Looks like two animals--two bunnies, and they are looking down to see	1. Ears, face.
		2. This little building up in the	
		3. Skies (clouds).	3. Skies all around the house.
Card VIII	2''	1. Looks like skies all over the world.	1. Clouds here and here and here.
		2. Looks like a skeleton's bone.	2. In here.
	10''		a. Fire down here.
Card IX	2''	1. Two angels fighting in the sky or	1. Two witches. This is the moon.
	24''	two witches fighting over the moon.	
Card X	3''	1. (Sighs) Crabs in the water.	1. He has tweezers. (side blue)
	14''	2. Bones on top. (upper D)	2. Peoples

When seen the following year, at the age of seven years and ten months, Johnny was timid, almost to the point of being withdrawn. However, he was overtly pleasant and cooperative. It was about this time that a baby brother, the youngest in the family of seven, was born. The second grade teacher thought he was falling behind in his work--tried hard but seemed to be preoccupied. When asked to draw a man, he produced the accompanying stick figure.

His Rorschach responses at this time were as follows:

Johnny's Rorschach Responses at the Seven Year Level

		Performance	Inquiry
Card I	8" 13"	1. Looks like a goat.	1. Horns, ears, eyes, mouth, nose, beard --a face.
Card II	20"	I don't know. (Encouraged) 1. Two bears.	1. I don't know--ears, mouth, head, paws and that's just the same as the other one.
Card III	6" 7"	1. Two men.	1. Stooping down holding something. a. Lightning around it. Q. The red.
Card IV	13" 14"	1. A giant.	1. Here's his feet and here's his club. Two hands and head. He's the other (turns his back) way.
Card V	4" 6"	1. A butterfly.	1. Two horns, head, wings and here's two feet. Q. Up in the air.
Card VI	7"	1. Hill. W	1. And here's the big hill. a. Clouds. Q. The black road going up to it.
Card VII	7" 8"	1. Lightning.	1. Black.
Card VIII	10" 11"	1. Clouds	1. When they go by they are all apart. a. Looks like two frogs--one on this one and one on this side. Q. Up on the (b) rock.
Card IX	8" 9"	1. Water. (D)	1. When it runs down to the creek--all this.
Card X	8" 10"	1. Two birds (red).	1. Here and here. a. These look like spiders. Here's their tail, head, feet. b. Here's two canaries.

At eight years and ten months of age, Johnny was a tall, smiling boy who had difficulty in understanding instructions but appeared to be trying. On the Monroe Diagnostic Reading Examination, he was a year below his third grade placement in reading and spelling. His arithmetic was up to grade, despite the fact that he volunteered his dislike of that subject. His third grade teacher saw him as a nice, quiet, polite boy who seemed to be doing average work in school. He was never a discipline problem.

At this time Johnny gave the following Rorschach responses:

Johnny's Rorschach Responses at the Eight Year Level

		Performance	Inquiry
Card I	5"	1. Looks like a butterfly. 2. Two men like that. (Holds hands out.)	1. W 2. Had coats going back (a cape).

Johnny, 11-25-47   7 yrs 10 mos   ①

Performance	Inquiry

		3. A woman--that is her dress. Her hands are up but she doesn't have no head.	3. (Center D)
	37"		
Card II	4"	1. Cat. See here's his mouth and that looks like two glassy eyes and this is the cheek.	1. Not no more--not a cat.
		2. Looks like two stones.	2. (denies)
		3. Looks like bear without no head. Holding two of them like that. (stretches hands out)	3. Noses here. Ears up like this (holds hands up).
	41"		a. They look like hens. (upper red)
Card III	2"	1. Looks like two men like this and	1. Head, nose and there there's things they're picking up.
		2. this is a bow tie.	2. Red bow tie.
		3. This is water coming down into stream	3. (inner grey)
		4. Looks like these two things are bowling things.	4. Bowling things to throw.
Card IV	5"	1. Looks like two legs right here.	1. A big giant--no just his leg.
		2. Looks like a big club right	2. His club. Q. Big needle.
		3. Looks like a little bird right	3. Wee, wee, little canary.
	37"	there. (S)	
Card V	3"	1. Looks like a bat.	1. Flying up in the air--legs here.
		2. This part right here looks like tweezers.	
		3. Looks like there are legs of sheep.	
		4. This leg looks like real skinny	
	40"	bird's leg.	
Card VI	10"	1. Looks like horse's head without this on it.	
		2. This looks like Indian head with feet.	2. (Side D)
		3. Looks like little waterfall coming	3. (Inner D)
	37"	together.	
Card VII	3"	1. Two sheep's heads with ears straight up.	
		2. This looks like a lion. Here's his	
	25"	ears--here's two cheeks.	
Card VIII	4"	1. Here's a lion up here and lion up here.	1. Four legs and thin.
		2. This looks like a little bunch of teeth. (S)	2. Lion's teeth.
		3. A rock there. Form looks like a rock. (Lower D)	3. Shape.
		4. This looks like a big, big, spider.	4. Lots of legs on top of it.
	31"	(upper grey)	
Card IX	5"	1. Here's reindeer's horns--two of them.	1. Just horns.
		2. Here's a man scrubbing his teeth (green). Two of them.	
		3. This looks like a real big rock.	3. (red)
			a. I see a little alligator snake like. (Inner D)
	30"		

	Performance	Inquiry

		Performance	Inquiry
Card X	3''	1. Two spiders.	1. Flying. You know sometimes spiders can fly.
			a. Sheep jumping (green).
			b. Big funny animal like that two horns; big eyes, two long parts of a tail. (green)
		2. Little doggie jumping. (brown)	
		3. Two animals kissing each other. (blue)	
	30''	4. These two look like real funny bugs, brown.	

At nine years and ten months of age Johnny was more friendly and timidly outgoing than on previous occasions. He was obviously pleased to see the examiner and was quietly spontaneous as he was being tested. On the Mare and Foal item of the Grace Arthur Performance test, he expressed his liking for it, adding, "I like horses, that's why." He grew weary on the last items but made no verbal protest. He achieved a P.Q. of 97, confirming the average intellectual rating found on the Binet.

Johnny gave the following Rorschach responses on this occasion:

Johnny's Rorschach Responses at the Nine Year Level

		Performance	Inquiry
Card I		Doesn't look like	
	56''	1. I just thought these are two witches.	1. Here are capes and that there--they are pulling somebody up.
	60''	2. And that was somebody.	2. Woman.
Card II	17''	1. Looks like two bears with noses together and they are bouncing	1. I don't know.
	26''	something on their noses.	
Card III	13''	1. Two men trying to pick up a	
		2. pot or something	
	26''	3. And there is a bow in the middle.	3. Goes on like a neck tie.
Card IV	2''	1. Looks like a big giant's boots.	1. Going after somebody.
		2. With his club.	
	12''	1. (Cont.) This is his head and hands.	
Card V	2''	1. Looks like a bat flying in the air.	
	5''		
Card VI		Doesn't look like anything. (Encouraged) Doesn't make me see	
	60''	a thing. I can't see a thing.	
Card VII	13''	1. Looks like two lambs standing on	1. Faces make me think of lambs.
	30''	something.	a. I thought it was a cloud.
Card VIII	3''	1. Two bears climbing	
	5''	2. a mountain.	
Card IX		(Laughs)	
	28''	1. This witch is here and this witch	a. Smoke is coming up and only shows their face. Red and Green smoke.
	36''	is here.	
Card X	2''	1. Two spiders and	
	6''	2. Some birds and things.	2. (Yellow) I don't know.

At ten years and ten months of age Johnny was a tall, thin, round-faced boy, very polite and pleasant. He enjoyed the test situation in his quiet way and was reluctant to terminate. His answers to questions and infrequent spontaneous remarks were given in a soft voice. On the WISC he achieved an average rating of 100 on Full scale, with performance slightly higher than verbal.

His Rorschach responses at this time were as follows:

Johnny's Rorschach Responses at the Ten Year Level

	Performance	Inquiry

Card I   9"
1. Two men up here like wings taking
2. somebody up--she has no head.

3. Looks like a cat sorta--a face of a cat.
  24"

Inquiry:
1. One foot and part of their dressing.
2. Of lady. Her legs, dress up here and two hands handing up there. Q. Dead.
3. Eyes, mouth, nose, his head. But I don't know what these would be (upper d).

Card II   5"
1. Two bears putting their noses together, with
2. bouncing balls.
  25"

Inquiry:
1. Noses and ears come down here and have paws as if they are begging.
2. Here are balls they are bouncing or juggling. Q. Pink. Q. Up in air.

Card III   3"
1. Two men with

2. a bow in the middle and each is holding
3. a pot and
4. something is falling down.
  22"

Inquiry:
1. Nose and it dents in and eyes and mouth--bending over.
2. Pink bow tie.

3. Two pots.
4. Looks like some kind of pink paint falling down.

Card IV   3"
1. Looks like a giant.

  10"   2. With a club in the middle.

Inquiry:
1. Here's hands, head. Q. Looks like he's in midair--there's on ground there.
2. Looks like he has it hidden behind him.

Card V   1"
1. Looks like a bat.
2. And a butterfly. When I turned it
  15"   upside down.

Inquiry:
1. Flying somewhere.
2. Sitting on something.

Card VI
(Slants) I can't figure anything out of the other one.
1. Looks like two men putting their
  50"   heads together with a big nose.

Inquiry:
1. Just the heads, big nose. Q. This is

Card VII   3"
1. Looks like two lambs dancing on a
  19"   2. Cloud

Inquiry:
1. Ears, eyes and nose gets real dark.
2. Gray and furry shaped.

Card VIII   4"
1. Looks like two bears climbing.
2. Up a mountain.
3. Looks like a man there with big
  18"   ears hanging down   WS

Inquiry:
3. Mouth (S) Nose (S) and here's his beard (grey).

Card IX   6"
1. Looks like a pink cloud and
2. carrots--two carrots.

  14"

Inquiry:
1. Here.
2. Orange and
a. Looks like a person. Q. Nose looks like witch. Has a pointed thing--big nose--just appearing in the cloud.

Card X   3"
1. Looks like two spiders and
2. two birds.

3. Pair of plowers (pliers).

Inquiry:
1. Spiders, legs. Q. Climbing somewhere.
2. (Brown) Baby robin. Q. Sorta brown and awful small.
3. Right here (green).

Performance	Inquiry
4. Pink cloud.	4. Sometimes at dawn it gets pink and all different shades.
	a. Here's dogs--looks like (yellow) sitting somewhere.
30"	

Johnny, at eleven years and ten months of age, was a tall, thin, soft-spoken boy, healthy in appearance and casually but neatly dressed. Despite his usual timid manner, it was obvious that he enjoyed the testing period and was eager to please the examiner. There was some spontaneity and he answered quickly, fully. He had decided he would like to be a farmer when he grew up. His worries included his fear of getting into trouble at school if he did not have his homework, concern about the two younger children when they went to play with neighbors' children and didn't tell the family, and disappointment when he did not have enough money to buy presents for his parents. He got angry when he heard the high school boys swearing or when he saw big kids fighting the little ones, but, "I just hold my fist and try not to do anything." He admitted that he sometimes hit his older sister when she hit him hard and meant it.

Following are the Rorschach responses which he gave at this time:

Johnny's Rorschach Responses at the Eleven Year Level

		Performance	Inquiry
Card I		Well.	
	4"	1. I see two giants like with wings-- holding	1. Here and here.
		2. a lady without no head.	2. She looks like she's straight. Here's her feet.
		3. Looks like a lamb and a cat. (Ad)	3. More like a cat but the way the ears go looks like a lamb. Q. Real mean and vicious thing like on Halloween.
	20"		
Card II	4"	1. Looks like two bears have	1. Here's ears and there's feet there and there's their paws--I mean the nose. Q. Looks like they are standing up like.
		2. a ball on their head.	2. Sorta like bouncing a ball on their head. A Something red that they are bouncing--not shaped too much like a ball.
	20"		
Card III	4"	1. Looks like there's a bow tie in the middle and	1. Red
		2. two men picking up	2. Two men holding a pot.
	14"	3. a pot.	
Card IV	3"	1. Looks like a giant with	1. Looks like he's walking sorta. Q. Looks like he might be holding the club.
		2. a real big club.	
	14"	1. (cont.) a silhouette of him.	
Card V	2"	1. Looks like a bat and a butterfly.	1. More like a butterfly. Q. Here's antennae, wings. Q. Looks like he's flying.
	14"		
Card VI	34"	(Shades his eyes) I can't figure anything out of that.	
		1. Looks like an Indian thing--feathers on his head--that's all I can see.	1. Just the feathers.
	50"		a. This might be a map of some sort.

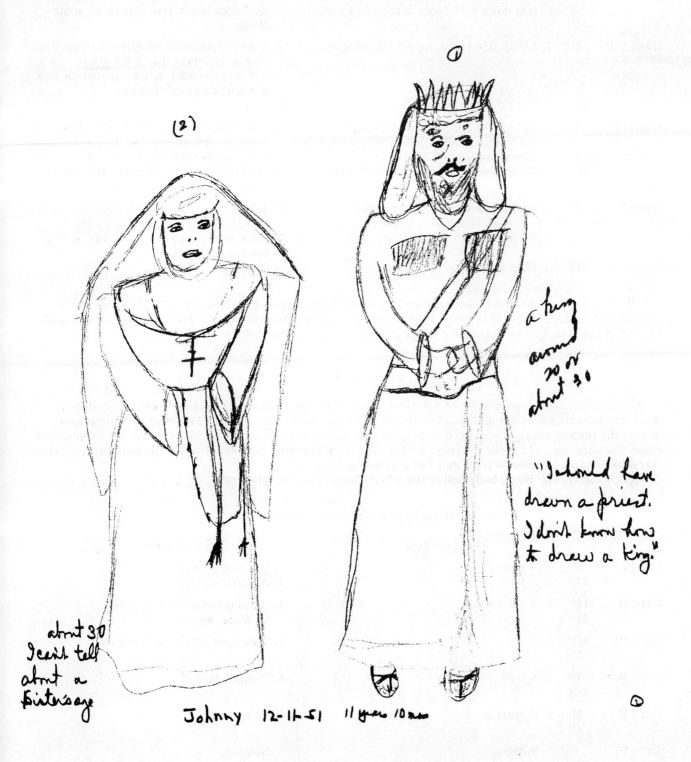

(2)

(1)

a king
around
20 or
about 30

"I should have
drawn a priest.
I don't know how
to draw a king."

about 30
I can't tell
about a
Sister's age

Johnny 12-14-51 11 years 10 mo

Performance			Inquiry
Card VII	4''	1. Looks like two ladies with hair up and putting hands opposite way, sitting down with faces turned to each other.	1. Hair sticking to each other, facing each other and hands the other way. Q. Looks sorta like a rock or something.
	21''		
Card VIII	6''	1. Looks like two animals climbing up.	1. Two red animals climbing up some of like a mountain that's far apart. He's not furry enough to be a mountain lion but sorta shaped that way.
	20''	2. the side of the mountain	
Card IX	6''	1. Looks like two witches looking at each other--sitting down with long noses and	1. Noses are shaped like a tree stem. (Orange and green) Q. Looks sorta like clouds they are sitting on.
	20''	2. Under them looks like there's fire.	2. Smoke's coming out here up between them.
Card X	4''	1. Looks like there's two crabs.	1. Looks like a female because they have one pincher bigger than the other.
		2. And a . . . two yellow dogs.	2. Have feet back here sorta like laying but are sitting up.
	27''	That's all.	

Johnny's mother and father, both dynamic personalities, expressed their concern about the boy's lack of aggression, saying that none of the other six children were at all like him. He was inordinately fond of animals and flowers and took complete care of their large lawn and flower beds.

GERTIE

At six years and seven months of age Gertie was a shy little flaxen-haired girl, with long pigtails down her back and dressed in a peasant blouse and navy skirt. She wispered most of her comments during the testing session, appeared to be apprehensive, but was seemingly cooperative--at least on the Binet Examination. Here she achieved an I.Q. of 111, suggesting high average intellectual ability. The Rorschach cards seemed to pose more of a problem for her.

Following are the Rorschach responses which Gertie gave at this time:

Gertie's Rorschach Responses at the Six Year Level

Performance			Inquiry
Card I	9''	1. A butterfly.	1. (No response.)
	25''	2. A face.	2. Animal--eyes.
Card II	11''	1. A butterfly.	1. (Denies butterfly.) A face. Q. Nose, eyes.
	25''		
Card III	10''	1. Face.	1. Two eyes (red). Q. Animals.
	25''		
Card IV	23''	1. A tree.	1. Trunk--leaves.
	24''		
Card V	2''	1. Butterfly.	1. Has wings.
	4''		
Card VI		Nothing.	Nothing.
Card VII	5''	1. Necklace.	1. A design necklace.
	10''		

	Performance	Inquiry
Card VIII	(Looks away from card.) Nothing.	Nothing.
Card IX	Nothing.	Nothing.
Card X	7'' 1. Design.	1. A paint design.
	9''	

Gertie at seven was the same physically attractive, exquisitely dressed little blond girl of the previous year. She was still very shy. Her second grade teacher saw her as average in all respects. While unable to make any spontaneous remarks, she was able to show pleasure on seeing the examiner and appeared to be cooperative. She made the accompanying drawing of a man--without facial features and somewhat distorted as to size of legs.

Her responses to the Rorschach cards at this time were as follows:

Gertie's Rorschach Responses at the Seven Year Level

		Performance	Inquiry
Card I	7''	1. Two men.	1. Cape on them, two feet and arms, the feather to his hat. Q. On that thing.
	20''		
Card II	1''	1. A face.	1. Two eyes (upper red), mouth (lower red), rest of face over here. Q. Cheeks. S is part but can't tell what. Q. A cat.
	5''		
Card III	5''	1. Two men and a	1. Leg, head, body, arms. Q. Inside.
	13''	2. Bow.	2. Red bow.
Card IV	8''	1. Great big feet.	1. (Lower part of outer D). A clown. Just see the feet.
	14''		
Card V	1''	1. A bat.	1. Two wings, feet, feelers. Q. In the air.
	7''		
Card VI	7''	1. A bug.	1. Head, two wings. Q. In the air. (Upper D).
	10''		
Card VII	3''	1. Two faces.	1. Upper third (without upper d). Q. A dog. Ears, tail and feet. Q. On a rock.
	9''		
Card VIII	8''	1. Two animals and a	1. He's walking up there.
		2. Tree.	2. Christmas tree--Christmas trees come out like that.
	12''		
Card IX	4''	1. A design.	1. All different colors on it.
	10''		
Card X	6''	1. Two bugs.	1. (Upper D). Climbing.
	12''	2. A design.	2. All different colors.

Gertie's blondness and healthy appearance at the age of eight years and eight months seemed to emphasize her German heritage. She remembered the examiner with evident pleasure, and was pleasant and cooperative in the test situation, despite an obvious tenseness. Her score on the Monroe Diagnostic Reading Examination at this time indicated that her reading and spelling achievement was above the average third grade expectation. Arithmetic was average. The third grade teacher was unable to individualize her--just one of the average, as was the situation the year before.

Gertie gave the following responses to the Rorschach cards at this time:

Gertie 2-3-48

7 yrs 7 month

Gertie's Rorschach Responses at the Eight Year Level

		Performance	Inquiry
Card I	12''	1. This could be two men.	1. There and there. Cape on them there. Their feet, head up here.
	16''	2. With a design in the middle.	2. Half a mouse, two ears.
Card II	10'' 36''	1. Looks like two lamb heads here.	1. Q. Out in the field.
Card III	5''	1. Here's two men and	1. & 3. Looks like they are picking up dishes.
		2. Here's a bow tie.	2. Put up on your neck.
	18''	3. Two dishes.	
Card IV	11'' 13''	1. Skin of an animal.	1. Feet, tail. Q. Fur. Q. Fuzzy and all that.
Card V	1'' 2''	1. A bat.	1. Wings, legs. Q. Up in the air. Q. Flying.
Card VI	10'' 22''	1. This looks like a bird up here.	1. Wings, head. Standing on a rock.
Card VII	6'' 13''	1. Two dogs or something standing on a rock.	
Card VIII	4''	1. Two tigers climbing up	
	8''	2. a tree.	2. A Christmas tree.
Card IX	5'' 6''	1. Design.	1. Nothing in it. (Not color).
Card X	4''	1. These two look like a spiders.	1. Out on the ground. (Brown.)
		2. And these are two bugs.	
	26''	3. Here's a bone (upper D).	

On the occasion of the fourth contact with Gertie, when she was nine and a half years old, she was a well built healthy-looking girl, whose blond, silky hair and blond eyelashes and eyebrows were her prominent facial features. She lacked spontaneity, but did not seem particularly shy--more constricted than shy. She watched the examiner's face for clues to her performance on the Grace Arthur Test, where she achieved the same high average rating as on the Binet at six years of age.

Her Rorschach responses at this time were as follows:

Gertie's Rorschach Responses at the Nine Year Level

		Performance	Inquiry
Card I	3'' 25''	1. I see two men hanging onto something.	1. A pole, head, cape.
Card II	3'' 18''	1. Looks like elephant heads.	1. Tell by their trunks. Q. Looks like they are sitting up.
Card III	3''	1. Here looks like two men.	1. & 3. They look like they are stooping down to get some water.
		2. Looks like a tie.	2. Bow tie.
	13''	3. This looks like two buckets.	
Card IV	6'' 32''	1. These look like feet. This looks like a post. This looks like two animals, leaning against holding their tails up.	1. Of animals that are leaning. (Heads?) (Upper d).

81

		Performance		Inquiry

Card V	1" 10"	1. Looks like a bat.	1. He looks like he's flying. Q. Has two feelers and little leg.
Card VI	8" 14"	1. These look like two people.	1. Head, arms. Looks like they are walking.
Card VII	3" 8"	1. Looks like two bunnies sitting on a rock.	
Card VIII	3" 14"	1. These look like two tigers or something trying to climb a tree. 2. These look like mountains (D).	1. Cause they are red. Branches come down. 2. Mountains are all the colors.
Card IX	5" 20"	1. These look like two heads (red). 2. These look like men (green). 3. These look like crabs (orange).	1. People. 2. Looks like he's sitting down. Hand. Knee. 3. They have sharp legs--the yellow and orange.
Card X	2" 34"	1. This is a spider. 2. This looks like a bunny face (green). 3. And worms--two worms. 4. People with heads. 5. And a dog--two dogs. That's all.	1. Looks like they are crawling. 3. Green. 4. They look like they are walking. 5. Looks like they are barking.

At ten and a half years of age Gertie was soft-spoken and seemingly shy, but she was alert and decisive in her replies on the WISC. Although lacking in spontaneity, it was obvious that she enjoyed the test and was reluctant to leave at the end of the hour. Here again she achieved a high average full scale rating, with the performance I.Q. 113 and verbal at 100. This discrepancy in favor of the performance may be related to her expressed dislike of school. She preferred to do things around the house, where she was helpful to mother, who worked outside the home. She also enjoyed rough games like football, and preferred to play with boys.

She gave the following Rorschach responses at this time:

Gertie's Rorschach Responses at the Ten Year Level

		Performance	Inquiry

Card I	9" 35"	1. I see two men here. (points). 2. Some kind of animal in the middle.	1. Head, feet come in here and cape on them. Q. Looks like they are fighting over something. 2. Looks like a little baby calf--horns up there--tail down.
Card II	9" 29"	1. This looks like an elephant here, there (points). 2. These look like funny heads (red).	1. Ears, trunk going up there and front paws. Q. Doing a trick in the circus. 2. Looks like faces with funny hairdos, sticking their tongues out at each other. Q. Women.
Card III	9" 27"	1. These look like two people with a 2. Bow in the middle. 3. With a design on the wall (outer red).	1. Face, body and here is legs. Men. Q. Looks like they are holding a a. pot or something. 2. Looks like a bow tie. 3. It wouldn't look like anything special.
Card IV	10" 16"	1. Looks like a bear rug real big here and little here.	1. Big feet and tail. Q. It's fur.

82

		Performance	Inquiry

		Performance	Inquiry
Card V	1''· 6''	1. Looks like a bat.	1. Horns, feet, legs and here's his wings. Q. Up in the air. Q. Flying.
Card VI	5'' 27''	1. This looks like a butterfly up here... with a big tail. (smiles).	1. Flying.
Card VII	3'' 7''	1. These look like two bunnies looking at each other on 2. Rocks.	1. Head, face, and little tail and feet standing on the end 2. Of the rock.
Card VIII	3'' 19''	1. This looks like a tree. 2. Looks like a bear or tiger. 3. This looks like a big rock.	1. Pine tree. Q. Comes out like a pine tree would. 2. Looks like they are crawling into the tree. 3. It could be two rocks with a big one in the background and some on in front. Q. Out in the country.
Card IX	5'' 22''	1. These look like crabs. (orange). 2. This looks like a dog with his hand paw itching his ears. (green).	1. Arms out here. Q. Crabs are orange in color. 2. Body with back leg coming up and here's his arm.
Card X	3'' 64''	1. These look like crabs (blue). 2. These look like dogs stretching (yellow). 3. These look like two people fighting. 4. This looks like a bow (blue). 5. This looks like a bunny face and 6. This looks like snakes. 7. This looks like a side of cliffs, with a face line in them.	1. His feet out here. 2. Some dogs are yellow. 3. Looks like dogs--I meant to say dogs-- legs, head, mouth. 4. It's a blue bow. 5. Ears and face. 6. I don't know. Green snakes. 7. Head and nose, neck and body. Q. Looks something like horses. Q. Come straight down.

At eleven and a half Gertie had blossomed into a beautiful blond, almost adolescent girl, soft-spoken and quiet but most cooperative, answering all questions fully and promptly, with a few additional spontaneous remarks. Her worries at this time were about her school marks and whether she was going to get through school. She was concerned about wars and things like that. She also worried when her mother or other family members failed to come home on time--afraid something had happened to them. She got angry when she couldn't have her way, got especially mad at her mother, but did nothing about it except "go off by myself and sit." Gertie had been told about menstruation and was not concerned about it. She made the accompanying human figure drawings.

Gertie gave the following Rorschach responses on this occasion:

Gertie's Rorschach Responses at the Eleven Year Level

		Performance	Inquiry
Card I	6'' 22''	1. Looks like two men standing on something. W That's about all.	1. These look like two men here. Q. Looks like something on a boat that you steer with. Q. Part of their coat swinging out. Q. In the breeze.
Card II	7'' 12''	1. Two elephants with their trunks together. W	1. Looks like two circus elephants. Q. Looks like they are doing a trick.
Card III	5''	1. Looks like two men standing there with	1. Looks like waiters. Q. Have tight fitting clothes. Q. Bending over. (D is not part.)

about as
old as I am

M#D

about in
Third grad

Gertie 1-22-52 11 yrs 7 months

84

		Performance	Inquiry

		Performance	Inquiry
		2. a bow tie in the middle.	2. Looks like one a man would put around his neck.
	12''		
Card IV	8''	1. Looks something like a fur rug or something--the skin.	1. Fur side. W
	18''		
Card V	5''	1. Looks like a bat. W	1. Flying.
	7''		
Card VI	10''	1. This looks something like a bird (upper D). Bottom just looks like something in back of it.	1. Looks like he's standing on something in the background. Q. Looks like a rock. Q. That's usually about what a bird stands on.
	31''		
Card VII	3''	1. This looks like two rabbits on a stone.	2. W. Standing on a stone.
	10''		
Card VIII	3''	1. Looks like two bears trying to get up in a tree. W	a. A Christmas tree. 1. Q. That looks just like a rock at the bottom. Q. Sometimes sees rocks around trees.
	10''		
Card IX	10''	1. This looks like a crab--these two (orange). 2. These look something like a dog scratching behind his ear (green).	
	25''		
Card X	9''	1. These look like two crayfish (blue). 2. These look like two rocks in the formation of a face (pink). 3. This looks like a bow (inner blue). 4. This looks like a rabbit face. 5. Two worms beside it. 6. These look like crayfish--little ones. (brown).	2. Looks like a baby. 3. Bow you put in your hair. 5. Green worms. 6. Baby ones. Q.

Gertie's family were more academically ambitious for her than she was for herself. She had already decided that college was not for her. All she hoped to do was squeeze through high school and then get married and have a home of her own.

BERNARD

Bernard, at six years and eight months of age, was a stockily built little Jewish boy, pleasant and confident in manner. His first grade teacher thought of him as good in numbers and doing satisfactory work in reading. On the Binet examination at this time he based at year VI and again at year VIII, failing the diamond and the repetition of digits at year VII. His highest success was Picture Absurdities on year X. The resulting I.Q. of 123 indicated slightly superior intellectual ability. In light of subsequent academic achievement, one wonders how much the mother's pre-school coaching and obvious academic ambitions for her only son could have influenced his attitude toward school.

Bernard's Rorschach responses on this occasion were as follows:

Bernard's Rorschach Responses at the Six Year Level

		Performance	Inquiry
Card I	25''	That one's a hard one. 1. A lady in back of it and a	1. This is the lady--can't see her head. Q. This part right here (rubs hand over chest and abdomen).

		Performance	Inquiry

<table>
<tr><td></td><td>60"</td><td>Fence right here where the gate opens. W</td><td>All of it is fence and the lady is in back of the gate.</td></tr>
<tr><td>Card II</td><td>3"</td><td>1. Two elephants with the trunks together. See? Up here it doesn't look like much of anything. (Red).</td><td>1. They're sitting down.</td></tr>
<tr><td></td><td>32"</td><td>2. Down here it looks like the sun.
3. and a butterfly.</td><td>2. Round - red.</td></tr>
<tr><td>Card III</td><td>6"</td><td>1. Two horses right here.</td><td>1. Look like horses, but one foot is not like the other one.</td></tr>
<tr><td></td><td>30"</td><td>2. This looks like fire or blood.
3. Here it looks like a bow tie.</td><td>2. Blood, because it is dripping.
3. Red one.</td></tr>
<tr><td>Card IV</td><td>3"</td><td>1. Looks like a big man sitting on something. Here's his two feet, head, arms and he's sitting on</td><td>1. Great big fat man.</td></tr>
<tr><td></td><td>18"</td><td>something.</td><td></td></tr>
<tr><td>Card V</td><td>2"</td><td>1. A butterfly.</td><td>1. That is all--just a butterfly--has things up here--cause butterfly have things up here.</td></tr>
<tr><td></td><td>6"</td><td></td><td></td></tr>
<tr><td>Card VI</td><td>5"</td><td>1. Looks like some kind of fly up here.
2. And down here (slanting) looks like a big butterfly, I think.</td><td>1. Has wings and a little whiskers.
2. I don't know what it is. (You said "big butterfly"). Butterfly doesn't have things sticking out.</td></tr>
<tr><td></td><td>16"</td><td></td><td></td></tr>
<tr><td>Card VII</td><td>20"</td><td>Don't look like nothing to me but I'll find out.</td><td></td></tr>
<tr><td></td><td>25"</td><td>1. Looks like two dogs standing on something right here.</td><td>1. Tail, feet are behind this, head and one ear.</td></tr>
<tr><td>Card VIII</td><td>7"</td><td>1. Looks like two mouses here and
2. right in here looks like bones.
3. Down here looks like fires.</td><td>1. Looks just like a mouse.
2. A skeleton. Q. Of a reindeer.
3. Color of fire.
  a. Here is a red and orange butterfly.</td></tr>
<tr><td></td><td>25"</td><td></td><td></td></tr>
<tr><td>Card IX</td><td>4"</td><td>1. Looks like the horns of a reindeer.
2. Down here looks like some more horns (green).
3. Just looks like red that they are</td><td>1. Just the horns and
2. These are horns too.

3. Looks like a lot of heads up on a pole.</td></tr>
<tr><td></td><td>23"</td><td>sitting on.</td><td>Q. All different animals.</td></tr>
<tr><td>Card X</td><td>6"</td><td>1. This looks like a big spider.
2. This looks like a head and
3. two snakes
4. This just looks like round heads.</td><td>1. Have things sticking out.
2. Rabbit's head and two snakes.
3. holding it. Q. Just snakes.
4. Dog's head and they are holding this thing in their mouth.</td></tr>
<tr><td></td><td></td><td>5. and this looks like right in your stomach (rubs stomach), your bones,</td><td>5. Something in a man's or woman's body.</td></tr>
<tr><td></td><td>29"</td><td>6. and this looks like bones.</td><td>(Just looks like this one.)</td></tr>
</table>

At seven years and eight months of age Bernard greeted the examiner with enthusiasm but was obviously ill-at-ease when asked to draw. He was apologetic about the accompanying figure of a man which he produced. The second grade teacher thought of him as an out-going little fellow who was slightly advanced in his school achievement. She felt, however, that his mother was putting undue pressure on him academically.

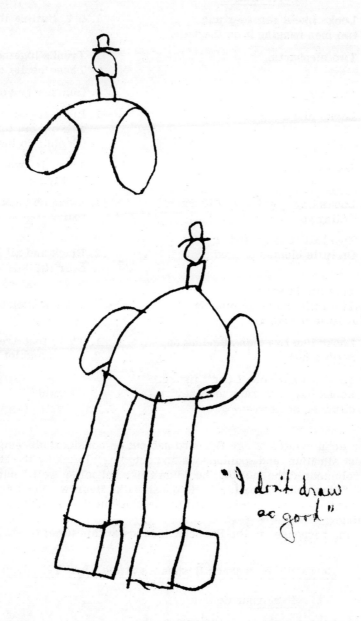

"I don't draw
as good"

Bernard 7-19-47   7yrs 8mos

87

He gave the following Rorschach responses at this time:

Bernard's Rorschach Responses at the Seven Year Level

		Performance	Inquiry
Card I	5''	1. Looks like a reindeer and	1. & 2. Nailing it to the wall.
	16''	2. two men hanging it on the wall.	
Card II	2''	1. Two elephants.	1. Trunks together and standing there.
	14''		These really do look like elephants.
Card III	3''	1. Two men.	1. (Runs finger over.) Q. Like skeletons.
Card IV	4''	1. Looks like a big gorilla.	1. Big feet--sitting on
			a. a big pin things.
	7''		1. (Contd.) So big and has a small head.
Card V	3''	1. Skeleton of an eagle.	1. An eagle, wings--a butterfly.
	7''		Q. Flying.
Card VI	3''	1. Looks like a wolf--a wolf that's	1. Lying on back. Has these things and
	7''	sitting up.	that.
Card VII	3''	1. Two little dogs standing	
		2. On little clumps of mud.	2. Black and all like that (rubs finger
	8''		over it).
Card VIII	6''	This one is hard.	
		1. Two little rats climbing up	a. Or a skeleton. Right there.
	10''	2. A little mountain.	
Card IX	9''	1. Looks like two men standing on	1. Their feet are down here.
	11''	2. A little hill.	2. Green and lot of grass.
Card X		This is a hard one I can't figure.	
	20''	1. Looks like two crabs and they're	(Brown)
	29''	climbing on something.	

At eight years and eight months of age Bernard had put on considerable weight. He was pleasant and cooperative in the test situation, and spontaneous and outgoing. In taking the Monroe Diagnostic Reading Examination he volunteered the fact that he "didn't like school so well," but now that he was going to Hebrew school, he "likes this one better." He doesn't like Hebrew school at all. On the MDRE he achieved slightly below the average for his third grade placement in reading and arithmetic, and fell a grade below in spelling.

He gave the following responses to the Rorschach cards at this time:

Bernard's Rorschach Responses at the Eight Year Level

		Performance	Inquiry
Card I	10''	Are there right or wrong answers?	
		1. Two guys and have	1. Hats, faces, legs.
		2. One those big things they were hunting	2. These two wings are part of the thing
	25''	and caught it.	they caught. They are holding onto it.
Card II	5''	1. Looks like a bear without a head or	1. Have red stuff on them.
		an ape. Two apes holding their hands	a. Two little things flying.
	20''	up together.	Q. Looks like roosters.
Card III	5''	1. Two men holding something and there's	a. Bones.
		a	
	15''	2. Bow tie in there.	2. Red.

88

		Performance		Inquiry

Card IV	4"	1. A big ape sitting on		Q. Big feet.
	11"	2. A stool.		
Card V	4"	1. That looks like a butterfly.		1. Two things a butterfly has. Wings and two other things on a butterfly. Flying, because wings are out.
	10"			
Card VI		1. That looks like a wolf laying down		1. Doesn't show face. Ears. Two paws out and body.
	10"	on his back.		
Card VII	3"	1. This one looks like two dogs with		1. Ears are together.
	10"	ears up there.		a. Dirt--looks like they are holding it.
Card VIII	5"	1. That one looks like these two red		a. Looks like some bones.
	13"	bugs climbing up this.		
Card IX	14"	1. That looks like two faces of a bear		1. Two bears (red). Looks like on top crawling down if you hold it this way.
	25"	down here.		
Card X		1. Two spiders and		1. Skinny.
		2. All these buts climbing up these		
	15"	things.		

During the year following the previous contact Bernard's family moved to a section of the city in which the majority of the Jewish population was centered, and the boy at nine years and eight months of age was attending a school where the average I.Q. was considerably higher than the first school he attended. He greeted the examiner with a broad, friendly smile and stated that he liked his new home and school very much. His obesity was even more evident than the year before--his hips were especially large. He enjoyed the Grace Arthur Performance Test and achieved the very superior rating of 141.

His responses to the Rorschach cards at this time were as follows:

Bernard's Rorschach Responses at the Nine Year Level

		Performance	Inquiry

Card I	15"	(Slants slightly.)	
		1. Looks like two people holding onto a	
		2. Skeleton or something.	
		1. (Contd.) Looks like it has wings on it. Looks like it has a hat.	
		2. (Contd.) Skeleton has sort of antlers on its head. Looks like the thing they are holding doesn't have a head.	
	87"		
Card II	10"	1. Looks like two people with red heads putting their hands together. Then here's their mouths and their head. Looks like there's red stuff on them-- looks like they	1. Sitting on fire beneath them.
		1. (Contd.) are wearing something and and their necks are white.	a. Deerskin on the furry side.
	62"		
Card III	10"	1. Looks like two things holding something and	1. People.
		2. Looks like a bow tie there.	2. Red one.
		3. That looks like a hatchet (upper red).	3. Handle and this.
		1. (Contd.) Looks like they are peeling the skin off of something and their	
	56"	body looks like it's cut in half.	

Performance		Inquiry

		Performance	Inquiry
Card IV	4''	1. That looks like an ape sitting on a	1. Big feet and looks like hair on him.
		2. Tree.	
		1. (Contd.) With big feet and little wee arms and just a stump for a head.	
	24''	2. (Contd.) That's a tree he's sittin' on.	
Card V	2''	1. Looks like a butterfly and things come out of head, feet, back and wings.	1. More like a butterfly.
	29''	Either looks like a butterfly or bat.	
Card VI	5''	1. Looks like a wolf laying down on his back--or fox. Looks like it's feet or paws are apart--has whiskers. You can see its ears. Looks like	
	47''	it's split open.	
Card VII	4''	1. Looks like two little rabbits sitting on a	
		2. Clump of grass.	
		1. (Contd.) Looking at each other with	
	26''	their tails out and their ears up.	
Card VIII	3''	1. Looks like a skeleton.	1. You can see bones.
		2. With bugs crawling up--rats or mice.	
		3. Looks like a skeleton or something.	3. Blood--makes them red.
	35''	It's red--the mice.	
Card IX	6''	1. This looks like a skeleton too--just plain skeleton looks like bones going across the top.	1. Green and orange.
		2. And looks like red down at the bottom is heads.	2. Man's head or something.
	32''	3. Looks like hands.	3. Things there and there.
Card X	5''	1. Looks like a skeleton.	1. Neck and down here.
		2. With all different kinds of bugs over it.	
		3. Looks like a spider.	3. (Blue).
		4. Mouse	4. (Brown).
		5. Snakes and	5. (Green).
		2. (Contd.) All kinds of different bugs.	
		1. (Contd.) Looks like a neck. Looks like a lot of different things around it.	
	58''	Blue like breasts.	1. (Contd.) Attached to skeleton.

At the age of ten years and nine months Bernard showed the results of his dieting during the preceding year. He looked quite handsome and was pleasantly outgoing. He was proud of being a patrol boy. Interested and persistent on the WISC, he achieved a full scale I.Q. of 120, with only one point difference between his verbal and performance I.Q.'s. He had found the work at the new school to be much more difficult than the previous school.

On this occasion, he gave the following Rorschach responses:

Bernard's Rorschach Responses at the Ten Year Level

		Performance	Inquiry
Card I	11''	1. This looks like two men holding onto something, ripping it apart. Looks like they have wings and whatever	
	49''	they are holding has horns.	2. A deer.

Performance			Inquiry
Card II	6"	1. That one looks like a bear's body with some kind of a red head with a pretty big nose.	1. Native head with ring around it--pretty big nose. Q. Looks like they are standing putting their hands together. Q. Feet, claws on end of it.
	29"		
Card III	3"	1. Looks like two people standing there--looks sorta like skeletons.	1. No hair--probably a man. Q. Looks like they are tearing some apart. a. Looks like bones.
		2. Then it looks like there's a bow tie in the middle.	2. A bow tie.
	28"	3. Looks like a shoe with a real skinny leg--with that looks the same.	3. Indian type moccasin. It could be either--but looks like a woman's shoe.
Card IV	5"	1. That one looks like a huge thing sitting on a log. Some kind of a monster--looks like it's turned around the opposite way with its back to you. Looks like the log has a lot of thorns growing out of it. Looks like the monster has a lot of hair on.	1. Could be an ape--arms are thin. Q. Big and big feet.
	59"		
Card V	4"	1. This looks like a bat or a butterfly--looks like the wings are like cut here. I guess that's all.	1. Looks like it's flying more like a butterfly.
	26"		
Card VI	3"	1. This looks like a wolf--a wolf rug--looks like it has whiskers on each side.	1. Looks like a rug.
	28"		
Card VII	7"	1. This looks like two little objects. Looks like rabbits with no feet and it looks like they are standing on 2. A rock.	2. Two of them. Q. Sort of color of rocks. Q. Gray and edges are like rock.
	26"		
Card VIII	3"	1. This looks like a skeleton with	1. Three D. Q. Bones and backbone. Q. Could be either. Q. Animal.
	29"	2. bugs climbing all over--mice.	
Card IX	9"	1. This looks like a skeleton too.	1. Right on here (middle). Could be your backbone.
		2. Looks like a head of something on either side.	2. Of a beaver or animal.
	31"		
Card X	6"	1. This looks like part of a skeleton with	1. (Gray and red). Has bones--looks like bones.
		2. Bugs crowding all over it.	
		3. These look like spiders and all little bugs.	3. Looks like they are crawling.
		4. This looks like a rabbit's head.	
		5. And something on either side.	5. Something green. Q. Could be snakes or little worms--little green ones.
	34"		

At eleven years and nine months of age Bernard had grown into a large, husky boy, who greeted the examiner with a confident "Hi," as he came into the examining room. This confidence, however, seemed somewhat superficial. He confided later that he found it uncomfortable living in this section of the city where most of his friends had more money and better homes than his family. He was not doing very well in school and he worried about his marks, because of his mother's disappointment in them. His grandparents lived with the family now, and that made four adults who seemed to be expecting more of him than he was able to do. He hoped he would not disappoint them.

On this occasion he gave the following Rorschach responses:

Bernard's Rorschach Responses at the Eleven Year Level

Performance	Inquiry

Card I   3"   1. These two men on the side of some-thing--looks like bones--maybe they killed something and they were hunters. Maybe they killed some-thing and are holding it--looks like they have wings and their hats are
43"   sort of pointed on the top.

1. No, but it looks like wings.

Card II   3"   1. Looks like two bear bodies--animal-- the skin of a bear and it looks like
2. People with red skin are under it and they have sort of pointed heads and a long nose and they
1. (Contd.) look like they are holding
36"   their hands together.

1. Fur side.

Card III   5"   1. This looks like two men that are split in the middle and it looks like they have bones and they are holding it and there's a
2. bow tie between them.
3. Looks like there's a hatchet over their heads--each one of them.

2. Red one.
3. Same if some other color.

Card IV   4"   1. This looks like a big ape sitting on a log--doesn't look like a head-- looks like he has his back on the picture, and he has real big feet
42"   and thin arms.

1. Looks like a furry creature and bigger than you would think a man would be in the picture.

Card V   2"   1. This looks like a butterfly and it has sort of like points on the head and the wings look like they are
30"   cut at the end.

1. Doesn't look alive. Q. They might have had something clamping the wings and it cut them and is holding them down in the case.

Card VI   2"   1. This looks like a wolf and he has whiskers and it looks like it could
34"   be a rug because it looks flat.

1. Looks like a wolf rug. This looks like the skin side--you can see the bone in here like.

Card VII   5"   1. This looks like two rabbit heads-- Looks like the tail and the body and they are attached on it looks like a
28"   rock.

1. The body and rock are together. Q. Sitting on the rock. Not exactly rabbits because they don't have any feet. Q. Just part.

Card VIII   3"   1. This looks like a skeleton in the middle.
2. On the outside looks like cloth-- different colored.
3. Looks like two red mice climbing up on the side of it and they have sort of purplish feet--the right front
48"   foot on each one is purplish.

2. Different colored cloth.

Card IX   6"   1. On the bottom of this red part looks like two heads laying on the ground face up.

1. Men.

92

about
my age

about
my age

Bernard — 10-9-51 — 11 yrs. 9 mos.

	Performance	Inquiry

| | 2. Looks like a backbone up the middle and then there | 2. An animal or person. Q. I guess it would be an animal. |
| | 3. are little things on top--they could be ground animals like mosquitoes or bugs. | 3. Looks like they are animals that crawl along (not crawling). |

Card X	2''	1. This looks like a lot of insects.	1. Whole thing.
		2. Two spiders.	2. Looks like they are blue.
		3. Couple of worms.	3. They are green. Q. They have
		4. Looks like a couple of crabs in the middle.	4. (Brown) On each side. Q. Hooks that come out.
		5. Some birds--green birds at the top.	5. Looks like birds because it has the beak on it.
		6. On the top looks like little octopuses.	6. Feet coming down and looks like their hands are on the little piece of wood.
		7. Then it looks like two little yellow dogs near the bottom with yellow spots on the chest.	7. Have tails, feet, looks like their chests are up--they're sitting up.

Bernard has continued through the years to drop in to see the examiner at frequent intervals just to talk. He is completing high school this year but has not decided what to do. His parents want him to be a doctor or a lawyer, but his grades have been too poor to get into the local universities. He continues to be concerned about his family trying to "keep up with the Joneses" in the new neighborhood, and he is especially uncomfortable with friends who own cars and have big allowances, when he must work if he has any money to spend.

NORA

Nora is as Irish as her name. At six years and ten months of age she was a round-faced, rosey-cheeked child with brown eyes and pigtails. It was evident during the testing session that she was trying to make a good impression with her deliberate speech and conforming manner. When confronted with a difficult question she would say, "I really don't know that." On the Binet examination she achieved an I.Q. of 100, which, however, due to her tenseness, seemed to be a minimal score.

Her Rorschach responses on this occasion were as follows:

Nora's Rorschach Responses at the Six Year Level

		Performance	Inquiry

Card I	5''	1. Butterfly.	1. In the sky.
	40''	2. I see some dots--dirt flying.	2. Here it is.
Card II	35''	I don't know that	
		1. I can see black and red--a fire and	1. It's red and black.
	45''	snake.	
Card III	9''	1. Looks like two ducks.	1. They're black--sitting on the snow. Q. White.
		2. I see the collar of a tie and	2. It's a bow--that you tie a tie on.
	60''	3. Two little red things--both chickens.	3. In a fire 'cause they're red.
Card IV	20''	1. Falling down a wall. We got a wall	1. Smoke falling down a wall.
	40''	at our house.	
Card V	2''	1. A butterfly.	1. Flying out of the smoke. Q. It's on his wings. Q. They're black.
	7''		

		Performance	Inquiry
Card VI	20''	1. I don't know that one. I don't know if it could be water--maybe it could	1. It's leaking down the wall from the pipe.
	50''	be.	
Card VII	8''	1. Sky.	1. Clouds in the sky.
	10''		
Card VIII	14''	1. Mountain with a bear climbing up	
	32''	it--two bears climbing up it.	
Card IX	4''	1. The world.	1. All different colors like a map.
	10''		
Card X	7''	1. Spiders.	1. On a spider web--not moving.
		2. Ducks.	2. Yellow ducks--on the ground.
	20''	3. Cocoanuts--two.	3. (Upper D) here and here.

At the age of seven years and seven months of age, Nora was a mature-looking, sober-faced little girl whose second grade teacher praised her responsible attitude in the classroom, her interest in her classmates, and her good academic achievement. She considered Nora a leader. Interested and cooperative in the test situation, Nora drew the accompanying figure of a man upon request. By Goodenough scoring standards, the figure suggests barely average intellectual ability.

Her responses to the Rorschach cards on this occasion were as follows:

Nora's Rorschach Responses at the Seven Year Level

		Performance	Inquiry
Card I	8''	1. I see a butterfly.	1. Body, tail, wings. Q. When he flies.
	11''		
Card II		(Encouraged).	
	58''	1. Looks like a body like.	1. (Of what?) A man. Q. Where the blood is. Q. Only half his legs.
	73''		
Card III	6''	1. Two birds like, with	1. Body, legs. Q. Pulling up something.
		2. A necktie.	2. Red.
Card IV	3''	1. Looks like a butterfly.	1. Q. Flying.
			a. dr Snail. Q. (Legs cut off).
	8''		Crawling on the ground.
Card V	7''	1. Looks like a rabbit flying.	a. A butterfly. Q. He's flying too.
	12''		
Card VI	5''	1. A snail.	1. Little baby snail. Here's the body.
	13''		Q. He crawls.
Card VII	8''	1. Looks like a castle and	d.
	20''	2. Snow over it.	2. Q. It's white.
Card VIII	3''	1. This looks like animals climbing up a mountain out of a	1. Bears.
	23''	2. Hole.	2. Round and big hole.
Card IX	7''	1. Looks like an animal with orange	1. Body (green), head (white), wings like
	9''	horns on it.	(red).
Card X	2''	1. Looks like flowers and	1. Red and yellow stuff.
		2. and 3. Spiders climbing up the	2. and 3. Spiders. Three (blue and
	10''	flowers.	upper D).

① Nora   6-15-48   7 yrs 10 months

At eight and a half years of age Nora was a very clean, neatly-dressed little girl with rather plain but not unattractive Irish facial features. While waiting for the third grade to return to the classroom after lunch hour, the examiner saw Nora run to the teacher and throw her arms about her. As she accompanied the examiner across the school yard to the examining room, she gently reminded a younger kindergarten sister that it was time for her to go into the building. In the testing situation she was conforming and attentive, but was somewhat slow in getting the instructions. On the Monroe Diagnostic Reading Examination she achieved better than average for her third grade placement, in both reading and arithmetic, but spelling was slightly below average for the grade.

Her responses to the Rorschach cards at this time were as follows:

Nora's Rorschach Responses at the Eight Year Level

		Performance	Inquiry
Card I	2''	1. Butterfly.	1. Got wings, got these two little hickies up there. Here's his face (lower d). Q. In the air. Q. Flying.
	12''		
Card II	3''	1. Looks like two bears.	1. Clapping hands. Sticking their hands out.
	34''		
Card III	14''	1. Two grasshoppers.	1. Jumping, putting their hands in the a. water.
		2. And a necktie.	2. Red.
	31''	3. And a dog.	3. Looks angry. Q. Going after his tail.
Card IV	15''	(Slants card).	
		1. Looks like a snail.	1. Shell, there's his head, ears. Q. He's crawling.
Card V	7''	1. This one looks like a butterfly too.	1. Looks like he's flying. Q. Black like
	15''	(Whispering to herself).	
Card VI		(Frowns, turns card, frowns and looks up at examiner).	
	55''	1. Looks like a turtle.	1. Got his shell. Head's sticking out on the ground.
	57''		
Card VII	14''	1. Looks like two doggies.	1. Barking at each other.
		2. And a little house.	2. a. Clouds over it.
Card VIII	8''	1. Looks like two polar bears climbing up on	1. How they climb.
		2. the hill.	
Card IX	11''	(Frowns).	
		1. This one looks like a map.	1. Got all different colors. a. Ground with grass on it. b. This water--water streams.
	17''		
Card X	19''	1. Looks like two spiders and	1. Climbing up a web.
		2. A cow or something.	2. (Upper gray).
	30''		1. (Contd.) He can't get off the spider web.

At nine years and eight months of age Nora was a neat, well-groomed, attractive, though not pretty, little girl who was more spontaneous and at ease than on other occasions and consequently seemed more alert. On the Grace Arthur Performance Test she achieved a high average rating.

Her Rorschach responses were as follows:

Performance		Inquiry

Card I   7"   1. That looks like they are dancing around a

2. Furnace or fire like--

2. Shaped and round

35"   1. (Contd.) two people.

Card II   2"   1. Two bears--they're stamping on

1. Q. Their head (red).

11"   2. Fire.

2. Here's fire.

Card III   5"   1. This looks like two grasshoppers getting

2. water out of a hole.

2. (Lower D).

3. A bow tie there.

3. That you put on your neck.

4. This looks like a mouse here--two little mouses it looks like (outer

4. Long tails like it. Q. Hanging

27"   red).

Card IV   5"   1. This looks like a man. He's sitting on a stone

2. like--some kind of stool. These are Roman numerals. (looking on the

16"   back of the card).

Card V   4"   1. This looks like a butterfly.

1. In the air. Flying.

14"

Card VI   (Shakes head).
This is something but I don't know what.

29"   1. Looks like a bear--but got a skinny

1. Two legs here. Q. His head like. On

37"   head--I'll say a bear.

the ground. Alive?--no dead.

Card VII   4"   1. This looks like two dogs looking back at each other and there's

2. A cloud under them.

2. Shape. Colored. Q. Dark and looks

15"   like a rain cloud.

Card VIII   6"   1. This looks like two mountain bears

2. climbing up that mountain.

2. Bright and dripping like. Color is real bright. Looks like it's shining here.

3. And wee tiny little fireballs coming

20"   down (lower red).

Card IX   12"   1. Looks like two witches.

1. Long hat. Q. Funny how they are acting. Putting hands on each other and long nose.
a. Big ball of fire here.

22"   2. On a cloud (green).

Card X   7"   1. There is two reindeer trying to jump over a

1. (Brown).

2. Log.

2. (Red is log).

3. Two little worms.

3. Can't tell any more.

4. Spiders on the side.

4. (Blue).

5. And one caught on

5. (Gray) Caught on stick and nearly fell off cliff. (Tells about dog and cliff).

30"   6. a stick.

At ten and a half years of age Nora, still quite neat in appearance, was outgoing in manner, but on this occasion less spontaneous than the year before. This lack of spontaneity was probably the result of the testing having deprived her of her gym period. She expressed her disappointment readily but accepted an apology graciously and became immediately interested and cooperative in the test situation. She volunteered the fact that her best friend was envious of her and wished she could come down and do these things too. On the WISC she scored high average on all three scaled, with an average scatter of test items. Information and vocabulary were the only items to fall below the scaled score of 10. Arithmetic was the highest at 14.

Nora's Rorschach responses at this time were as follows:

Nora's Rorschach Responses at the Ten Year Level

		Performance	Inquiry
Card I	5''	1. Looks like two witches with wings.	1. Long hat, dressed all in black. That looks like wings. They're on something. Q. Maybe sitting on it.
	19''		
Card II	1''	1. This one looks like two bears.	1. Bears look like they are slapping each other (red heads).
	7''		
Card III	3''	1. This one looks like there's two grasshoppers and	1. Looks like they are putting their hands in the water.
		2. Two mouses hanging next to them.	2. They are hanging from something like a tree.
		3. And a bow tie in the middle and it looks like there's	3. I don't know.
		4. Water there.	4. Color black and white and how it's shaped. Q. Looks like moon's shivering on it.
	23''		
Card IV	4''	1. This looks like a bear skin.	1. Looks like the fur side. (Rubs finger over). Wrinkled makes it look like fur--head like here.
	19''	2. Outside it looks like a snail (points to bottom).	
Card V	1''	1. This looks like a rabbit.	1. Two ears. Q. In the woods trying to jump over something.
	6''		
Card VI	13''	1. Looks like a giraffe with a long neck.	1. Looks like he's got a long neck and he's reaching for something or going down for something because hind legs are bigger than his front ones.
	20''		
Card VII	2''	1. This one looks like two dogs--they're sitting on a	1. Ears and here's the tail. Here's the face.
	12''	2. Rock.	2. The way it's shaped.
Card VIII	2''	1. This looks like two bears climbing up on a	
		2. Mountain. In the middle of the mountain looks like	2. All different colors makes it look like a mountain.
	18''	3. There's skeletons there.	I don't know.
Card IX	6''	1. This just looks like a mountain.	1. Color. Q. I don't know.
	13''		
Card X	2''	1. This looks like two spiders on the side.	1. I don't know.
		2. Two reindeer (brown).	2. Looks like their horns.
		3. Worms and	3. Green. I think they are earthworms.
		4. Two lions.	4. Got like a small tip of a tail and looks like they got their mouth open.
	23''		

At eleven and a half years of age Nora had changed little in appearance except to look adolescent. She was enthusiastic in greeting the examiner and wanted to know at the end of the testing period when she would be coming again. She was very talkative, and one of her main topics of discussion was the new man teacher. She denied ever having heard of menstruation, and seemed to want to change the subject immediately. When asked to draw a person Nora cheerfully produced the accompanying pictures. She was disappointed when the test session was over.

Her Rorschach responses on this occasion were as follows:

Nora's Rorschach Responses at the Eleven Year Level

	Performance	Inquiry
Card I 5''	1. Looks like two witches. Uh huh.	1. Witches look like they are fighting over something. Q. Don't know. Looks like a dress.
16''		
Card II 1''	1. Two bears--they are clapping hands. Looks like they are	
11''	dancing.	
Card III 2''	1. This is two grasshoppers.	1. Looks like they have a. Buckets and dipping into water.
	2. There's two mice on the side and	2. Tail up, hanging from their tail.
	3. a bow tie and looks like	3. It's red.
	4. there's a puddle of water there. DX	4. Shadow like and can see the white paper.
19''		
Card IV 6''	Uhh.	
	1. This looks like a snail like (side d).	1. Head of a snail.
	2. A raccoon skin (upper d).	2. Just the head, white split and ear and nose coming up.
15''		
Card V 3''	1. This looks like a bunny. He's got his skin torn off him, hanging on	1. Fur spread apart. Somebody pulled it. Q. Looks like he's hopping.
13''	its side.	
Card VI 7''	I don't know what this looks like.	
	1. Looks like a rug--that's all I can see on that.	1. Animal rug you know--a. . .
Card VII 2''	1. This looks like two dogs and they are	1. Shape of a rock.
	2. on a rock and	
	1. (Contd.) Looks like they are barking	
12''	at each other.	
Card VIII 2''	1. This looks like two bears climbing up	1. Here and here.
	2. a hill.	2. Point of it makes it look more like-- and the color. Q. Out in the west.
	3. Looks like there's a skeleton or	3. Just looks like a skeleton. Q. Like a
16''	something in the center.	camel's.
Card IX 4''	1. This is two witches pointing their hands at each other. They	1. Their fingers here.
	2. are standing on rocks just like on a mountainside.	2. Rocks are on top of each other. Q. I don't know.
Card X 2''	1. Here's two spiders.	1. Looks like they are on a web (doesn't see the web).
	2. Looks like a worm.	2. Got his head up. Q. I don't know. a. With a face like a bunny.

about
13, I suppose

about the
same age

Q Nora 5-22-52 11 years 6 months

101

Performance	Inquiry
3. Here's two dogs on the (inner yellow).	3. They look like they are begging for something.
4. A wishbone. (Am I going too fast?)	4. Up here.
5. On the side, there are all like mountains.	5. (Red) Bumpy and rough like a stone.
6. Looks like two reindeer jumping off the side. (brown).	6. Body and back legs. When a reindeer jumps he spreads his back leg.

Of the six children whose Rorschachs were presented in this chapter, Nora comes nearer following the Rorschach norms as outlined in previous chapters. She too was the one who seemed to develop with the least number of neurotic incidents. She, like Bernard, has continued to contact the examiner during her high school years. Having decided early to become a nurse, she enters training in the spring after her graduation from high school next February, and has asked the examiner to be one of her sponsors.

Among the remaining one hundred and thirty-two children in the longitudinal study, just as in the six introduced here, there are as many variations of Rorschach as there are children. At the same time, there is a common path of development mirrored in these records. Some enter this path at a more advanced stage than others, some stray farther away before returning, but each child approximates to some degree the path determined by the Rorschach norms derived from the study of the children as a group.

It is the author's plan to make available the serial Rorschach records of all the children, together with a brief summary of other psychological data about each child, in the form of a source book, in order that other investigators may use this material as they may see fit.

Appendix

The appendix to this book is comprised of master tables, excerpts from each of which appear in the discussion of the Rorschach norms for children, Chapter III. Each of these master tables, A through T, contains the statistical measures of one Rorschach scoring category, beginning with treatment of $\underline{R}$ or Total Number of Responses in Table A and ending with $\underline{P}$, Popular Responses in Table T.

In each of these tables are found the range, quartiles, medians, means, and standard deviations of a particular scoring category, distributed according to age, sex, and intelligence of both the longitudinal and control groups. A careful study of these tables gives more meaning to the discussion in the text than can be found in the smaller tables included therein.

TABLE A

R, OR TOTAL NUMBER OF RESPONSES
GIVEN TO THE RORSCHACH CARDS BY LONGITUDINAL AND CONTROL GROUPS

(Read across pages 104 and 105.)

	Superior (125 I.Q. and up)			Bright (110-124 I.Q.)			

SIX YEAR OLD LONGITUDINAL GROUP

	Boys N 6	Girls N 7	Both N 13	Boys N 17	Girls N 15	Both N 32	Boys N 36
Range	16-40	13-21	13-40	10-50	7-42	7-50	9-52
Q_1	19.8	14.0	15.0	12.5	10.0	12.0	12.0
Mdn	22.5	15.0	18.0	15.0	15.0	15.0	15.0
Q_3	32.8	18.0	22.5	25.5	23.0	23.0	18.0
Mean	25.5	16.0	20.4	19.8	17.8	18.9	16.2
SD	7.9	2.5	7.4	10.9	8.8	9.9	4.2

SEVEN YEAR OLD LONGITUDINAL GROUP

	Boys N 6	Girls N 7	Both N 13	Boys N 17	Girls N 15	Both N 32	Boys N 36
Range	12-37	7-30	7-37	10-33	10-33	10-33	9-38
Q_1	12.0	15.0	13.0	12.0	13.0	13.2	11.2
Mdn	16.5	20.0	19.0	15.0	16.0	15.5	15.5
Q_3	28.5	22.0	24.0	22.0	20.0	21.5	18.8
Mean	20.0	19.1	19.5	17.8	17.4	17.6	16.3
SD	9.1	6.6	7.8	7.2	6.5	6.8	6.4

SEVEN YEAR OLD CONTROL GROUP

	Boys N 6	Girls N 3	Both N 9	Boys N 9	Girls N 9	Both N 18	Boys N 19
Range	9-44	10-18	9-44	9-21	10-28	9-28	8-31
Q_1	13.5	10.0	12.0	11.5	11.5	11.8	10.0
Mdn	28.0	14.0	18.0	16.0	15.0	15.0	14.0
Q_3	41.0	18.0	38.0	19.5	21.5	19.2	23.0
Mean	27.3	14.0	22.9	15.7	16.6	16.1	17.1
SD	13.3	3.3	12.6	4.0	6.0	5.2	7.6

EIGHT YEAR OLD LONGITUDINAL GROUP

	Boys N 6	Girls N 7	Both N 13	Boys N 17	Girls N 15	Both N 32	Boys N 36
Range	15-34	16-48	15-48	11-37	15-36	11-37	11-67
Q_1	19.5	20.0	20.5	13.5	20.0	15.0	13.0
Mdn	28.5	28.0	28.0	22.0	21.0	21.0	17.0
Q_3	32.2	38.0	34.5	27.5	30.0	29.5	22.8

OF ELEMENTARY SCHOOL CHILDREN FROM SIX THROUGH ELEVEN YEARS OF AGE
REPORTED ACCORDING TO INTELLIGENCE LEVELS AND SEX

(Read across pages 104 and 105.)

Average (90-109 I.Q.)		Dull (89 I.Q. and below)			Total (74-140 I.Q.)		

SIX YEAR OLD LONGITUDINAL GROUP

Girls	Both	Boys	Girls	Both	Boys	Girls	Both
N 39	N 75	N 9	N 9	N 18	N 68	N 70	N 138
5-40	5-40	10-23	9-19	9-23	9-50	5-42	5-50
12.0	12.0	10.5	10.0	10.0	12.2	12.0	12.0
14.0	15.0	14.0	12.0	12.0	15.0	14.0	15.0
18.0	18.0	16.0	13.5	14.0	21.0	18.0	19.0
15.2	15.7	14.0	12.2	13.1	17.6	15.5	16.5
5.8	5.0	4.0	2.8	3.6	7.6	6.1	6.7

SEVEN YEAR OLD LONGITUDINAL GROUP

Girls	Both	Boys	Girls	Both	Boys	Girls	Both
N 39	N 75	N 9	N 9	N 18	N 68	N 70	N 138
7-29	7-38	10-27	10-21	10-27	9-38	7-21	7-38
11.0	11.0	10.5	10.0	10.0	12.0	11.0	11.8
14.0	15.0	14.0	12.0	13.0	15.0	15.0	15.0
17.0	17.0	18.0	16.0	18.0	19.0	18.0	19.0
14.9	15.6	15.1	13.3	14.2	16.9	15.7	16.3
5.1	5.6	5.1	3.7	4.6	7.0	5.6	6.1

SEVEN YEAR OLD CONTROL GROUP

Girls	Both	Boys	Girls	Both	Boys	Girls	Both
N 15	N 34	N 4	N 8	N 12	N 38	N 35	N 73
7-26	7-31	12-17	5-24	5-24	8-44	5-28	5-44
13.0	10.8	12.2	10.2	11.2	11.0	12.0	11.5
15.0	15.0	13.5	15.0	13.5	15.5	15.0	15.0
20.0	23.0	16.2	21.0	17.8	22.8	19.0	20.5
16.3	16.7	14.0	14.9	14.6	18.0	15.9	17.0
5.0	6.5	1.9	6.1	5.1	8.7	5.6	7.6

EIGHT YEAR OLD LONGITUDINAL GROUP

Girls	Both	Boys	Girls	Both	Boys	Girls	Both
N 39	N 75	N 9	N 9	N 18	N 68	N 70	N 138
6-35	6-67	11-25	10-22	10-25	11-67	6-48	6-67
14.0	14.0	11.0	10.5	12.0	14.0	15.0	14.0
17.0	17.0	15.0	17.0	15.0	19.0	18.0	18.0
19.0	21.0	22.5	20.0	20.0	25.5	22.0	24.0

	Superior (125 I.Q. and up)			Bright (110-124 I.Q.)			

EIGHT YEAR OLD LONGITUDINAL GROUP (Continued)

Mean	26.7	30.0	28.5	21.1	24.3	22.6	20.0
SD	6.7	10.3	9.0	7.8	7.0	7.5	9.9

NINE YEAR OLD LONGITUDINAL GROUP

	Boys N 6	Girls N 7	Both N 13	Boys N 17	Girls N 15	Both N 32	Boys N 36
Range	22-44	16-62	16-62	14-54	14-48	14-54	8-49
Q_1	27.2	20.0	22.0	20.5	22.0	21.2	15.2
Mdn	32.0	36.0	32.0	28.0	26.0	27.5	19.5
Q_3	42.5	58.0	45.0	35.5	34.0	34.0	24.8
Mean	33.5	37.3	35.5	29.1	27.9	28.5	21.1
SD	7.5	17.6	14.0	11.0	9.1	10.1	8.2

TEN YEAR OLD LONGITUDINAL GROUP

	Boys N 6	Girls N 7	Both N 13	Boys N 17	Girls N 15	Both N 32	Boys N 36
Range	24-39	16-106	16-106	15-141	15-71	15-141	13-57
Q_1	25.5	18.0	25.0	19.5	18.0	18.8	17.2
Mdn	30.5	32.0	32.0	30.0	28.0	28.0	21.0
Q_3	38.2	46.0	45.0	55.0	41.0	47.8	27.8
Mean	31.3	41.9	37.0	41.2	32.3	37.0	24.1
SD	5.7	28.3	21.8	31.8	15.4	25.6	9.9

ELEVEN YEAR OLD LONGITUDINAL GROUP

	Boys N 6	Girls N 7	Both N 13	Boys N 17	Girls N 15	Both N 32	Boys N 36
Range	22-88	19-150	19-150	14-167	13-159	13-167	12-78
Q_1	37.0	21.0	24.0	20.0	21.0	21.0	19.0
Mdn	38.0	27.0	37.0	30.0	26.0	27.0	23.0
Q_3	73.8	74.0	61.5	49.5	39.0	44.5	32.5
Mean	41.0	50.6	46.1	42.1	37.2	39.8	26.7
SD	14.3	44.2	34.2	36.1	34.8	35.2	12.8

ELEVEN YEAR OLD CONTROL GROUP

	Boys N 3	Girls N 5	Both N 8	Boys N 7	Girls N 11	Both N 18	Boys N 22
Range	15-40	14-70	14-70	12-112	10-55	10-112	10-41
Q_1	15.0	16.0	18.8	17.0	19.0	17.8	15.8
Mdn	36.0	21.0	25.0	18.0	27.0	26.5	18.0
Q_3	40.0	49.0	39.0	35.0	30.0	46.0	31.2
Mean	30.3	30.2	30.2	35.1	28.0	30.8	22.7
SD	10.9	20.4	17.5	32.5	11.9	22.7	9.0

TABLE A (Continued)
(Read across pages 106 and 107.)

Average (90-109 I.Q.)		Dull (89 I.Q. and below)			Total (74-140 I.Q.)		

EIGHT YEAR OLD LONGITUDINAL GROUP (Continued)

17.0	18.4	16.9	15.4	16.2	20.4	19.7	20.1
5.3	7.7	5.3	3.5	5.1	9.1	7.6	8.1

NINE YEAR OLD LONGITUDINAL GROUP

Girls	Both	Boys	Girls	Both	Boys	Girls	Both
N 39	N 75	N 9	N 9	N 18	N 68	N 70	N 138
9-44	8-49	11-28	12-38	11-38	8-54	9-62	8-62
16.0	16.0	14.5	13.5	14.8	16.0	16.0	16.0
19.0	19.0	17.0	18.0	17.5	22.0	21.0	22.0
23.0	24.0	24.5	24.5	27.5	29.0	26.5	28.2
20.2	20.6	19.3	19.9	19.6	24.0	23.5	23.7
6.9	7.3	5.5	7.9	6.9	10.0	10.4	9.9

TEN YEAR OLD LONGITUDINAL GROUP

Girls	Both	Boys	Girls	Both	Boys	Girls	Both
N 39	N 75	N 9	N 9	N 18	N 68	N 70	N 138
11-38	11-57	12-56	10-35	10-56	12-141	10-106	10-141
16.0	17.0	14.0	15.0	14.0	18.0	18.0	18.0
24.0	22.0	19.0	19.0	19.0	24.0	24.0	24.0
28.0	28.0	27.5	24.0	26.2	32.0	30.2	31.2
23.2	23.6	23.3	20.0	21.6	28.9	26.6	27.7
7.5	8.4	12.7	6.8	10.5	19.9	14.2	16.6

ELEVEN YEAR OLD LONGITUDINAL GROUP

Girls	Both	Boys	Girls	Both	Boys	Girls	Both
N 39	N 75	N 9	N 9	N 18	N 68	N 70	N 138
11-53	11-78	17-42	11-38	11-42	12-167	11-159	11-167
17.0	18.0	20.0	11.5	17.0	20.0	18.0	19.0
22.0	23.0	23.0	18.0	21.5	25.5	23.0	24.0
28.0	29.0	32.5	23.0	26.5	38.0	29.0	33.2
23.4	25.0	26.2	19.2	22.7	31.8	28.6	30.1
8.5	10.5	7.9	8.0	8.7	22.5	23.8	22.5

ELEVEN YEAR OLD CONTROL GROUP

Girls	Both	Boys	Girls	Both	Boys	Girls	Both
N 18	N 40	N 8	N 6	N 14	N 40	N 40	N 80
12-87	10-87	12-54	17-26	12-54	10-112	10-87	10-112
14.8	15.0	14.2	17.0	16.5	15.2	17.0	16.0
19.5	19.0	29.0	21.5	23.0	19.5	21.5	21.0
25.5	30.5	49.5	26.0	37.5	35.0	28.0	32.8
25.2	23.8	30.6	21.5	26.7	27.0	26.0	26.5
17.7	13.7	16.3	4.2	13.3	17.8	15.5	16.0

TABLE B

W%, OR PERCENTAGE OF WHOLE RESPONSES
GIVEN TO THE RORSCHACH CARDS BY LONGITUDINAL AND CONTROL GROUPS

(Read across pages 108 and 109.)

	Superior (125 I.Q. and up)			Bright (110-124 I.Q.)			

SIX YEAR OLD LONGITUDINAL GROUP

	Boys N 6	Girls N 7	Both N 13	Boys N 17	Girls N 15	Both N 32	Boys N 36
Range	10-54	23-67	10-67	11-73	10-100	10-100	13-67
Q_1	12.2	23.0	23.0	26.0	33.0	30.2	36.0
Mdn	38.0	43.0	43.0	40.0	43.0	42.0	44.0
Q_3	46.5	50.0	47.0	55.5	64.0	59.5	53.0
Mn	32.8	44.1	38.9	40.6	51.9	45.9	42.9
SD	16.3	10.9	14.8	18.5	26.2	22.9	14.4

SEVEN YEAR OLD LONGITUDINAL GROUP

	Boys N 6	Girls N 7	Both N 13	Boys N 17	Girls N 15	Both N 32	Boys N 36
Range	8-75	18-86	8-86	7-75	18-54	7-75	0-82
Q_1	24.5	20.0	22.5	18.0	25.0	22.2	28.2
Mdn	44.5	41.0	41.0	38.0	36.0	36.0	39.0
Q_3	62.2	53.0	57.5	60.0	47.0	50.0	50.0
Mn	43.3	41.0	42.1	39.0	36.1	37.6	40.2
SD	22.2	22.1	22.2	22.7	11.2	18.1	17.7

SEVEN YEAR OLD CONTROL GROUP

	Boys N 6	Girls N 3	Both N 9	Boys N 9	Girls N 9	Both N 18	Boys N 19
Range	7-88	39-80	7-88	29-100	27-75	27-100	13-75
Q_1	20.5	39.0	26.5	31.5	31.0	32.2	17.0
Mdn	29.0	43.0	39.0	50.0	42.0	46.0	30.0
Q_3	61.8	80.0	66.5	61.0	58.0	59.5	70.0
Mn	38.5	54.0	43.7	51.2	45.2	48.2	42.3
SD	25.9	18.4	24.7	20.8	15.8	18.8	24.8

EIGHT YEAR OLD LONGITUDINAL GROUP

	Boys N 6	Girls N 7	Both N 13	Boys N 17	Girls N 15	Both N 32	Boys N 36
Range	9-47	11-45	9-47	0-54	11-44	0-54	6-62
Q_1	20.2	11.0	12.0	17.5	14.0	16.2	24.5
Mdn	31.5	16.0	25.0	27.0	22.0	25.5	32.5
Q_3	42.5	38.0	40.0	38.0	33.0	33.0	46.8

TABLE B (Continued)

OF ELEMENTARY SCHOOL CHILDREN FROM SIX THROUGH ELEVEN YEARS OF AGE REPORTED ACCORDING TO INTELLIGENCE LEVELS AND SEX

(Read across pages 108 and 109.)

Average (90–109 I.Q.)		Dull (75–89 I.Q.)			Total (74–140 I.Q.)		

SIX YEAR OLD LONGITUDINAL GROUP

Girls	Both	Boys	Girls	Both	Boys	Girls	Both
N 39	N 75	N 9	N 9	N 18	N 68	N 70	N 138
11-100	11-100	14-73	20-100	14-100	10-73	10-100	10-100
28.0	30.0	19.5	37.5	29.5	28.0	32.8	31.8
42.0	42.0	43.0	50.0	48.0	42.0	43.5	43.0
54.0	54.0	59.0	63.0	58.5	53.0	55.2	54.2
43.5	43.2	42.7	51.9	47.3	41.4	46.5	44.0
19.7	16.7	19.9	21.6	21.4	17.0	20.6	18.5

SEVEN YEAR OLD LONGITUDINAL GROUP

Girls	Both	Boys	Girls	Both	Boys	Girls	Both
N 39	N 75	N 9	N 9	N 18	N 68	N 70	N 138
7-80	0-82	11-50	17-100	11-100	0-82	7-100	0-100
30.0	29.0	26.5	27.0	27.2	25.8	29.0	28.0
36.0	38.0	36.0	43.0	38.0	38.0	36.5	38.0
50.0	50.0	50.0	70.0	50.0	50.0	50.0	50.0
39.0	39.6	35.1	49.2	42.2	39.5	39.9	39.7
16.3	17.0	12.6	25.1	21.3	20.0	17.4	18.1

SEVEN YEAR OLD CONTROL GROUP

Girls	Both	Boys	Girls	Both	Boys	Girls	Both
N 15	N 34	N 4	N 8	N 12	N 38	N 35	N 73
17-67	13-75	29-67	18-60	18-67	7-100	17-80	7-100
25.0	22.0	29.5	23.0	24.5	27.0	27.0	27.0
36.0	32.5	42.0	36.5	36.5	33.0	40.0	39.0
57.0	64.8	63.5	43.0	60.8	67.8	56.0	59.0
40.1	41.3	45.0	35.1	38.4	44.1	41.5	42.8
16.8	21.2	15.8	12.9	14.6	23.3	15.8	21.1

EIGHT YEAR OLD LONGITUDINAL GROUP

Girls	Both	Boys	Girls	Both	Boys	Girls	Both
N 39	N 75	N 9	N 9	N 18	N 68	N 70	N 138
19-67	6-67	16-82	14-73	14-82	0-82	11-73	0-82
31.0	29.0	24.5	21.0	23.5	22.5	21.8	22.0
35.0	35.0	27.0	45.0	38.5	31.0	33.0	33.0
42.0	45.0	64.0	60.0	60.0	45.8	42.0	42.2

	Superior (125 I.Q. and up)			Bright (110-124 I.Q.)			

EIGHT YEAR OLD LONGITUDINAL GROUP (Continued)

	Superior			Bright			
Mn	30.7	24.3	27.2	28.0	24.0	26.1	34.6
SD	12.8	13.7	13.6	15.0	10.3	13.0	14.8

NINE YEAR OLD LONGITUDINAL GROUP

	Boys N 6	Girls N 7	Both N 13	Boys N 17	Girls N 15	Both N 32	Boys N 36
Range	7-28	5-44	5-44	4-57	8-57	4-57	6-64
Q_1	15.2	9.0	9.0	11.5	15.0	12.0	25.0
Mdn	22.0	17.0	21.0	18.0	21.0	19.0	31.0
Q_3	25.8	32.0	29.0	26.0	32.0	28.2	40.2
Mn	20.3	20.9	20.6	21.2	23.4	22.2	32.9
SD	6.7	13.6	11.0	13.5	13.1	13.2	13.8

TEN YEAR OLD LONGITUDINAL GROUP

	Boys N 6	Girls N 7	Both N 13	Boys N 17	Girls N 15	Both N 32	Boys N 36
Range	15-35	7-46	7-46	6-53	4-53	4-53	11-65
Q_1	15.8	8.0	15.5	10.0	15.0	12.0	22.2
Mdn	22.5	29.0	24.0	20.0	21.0	20.5	32.0
Q_3	32.0	44.0	34.0	32.0	25.0	29.0	39.0
Mn	23.7	27.0	25.5	22.8	22.3	22.6	32.2
SD	7.4	14.5	11.9	14.7	12.8	13.7	12.1

ELEVEN YEAR OLD LONGITUDINAL GROUP

	Boys N 6	Girls N 7	Both N 13	Boys N 17	Girls N 15	Both N 32	Boys N 36
Range	16-45	3-38	3-45	5-60	5-53	5-60	5-69
Q_1	16.0	8.0	12.5	11.5	15.0	12.0	17.2
Mdn	24.0	14.0	16.0	17.0	22.0	17.5	28.5
Q_3	38.2	23.0	34.5	26.0	30.0	29.8	38.8
Mn	26.3	19.9	23.1	21.9	24.0	22.9	28.8
SD	11.5	13.0	12.8	15.6	13.5	14.2	15.2

ELEVEN YEAR OLD CONTROL GROUP

	Boys N 3	Girls N 5	Both N 8	Boys N 7	Girls N 11	Both N 18	Boys N 22
Range	17-80	17-50	17-80	17-83	5-100	5-100	6-90
Q_1	17.0	17.5	17.2	23.0	26.0	25.2	18.0
Mdn	40.0	33.0	36.5	32.0	32.0	32.0	36.0
Q_3	80.0	46.5	48.2	61.0	53.0	54.5	53.8
Mn	45.7	32.2	37.2	41.3	38.7	39.7	37.8
SD	26.0	13.2	20.1	21.7	23.6	23.1	21.5

Average (90-109 I.Q.)		Dull (75-89 I.Q.)			Total (74-140 I.Q.)		

EIGHT YEAR OLD LONGITUDINAL GROUP (Continued)

37.3	36.0	40.7	43.0	41.8	33.4	33.9	33.6
11.0	12.6	22.3	19.4	21.1	16.6	14.0	14.8

NINE YEAR OLD LONGITUDINAL GROUP

Girls	Both	Boys	Girls	Both	Boys	Girls	Both
N 39	N 75	N 9	N 9	N 18	N 68	N 70	N 138
8-78	6-78	9-55	18-62	9-62	4-64	5-78	4-78
20.0	23.0	17.5	21.5	20.5	18.0	18.0	18.0
28.0	30.0	23.0	28.0	25.0	25.0	24.5	25.0
37.0	38.0	41.0	46.0	44.5	36.8	36.0	36.0
29.9	31.4	27.8	33.3	30.6	28.2	28.1	28.1
14.0	13.5	14.2	14.1	14.6	14.6	13.9	13.8

TEN YEAR OLD LONGITUDINAL GROUP

Girls	Both	Boys	Girls	Both	Boys	Girls	Both
N 39	N 75	N 9	N 9	N 18	N 68	N 70	N 138
0-50	0-65	2-43	13-64	2-64	2-65	0-64	0-65
15.0	19.0	19.0	22.0	21.2	19.0	15.0	17.8
25.0	29.0	30.0	32.0	32.0	29.0	25.0	26.5
33.0	38.0	39.0	40.0	39.5	37.8	33.0	35.0
25.3	28.6	27.4	35.9	31.7	28.5	26.2	27.3
12.0	12.1	12.3	15.0	14.5	13.4	13.1	12.8

ELEVEN YEAR OLD LONGITUDINAL GROUP

Girls	Both	Boys	Girls	Both	Boys	Girls	Both
N 39	N 75	N 9	N 9	N 18	N 68	N 70	N 138
0-73	0-73	8-35	13-64	8-64	5-69	0-73	0-73
17.0	17.0	13.0	22.0	14.8	15.0	16.0	15.8
24.0	25.0	22.0	27.0	26.5	24.0	24.5	24.0
32.0	35.0	31.5	40.0	33.5	35.0	33.0	33.0
26.0	27.4	21.8	31.9	26.8	26.0	25.7	25.9
14.1	14.1	9.4	14.1	13.1	14.9	13.8	13.8

ELEVEN YEAR OLD CONTROL GROUP

Girls	Both	Boys	Girls	Both	Boys	Girls	Both
N 18	N 40	N 8	N 6	N 14	N 40	N 40	N 80
4-63	4-90	11-60	8-60	8-60	6-90	4-100	4-100
22.2	19.2	19.5	11.0	16.5	19.0	20.8	19.2
36.5	36.5	27.0	20.5	23.5	32.5	32.5	32.5
41.0	49.2	48.2	30.0	37.8	52.2	39.0	46.2
33.8	36.0	32.2	20.8	27.4	37.9	33.0	35.4
15.4	19.2	15.9	9.5	14.6	21.3	18.0	19.1

TABLE C

D%, OR PERCENTAGE OF LARGE DETAIL RESPONSES
GIVEN TO THE RORSCHACH CARDS BY LONGITUDINAL AND CONTROL GROUPS

(Read across pages 112 and 113.)

	Superior (125 I.Q. and up)			Bright (110–124 I.Q.)			

SIX YEAR OLD LONGITUDINAL GROUP

	Boys N 6	Girls N 7	Both N 13	Boys N 17	Girls N 15	Both N 32	Boys N 36
Range	31-78	27-67	27-78	27-83	0-67	0-83	25-86
Q_1	39.2	50.0	46.0	41.0	27.0	36.8	42.2
Mdn	57.0	57.0	57.0	52.0	42.0	50.0	53.0
Q_3	72.8	62.0	64.5	59.5	61.0	60.0	60.8
Mn	56.0	54.3	55.1	50.9	41.4	46.4	52.8
SD	16.3	12.2	14.2	14.1	22.6	18.9	14.6

SEVEN YEAR OLD LONGITUDINAL GROUP

	Boys N 6	Girls N 7	Both N 13	Boys N 17	Girls N 15	Both N 32	Boys N 36
Range	25-69	14-67	14-69	18-75	41-77	18-77	18-78
Q_1	31.0	40.0	36.5	33.0	50.0	44.0	43.2
Mdn	50.0	55.0	55.0	52.0	62.0	56.0	58.0
Q_3	68.2	65.0	66.0	64.0	64.0	64.0	66.2
Mn	49.2	50.0	49.6	49.6	58.1	53.6	53.2
SD	16.8	17.0	16.9	16.8	10.0	14.5	16.4

SEVEN YEAR OLD CONTROL GROUP

	Boys N 6	Girls N 3	Both N 9	Boys N 9	Girls N 9	Both N 18	Boys N 19
Range	11-70	0-61	0-70	0-71	25-73	0-73	25-86
Q_1	38.0	0	29.0	34.5	30.0	32.5	30.0
Mdn	59.5	57.0	59.0	42.0	58.0	50.5	58.0
Q_3	63.2	61.0	61.0	68.5	62.5	65.5	72.0
Mn	51.3	39.3	47.3	44.8	50.7	47.7	51.8
SD	19.3	27.8	23.2	21.5	18.4	20.3	20.5

EIGHT YEAR OLD LONGITUDINAL GROUP

	Boys N 6	Girls N 7	Both N 13	Boys N 17	Girls N 15	Both N 32	Boys N 36
Range	47-75	58-82	47-82	30-73	57-81	30-81	39-90
Q_1	50.8	55.0	53.5	51.0	62.0	60.2	50.0
Mdn	57.5	63.0	60.0	65.0	67.0	67.0	61.5
Q_3	66.8	66.0	65.0	68.5	71.0	69.0	68.5

TABLE C (Continued)

OF ELEMENTARY SCHOOL CHILDREN FROM SIX THROUGH ELEVEN YEARS OF AGE
REPORTED ACCORDING TO INTELLIGENCE LEVELS AND SEX

(Read across pages 112 and 113.)

Average (90-109 I.Q.)		Dull (75-89 I.Q.)			Total (74-140 I.Q.)		

SIX YEAR OLD LONGITUDINAL GROUP

Girls	Both	Boys	Girls	Both	Boys	Girls	Both
N 39	N 75	N 9	N 9	N 18	N 68	N 70	N 138
0-89	0-89	17-86	0-80	0-86	17-86	0-89	0-89
39.0	41.0	38.0	33.5	36.8	42.0	37.5	40.0
53.0	53.0	50.0	44.0	45.0	52.0	50.0	51.0
64.0	61.0	71.0	53.0	62.5	61.8	61.0	61.0
51.2	51.9	52.6	42.9	47.7	52.5	48.3	50.4
19.1	16.5	20.2	20.2	20.9	15.8	19.5	17.4

SEVEN YEAR OLD LONGITUDINAL GROUP

Girls	Both	Boys	Girls	Both	Boys	Girls	Both
N 39	N 75	N 9	N 9	N 18	N 68	N 70	N 138
20-87	18-87	25-89	0-72	0-89	18-89	0-87	0-89
46.0	44.0	47.5	30.0	42.0	42.2	46.0	44.0
58.0	58.0	59.0	50.0	50.0	56.5	57.0	56.0
69.0	67.0	73.0	69.0	71.0	67.0	65.5	67.0
58.0	55.7	59.0	46.7	52.8	52.7	55.8	54.3
16.0	15.8	17.9	22.2	21.2	17.3	16.1	16.2

SEVEN YEAR OLD CONTROL GROUP

Girls	Both	Boys	Girls	Both	Boys	Girls	Both
N 15	N 34	N 4	N 8	N 12	N 38	N 35	N 73
31-80	25-86	25-64	40-76	25-76	0-86	0-80	0-86
38.0	32.5	30.5	57.0	48.8	30.0	40.0	36.0
60.0	59.0	50.5	61.0	60.0	52.0	60.0	58.0
70.0	70.5	61.5	67.8	66.2	67.8	65.0	65.5
55.6	53.5	47.5	61.1	56.6	49.6	53.7	51.8
15.6	18.3	14.3	9.9	13.2	19.9	18.0	19.6

EIGHT YEAR OLD LONGITUDINAL GROUP

Girls	Both	Boys	Girls	Both	Boys	Girls	Both
N 39	N 75	N 9	N 9	N 18	N 68	N 70	N 138
33-80	33-90	18-72	27-80	18-80	18-90	27-82	18-90
53.0	52.0	36.0	40.0	40.0	50.0	53.0	52.0
61.0	61.0	64.0	50.0	55.0	62.0	62.0	62.0
67.0	67.0	69.5	66.5	68.2	68.0	67.0	67.2

TABLE C (Continued)

(Read across pages 114 and 115.)

	Superior (125 I.Q. and up)			Bright (110-124 I.Q.)			

EIGHT YEAR OLD LONGITUDINAL GROUP (Continued)

Mn	58.8	62.6	60.8	60.1	68.2	63.9	60.2
SD	9.0	9.8	9.6	11.2	7.5	10.4	12.8

NINE YEAR OLD LONGITUDINAL GROUP

	Boys N 6	Girls N 7	Both N 13	Boys N 17	Girls N 15	Both N 32	Boys N 36
Range	47-71	27-70	27-71	35-76	36-88	35-88	36-78
Q_1	53.8	56.0	56.0	52.5	50.0	50.5	54.2
Mdn	68.0	59.0	61.0	64.0	55.0	60.0	63.0
Q_3	69.5	68.0	68.5	69.5	76.0	72.8	70.8
Mn	63.2	57.0	59.8	60.2	61.0	60.6	61.2
SD	8.7	13.2	11.7	11.4	14.8	13.0	11.8

TEN YEAR OLD LONGITUDINAL GROUP

	Boys N 6	Girls N 7	Both N 13	Boys N 17	Girls N 15	Both N 32	Boys N 36
Range	58-71	36-68	36-71	33-73	37-83	33-83	30-76
Q_1	58.8	50.0	57.5	46.5	50.0	47.0	50.5
Mdn	65.5	59.0	65.0	59.0	61.0	60.5	61.0
Q_3	69.5	67.0	67.5	64.5	75.0	67.8	65.0
Mn	64.7	57.4	60.8	55.4	60.8	57.9	57.8
SD	4.8	10.6	9.1	11.7	13.4	12.6	10.3

ELEVEN YEAR OLD LONGITUDINAL GROUP

	Boys N 6	Girls N 7	Both N 13	Boys N 17	Girls N 15	Both N 32	Boys N 36
Range	50-74	26-84	26-84	26-83	23-73	23-83	31-85
Q_1	52.2	49.0	51.0	41.5	45.0	43.2	50.0
Mdn	57.5	63.0	59.0	50.0	54.0	50.5	61.5
Q_3	65.8	68.0	66.5	70.0	65.0	68.0	67.8
Mn	59.2	58.1	58.6	52.9	53.9	53.4	59.4
SD	7.8	16.9	13.5	17.0	13.2	15.2	11.9

ELEVEN YEAR OLD CONTROL GROUP

	Boys N 3	Girls N 5	Both N 8	Boys N 7	Girls N 11	Both N 18	Boys N 22
Range	20-78	36-71	20-78	17-71	0-74	0-74	10-68
Q_1	20.0	40.0	38.0	31.0	37.0	34.5	42.2
Mdn	50.0	61.0	55.5	47.0	54.0	52.0	53.0
Q_3	78.0	69.0	70.0	66.0	63.0	63.5	62.0
Mn	49.3	55.8	53.4	45.9	48.6	47.6	49.4
SD	23.7	13.5	18.3	18.4	19.1	20.4	14.1

114

TABLE C (Continued)
(Read across pages 114 and 115.)

Average (90-109 I.Q.)		Dull (75-89 I.Q.)			Total (74-140 I.Q.)		

EIGHT YEAR OLD LONGITUDINAL GROUP (Continued)

Average (90-109 I.Q.)		Dull (75-89 I.Q.)			Total (74-140 I.Q.)		
58.9	59.5	54.3	52.4	53.4	59.3	60.4	59.9
9.6	10.9	18.8	16.4	17.8	13.5	11.1	11.9

NINE YEAR OLD LONGITUDINAL GROUP

Girls N 39	Both N 75	Boys N 9	Girls N 9	Both N 18	Boys N 68	Girls N 70	Both N 138
22-83	22-83	44-79	38-81	38-81	35-79	22-88	22-88
55.0	56.0	54.0	48.0	49.2	54.2	54.5	54.8
64.0	63.0	69.0	58.0	65.5	64.0	61.5	63.0
70.0	70.0	75.0	70.5	68.2	71.0	70.2	71.0
63.0	62.2	65.2	59.9	62.6	61.7	61.6	61.6
11.1	11.1	11.5	12.7	12.5	11.7	12.2	11.6

TEN YEAR OLD LONGITUDINAL GROUP

Girls N 39	Both N 75	Boys N 9	Girls N 9	Both N 18	Boys N 68	Girls N 70	Both N 138
47-86	30-86	54-68	40-68	40-68	30-76	36-86	30-86
58.0	54.0	57.0	45.0	53.0	52.0	55.5	53.0
67.0	63.0	59.0	60.0	59.0	61.0	63.5	61.5
72.0	69.0	62.5	65.6	64.0	65.0	69.2	68.0
66.2	62.2	59.7	55.8	57.7	58.1	62.8	60.5
10.0	10.6	4.0	10.2	8.0	10.1	11.3	10.7

ELEVEN YEAR OLD LONGITUDINAL GROUP

Girls N 39	Both N 75	Boys N 9	Girls N 9	Both N 18	Boys N 68	Girls N 70	Both N 138
27-84	27-85	50-79	36-76	36-79	28-85	23-84	23-85
58.0	55.0	59.0	54.5	55.8	50.0	54.0	50.0
64.0	63.0	67.0	59.0	66.0	59.0	62.5	61.0
71.0	69.0	73.0	74.0	73.5	68.0	70.2	69.0
63.8	61.7	65.9	61.2	63.6	58.6	60.8	59.7
11.3	11.4	8.5	12.2	10.8	13.5	12.8	12.7

ELEVEN YEAR OLD CONTROL GROUP

Girls N 18	Both N 40	Boys N 8	Girls N 6	Both N 14	Boys N 40	Girls N 40	Both N 80
33-70	10-70	25-76	60-81	25-81	10-78	0-81	0-81
39.8	40.8	33.5	65.2	52.5	33.5	42.2	39.2
54.0	53.5	59.5	72.0	64.5	53.0	58.0	55.0
65.0	62.0	69.5	77.2	73.8	62.0	67.0	65.0
52.9	51.0	52.9	71.3	60.8	49.5	54.8	52.2
12.0	13.4	18.1	6.7	16.9	16.8	15.7	15.8

TABLE D

d%, OR PERCENTAGE OF SMALL DETAIL RESPONSES
GIVEN TO THE RORSCHACH CARDS BY LONGITUDINAL AND CONTROL GROUPS

(Read across pages 116 and 117.)

	Superior (125 I.Q. and up)			Bright (110-124 I.Q.)			

SIX YEAR OLD LONGITUDINAL GROUP

	Boys N 6	Girls N 7	Both N 13	Boys N 17	Girls N 15	Both N 32	Boys N 36
Range	0-8	0-6	0-8	0-26	0-17	0-26	0-13
Q_1	0	0	0	0	0	0	0
Mdn	2.0	0	0	0	4.0	2.0	0
Q_3	6.5	0	5.0	10.0	7.0	8.0	4.0
Mn	3.0	0.9	1.8	5.9	4.6	5.3	2.3
SD	3.2	2.1	2.9	7.7	5.2	6.6	4.1

SEVEN YEAR OLD LONGITUDINAL GROUP

	Boys N 6	Girls N 7	Both N 13	Boys N 17	Girls N 15	Both N 32	Boys N 36
Range	0-15	0-10	0-15	0-24	0-20	0-24	0-41
Q_1	0	0	0	0	0	0	0
Mdn	0	7.0	5.0	5.0	0	1.5	0
Q_3	9.8	9.0	8.5	9.0	6.0	5.8	5.8
Mn	3.8	5.4	4.7	5.9	3.7	4.9	3.6
SD	5.8	3.7	4.9	7.1	6.2	6.7	7.9

SEVEN YEAR OLD CONTROL GROUP

	Boys N 6	Girls N 3	Both N 9	Boys N 9	Girls N 9	Both N 18	Boys N 19
Range	0-15	0-10	0-15	0-13	0-18	0-18	0-27
Q_1	0	0	0	0	0	0	0
Mdn	4.0	0	0	0	0	0	0
Q_3	14.2	10.0	12.0	0	3.0	0	3.0
Mn	6.2	3.3	5.2	1.4	2.7	2.1	3.5
SD	6.2	4.7	6.1	4.1	4.6	5.1	7.2

EIGHT YEAR OLD LONGITUDINAL GROUP

	Boys N 6	Girls N 7	Both N 13	Boys N 17	Girls N 15	Both N 32	Boys N 36
Range	0-24	0-14	0-24	0-37	0-25	0-37	0-19
Q_1	4.5	0	1.5	0	0	0	0
Mdn	8.0	11.0	10.0	5.0	3.0	3.5	0
Q_3	15.0	13.0	12.5	10.5	6.0	8.0	6.0

OF ELEMENTARY SCHOOL CHILDREN FROM SIX THROUGH ELEVEN YEARS OF AGE REPORTED ACCORDING TO INTELLIGENCE LEVELS AND SEX

(Read across pages 116 and 117.)

Average (90–109 I.Q.)		Dull (75–89 I.Q.)			Total (74–140 I.Q.)		

SIX YEAR OLD LONGITUDINAL GROUP

Girls	Both	Boys	Girls	Both	Boys	Girls	Both
N 39	N 75	N 9	N 9	N 18	N 68	N 70	N 138
0–19	0–19	0–7	0–26	0–26	0–26	0–26	0–26
0	0	0	0	0	0	0	0
0	0	0	0	0	0	0	0
6.0	5.0	5.5	4.0	4.8	7.0	6.0	7.0
3.1	2.7	2.0	3.8	2.9	3.2	3.3	3.2
5.7	4.8	2.9	8.2	6.3	5.4	5.7	5.4

SEVEN YEAR OLD LONGITUDINAL GROUP

Girls	Both	Boys	Girls	Both	Boys	Girls	Both
N 39	N 75	N 9	N 9	N 18	N 68	N 70	N 138
0–12	0–41	0–18	0–11	0–18	0–41	0–20	0–41
0	0	0	0	0	0	0	0
0	0	0	0	0	0	0	0
0	5.0	7.5	0	1.5	6.8	5.0	6.0
1.7	2.6	3.6	1.2	2.4	4.2	2.4	3.3
3.5	5.9	5.7	3.4	4.9	7.4	4.3	5.9

SEVEN YEAR OLD CONTROL GROUP

Girls	Both	Boys	Girls	Both	Boys	Girls	Both
N 15	N 34	N 4	N 8	N 12	N 38	N 35	N 73
0–11	0–27	0–8	0–9	0–9	0–27	0–18	0–27
0	0	0	0	0	0	0	0
0	0	0	0	0	0	0	0
5.0	4.2	6.0	7.5	7.5	4.2	6.0	5.5
2.7	3.1	2.0	2.9	2.6	3.3	2.8	3.0
3.7	5.8	3.5	3.8	3.7	6.2	4.5	5.6

EIGHT YEAR OLD LONGITUDINAL GROUP

Girls	Both	Boys	Girls	Both	Boys	Girls	Both
N 39	N 75	N 9	N 9	N 18	N 68	N 70	N 138
0–14	0–19	0–8	0–23	0–23	0–37	0–25	0–37
0	0	0	0	0	0	0	0
0	0	0	0	0	0	0	0
6.0	6.0	5.0	2.5	5.0	8.8	6.0	6.0

	Superior (125 I.Q. and up)			Bright (110-124 I.Q.)			

EIGHT YEAR OLD LONGITUDINAL GROUP (Continued)

Mn	8.7	7.6	8.1	7.9	4.5	6.3	3.1
SD	8.2	5.8	7.1	10.5	6.3	8.9	4.7

NINE YEAR OLD LONGITUDINAL GROUP

	Boys N 6	Girls N 7	Both N 13	Boys N 17	Girls N 15	Both N 32	Boys N 36
Range	5-17	0-29	0-29	0-29	0-31	0-31	0-22
Q_1	6.5	0	2.5	2.5	4.0	4.2	0
Mdn	12.0	13.0	13.0	7.0	7.0	7.0	0
Q_3	16.2	16.0	16.0	18.5	19.0	18.5	6.0
Mn	11.5	10.3	10.8	10.2	11.0	10.6	3.5
SD	4.4	10.2	8.1	8.9	9.0	8.8	5.2

TEN YEAR OLD LONGITUDINAL GROUP

	Boys N 6	Girls N 7	Both N 13	Boys N 17	Girls N 15	Both N 32	Boys N 36
Range	0-21	0-20	0-21	0-25	0-25	0-25	0-21
Q_1	2.2	2.0	1.5	1.5	3.0	3.0	0
Mdn	6.5	13.0	8.0	9.0	10.4	8.4	2.0
Q_3	12.8	15.0	17.5	19.0	17.0	18.5	11.0
Mn	7.8	9.1	8.5	10.4	10.9	10.7	6.1
SD	6.7	7.4	7.2	8.4	7.9	8.1	7.9

ELEVEN YEAR OLD LONGITUDINAL GROUP

	Boys N 6	Girls N 7	Both N 13	Boys N 17	Girls N 15	Both N 32	Boys N 36
Range	5-18	0-19	0-19	0-29	0-31	0-31	0-24
Q_1	6.5	0	4.5	0	4.0	0.8	0
Mdn	10.0	5.0	8.0	6.0	9.0	8.5	5.0
Q_3	15.0	16.0	15.0	16.5	20.0	17.0	10.0
Mn	10.7	7.9	9.2	9.6	11.7	10.6	5.9
SD	4.5	7.1	6.2	9.1	9.1	9.1	6.3

ELEVEN YEAR OLD CONTROL GROUP

	Boys N 3	Girls N 5	Both N 8	Boys N 7	Girls N 11	Both N 18	Boys N 22
Range	0-6	0-21	0-21	0-23	0-22	0-23	0-29
Q_1	0	0	0	0	0	0	0
Mdn	3.0	7.0	4.0	6.0	4.0	5.0	1.5
Q_3	6.0	17.5	12.2	6.0	10.0	7.8	14.5
Mn	3.0	8.4	6.4	5.9	5.5	5.7	7.4
SD	2.4	8.2	7.1	7.5	6.5	7.0	9.6

Average (90–109 I.Q.)		Dull (75–89 I.Q.)			Total (74–140 I.Q.)		

EIGHT YEAR OLD LONGITUDINAL GROUP (Continued)

3.1	3.1	2.4	3.1	2.8	4.7	3.8	4.3
4.1	4.3	2.9	7.2	5.6	7.4	5.3	6.2

NINE YEAR OLD LONGITUDINAL GROUP

Girls N 39	Both N 75	Boys N 9	Girls N 9	Both N 18	Boys N 68	Girls N 70	Both N 138
0–18	0–22	0–8	0–36	0–36	0–29	0–36	0–36
0	0	0	0	0	0	0	0
4.0	0	0	0	0	4.0	5.0	5.0
9.0	8.0	6.0	8.0	5.8	9.8	11.0	11.0
4.8	4.2	4.3	5.8	5.1	6.0	6.8	6.5
5.5	5.2	8.4	11.2	10.1	7.6	8.1	7.6

TEN YEAR OLD LONGITUDINAL GROUP

Girls N 39	Both N 75	Boys N 9	Girls N 9	Both N 18	Boys N 68	Girls N 70	Both N 138
0–21	0–21	0–20	0–35	0–35	0–25	0–35	0–35
0	0	0	0	0	0	0	0
5.0	4.0	11.0	0	4.5	5.5	6.0	6.0
9.0	9.0	16.5	8.5	12.5	12.8	11.0	12.0
5.4	5.7	8.9	6.3	7.6	7.7	7.1	7.4
5.8	6.6	7.6	10.8	9.5	8.2	7.4	7.6

ELEVEN YEAR OLD LONGITUDINAL GROUP

Girls N 39	Both N 75	Boys N 9	Girls N 9	Both N 18	Boys N 68	Girls N 70	Both N 138
0–21	0–24	0–27	0–33	0–33	0–29	0–33	0–33
0	0	0	0	0	0	0	0
3.0	4.0	5.0	0	2.0	5.0	4.0	5.0
11.0	10.0	18.5	5.0	8.5	14.0	15.2	14.0
6.4	6.2	8.9	4.8	6.8	7.6	7.5	7.6
8.3	7.2	9.7	10.2	10.2	7.8	8.7	8.0

ELEVEN YEAR OLD CONTROL GROUP

Girls N 18	Both N 40	Boys N 8	Girls N 6	Both N 14	Boys N 40	Girls N 40	Both N 80
0–26	0–29	0–22	0–8	0–22	0–29	0–26	0–29
0	0	0	0	0	0	0	0
5.0	4.5	4.0	6.0	5.5	3.0	5.5	5.0
9.8	10.8	7.8	6.5	7.2	7.8	8.0	8.0
6.8	7.1	5.6	5.0	5.4	6.4	6.4	6.4
7.9	8.9	6.9	2.5	5.4	8.6	7.1	7.5

TABLE E

Dd%, OR PERCENTAGE OF UNUSUAL DETAIL RESPONSES GIVEN TO THE RORSCHACH CARDS BY LONGITUDINAL AND CONTROL GROUPS

(Read across pages 120 and 121.)

	Superior (125 I.Q. and up)			Bright (110-124 I.Q.)			

SIX YEAR OLD LONGITUDINAL GROUP

	Boys N 6	Girls N 7	Both N 13	Boys N 17	Girls N 15	Both N 32	Boys N 36
Range	0-13	0-0	0-13	0-17	0-7	0-17	0-6
Q_1	0	0	0	0	0	0	0
Mdn	4.0	0	0	0	0	0	0
Q_3	7.8	0	4.0	3.0	0	0	0
Mn	4.5	0	2.1	2.4	0.9	1.7	0.4
SD	4.4	0	3.8	4.7	2.4	3.8	1.3

SEVEN YEAR OLD LONGITUDINAL GROUP

	Boys N 6	Girls N 7	Both N 13	Boys N 17	Girls N 15	Both N 32	Boys N 36
Range	0-5	0-10	0-10	0-27	0-7	0-27	0-31
Q_1	0	0	0	0	0	0	0
Mdn	0	0	0	0	0	0	0
Q_3	4.2	9.0	5.5	7.5	0	5.8	0
Mn	1.5	4.0	2.8	4.8	1.2	3.1	2.4
SD	2.2	4.0	3.5	7.4	2.4	5.8	5.9

SEVEN YEAR OLD CONTROL GROUP

	Boys N 6	Girls N 3	Both N 9	Boys N 9	Girls N 9	Both N 18	Boys N 19
Range	0-11	0-0	0-11	0-8	0-7	0-8	0-7
Q_1	0	0	0	0	0	0	0
Mdn	0	0	0	0	0	0	0
Q_3	5.0	0	1.5	0	3.0	0	0
Mn	2.3	0	1.6	0.9	1.4	1.2	1.1
SD	4.0	0	3.5	2.5	2.7	2.6	2.2

EIGHT YEAR OLD LONGITUDINAL GROUP

	Boys N 6	Girls N 7	Both N 13	Boys N 17	Girls N 15	Both N 32	Boys N 36
Range	0-12	0-11	0-12	0-22	0-9	0-22	0-22
Q_1	0	0	0	0	0	0	0
Mdn	0	4.0	0	0	0	0	0
Q_3	3.0	8.0	7.5	5.0	4.0	3.8	0

TABLE E (Continued)

OF ELEMENTARY SCHOOL CHILDREN FROM SIX THROUGH ELEVEN YEARS OF AGE REPORTED ACCORDING TO INTELLIGENCE LEVELS AND SEX

(Read across pages 120 and 121.)

Average (90-109 I.Q.)		Dull (75-89 I.Q.)			Total (74-140 I.Q.)		

SIX YEAR OLD LONGITUDINAL GROUP

Girls	Both	Boys	Girls	Both	Boys	Girls	Both
N 39	N 75	N 9	N 9	N 18	N 68	N 70	N 138
0-20	0-20	0-6	0-10	0-10	0-17	0-20	0-20
0	0	0	0	0	0	0	0
0	0	0	0	0	0	0	0
0	0	2.0	0	0	0	0	0
1.8	1.2	1.1	1.1	1.1	1.3	1.4	1.4
4.0	3.0	2.1	3.1	2.7	3.3	3.4	3.2

SEVEN YEAR OLD LONGITUDINAL GROUP

Girls	Both	Boys	Girls	Both	Boys	Girls	Both
N 39	N 75	N 9	N 9	N 18	N 68	N 70	N 138
0-13	0-31	0-8	0-7	0-8	0-31	0-13	0-31
0	0	0	0	0	0	0	0
0	0	0	0	0	0	0	0
0	0	0	0	0	6.0	0	0
0.9	1.6	0.9	0.8	0.8	2.7	1.3	2.0
3.0	4.5	2.5	2.2	2.4	6.0	3.0	4.6

SEVEN YEAR OLD CONTROL GROUP

Girls	Both	Boys	Girls	Both	Boys	Girls	Both
N 15	N 34	N 4	N 8	N 12	N 38	N 35	N 73
0-8	0-8	0-8	0-8	0-8	0-11	0-8	0-11
0	0	0	0	0	0	0	0
0	0	0	0	0	0	0	0
0	0	7.8	0	5.2	0.8	0	0
0.9	1.0	3.8	1.0	1.9	1.5	1.0	1.3
2.4	2.3	3.8	2.6	3.3	2.9	2.5	2.8

EIGHT YEAR OLD LONGITUDINAL GROUP

Girls	Both	Boys	Girls	Both	Boys	Girls	Both
N 39	N 75	N 9	N 9	N 18	N 68	N 70	N 138
0-7	0-22	0-12	0-14	0-14	0-22	0-14	0-22
0	0	0	0	0	0	0	0
0	0	0	0	0	0	0	0
0	0	6.0	0	1.2	0	0	0

	Superior (125 I.Q. and up)			Bright (110-124 I.Q.)			

EIGHT YEAR OLD LONGITUDINAL GROUP (Continued)

Mn	2.0	4.7	3.5	3.7	1.7	2.8	1.6
SD	4.5	3.8	4.4	7.0	2.7	5.5	4.2

NINE YEAR OLD LONGITUDINAL GROUP

	Boys N 6	Girls N 7	Both N 13	Boys N 17	Girls N 15	Both N 32	Boys N 36
Range	0-5	0-37	0-37	0-20	0-12	0-20	0-14
Q_1	0	0	0	0	0	0	0
Mdn	3.0	6.0	3.0	4.0	0	3.0	0
Q_3	3.5	16.0	9.5	14.0	6.0	6.8	2.5
Mn	3.5	10.3	7.2	6.3	2.9	4.7	1.7
SD	1.1	12.5	9.8	6.8	4.2	5.9	3.5

TEN YEAR OLD LONGITUDINAL GROUP

	Boys N 6	Girls N 7	Both N 13	Boys N 17	Girls N 15	Both N 32	Boys N 36
Range	0-5	0-38	0-38	0-44	0-18	0-44	0-21
Q_1	0	0	0	0	0	0	0
Mdn	0	6.0	3.0	6.0	0	3.5	0
Q_3	3.5	16.0	6.5	19.5	6.0	11.8	5.0
Mn	1.3	10.0	6.0	10.5	4.3	7.6	3.3
SD	2.0	12.5	10.2	12.9	5.8	10.5	5.7

ELEVEN YEAR OLD LONGITUDINAL GROUP

	Boys N 6	Girls N 7	Both N 13	Boys N 17	Girls N 15	Both N 32	Boys N 36
Range	0-12	0-49	0-49	0-52	0-35	0-52	0-26
Q_1	0	0	0	0	0	0	0
Mdn	2.5	5.0	3.0	12.0	6.0	6.0	3.5
Q_3	4.8	23.0	10.5	21.5	13.0	15.0	8.5
Mn	3.0	12.6	8.2	14.0	7.4	10.9	5.6
SD	3.4	16.8	13.4	15.2	9.2	13.0	7.1

ELEVEN YEAR OLD CONTROL GROUP

	Boys N 3	Girls N 5	Both N 8	Boys N 7	Girls N 11	Both N 18	Boys N 22
Range	0-8	0-7	0-8	0-26	0-31	0-31	0-24
Q_1	0	0	0	0	0	0	0
Mdn	0	4.0	2.0	0	3.0	1.5	0
Q_3	8.0	6.5	6.8	9.0	7.0	7.5	7.0
Mn	2.7	3.4	3.1	5.9	5.7	5.8	3.8
SD	3.8	2.9	3.3	8.9	8.7	8.8	6.1

Average (90-109 I.Q.)		Dull (75-89 I.Q.)			Total (74-140 I.Q.)		

EIGHT YEAR OLD LONGITUDINAL GROUP (Continued)

| 0.5 | 1.0 | 2.7 | 1.6 | 2.1 | 2.3 | 1.3 | 1.8 |
| 1.7 | 3.1 | 4.1 | 4.4 | 4.3 | 5.2 | 2.9 | 4.0 |

NINE YEAR OLD LONGITUDINAL GROUP

Girls	Both	Boys	Girls	Both	Boys	Girls	Both
N 39	N 75	N 9	N 9	N 18	N 68	N 70	N 138
0-11	0-14	0-7	0-5	0-7	0-20	0-37	0-37
0	0	0	0	0	0	0	0
0	0	0	0	0	0	0	0
0	1.0	7.0	2.5	5.0	4.0	5.0	4.2
1.6	1.6	2.7	1.1	1.9	3.1	2.7	2.9
3.2	3.2	3.2	2.1	2.8	4.9	5.6	5.1

TEN YEAR OLD LONGITUDINAL GROUP

Girls	Both	Boys	Girls	Both	Boys	Girls	Both
N 39	N 75	N 9	N 9	N 18	N 68	N 70	N 138
0-18	0-21	0-10	0-23	0-23	0-44	0-38	0-44
0	0	0	0	0	0	0	0
0	0	0	0	0	0	0	0
4.0	5.0	7.5	4.5	5.2	6.8	6.0	6.0
2.9	3.1	4.2	1.8	3.0	5.0	3.8	4.4
5.1	5.2	5.8	2.8	4.8	8.7	6.4	7.4

ELEVEN YEAR OLD LONGITUDINAL GROUP

Girls	Both	Boys	Girls	Both	Boys	Girls	Both
N 39	N 75	N 9	N 9	N 18	N 68	N 70	N 138
0-23	0-26	0-14	0-11	0-14	0-52	0-49	0-52
0	0	0	0	0	0	0	0
0	0	0	0	0	4.0	0	3.0
7.0	7.0	7.0	3.0	5.2	9.8	7.2	9.0
3.2	4.3	3.6	1.9	2.7	7.2	4.9	6.0
5.1	6.0	4.8	3.7	4.4	10.4	8.3	9.1

ELEVEN YEAR OLD CONTROL GROUP

Girls	Both	Boys	Girls	Both	Boys	Girls	Both
N 18	N 40	N 8	N 6	N 14	N 40	N 40	N 80
0-22	0-24	0-24	0-6	0-24	0-26	0-31	0-31
0	0	0	0	0	0	0	0
0	0	6.5	4.0	4.5	0	3.5	0
8.2	7.0	15.2	6.0	8.5	8.0	6.8	7.0
4.3	4.0	8.0	3.3	6.0	4.9	4.4	4.7
6.1	6.1	8.2	2.5	6.8	7.2	6.3	6.5

S% OR PERCENTAGE OF WHITE SPACE RESPONSES
GIVEN TO THE RORSCHACH CARDS BY LONGITUDINAL AND CONTROL GROUPS

(Read across pages 124 and 125.)

	Superior (125 I.Q. and up)			Bright (110–124 I.Q.)			

SIX YEAR OLD LONGITUDINAL GROUP

	Boys N 6	Girls N 7	Both N 13	Boys N 17	Girls N 15	Both N 32	Boys N 36
Range	0-10	0-7	0-10	0-5	0-7	0-7	0-8
Q_1	0	0	0	0	0	0	0
Mdn	4.0	0	0	0	0	0	0
Q_3	7.0	0	5.5	0	0	0	0
Mean	4.0	1.0	2.4	0.3	1.3	0.8	1.4
SD	3.5	2.4	3.3	1.2	2.6	2.0	3.0

SEVEN YEAR OLD LONGITUDINAL GROUP

	Boys N 6	Girls N 7	Both N 13	Boys N 17	Girls N 15	Both N 32	Boys N 36
Range	0-8	0-5	0-8	0-5	0-12	0-12	0-8
Q_1	0	0	0	0	0	0	0
Mdn	0	0	0	0	0	0	0
Q_3	5.0	3.0	3.5	0	0	0	0
Mean	6.0	1.1	1.5	0.8	1.1	0.9	0.6
SD	3.1	1.9	2.5	1.7	3.1	2.4	1.9

SEVEN YEAR OLD CONTROL GROUP

	Boys N 6	Girls N 3	Both N 9	Boys N 9	Girls N 9	Both N 18	Boys N 19
Range	0-9	0-10	0-10	0-8	0-0	0-8	0-9
Q_1	0	0	0	0	0	0	0
Mdn	0	0	0	0	0	0	0
Q_3	2.2	10.0	4.5	3.0	0	0	0
Mean	1.5	3.3	2.1	1.6	0	0.8	0.6
SD	3.4	4.7	4.0	2.9	0	2.2	2.1

EIGHT YEAR OLD LONGITUDINAL GROUP

	Boys N 6	Girls N 7	Both N 13	Boys N 17	Girls N 15	Both N 32	Boys N 36
Range	0-0	0-6	0-6	0-4	0-10	0-10	0-9
Q_1	0	0	0	0	0	0	0
Mdn	0	0	0	0	0	0	0
Q_3	0	4.0	0	0	0	0	0

OF ELEMENTARY SCHOOL CHILDREN FROM SIX THROUGH ELEVEN YEARS OF AGE REPORTED ACCORDING TO INTELLIGENCE LEVELS AND SEX

(Read across pages 124 and 125.)

Average (90-109 I.Q.)		Dull (89 I.Q. and below)			Total (74-140 I.Q.)		

SIX YEAR OLD LONGITUDINAL GROUP

Girls	Both	Boys	Girls	Both	Boys	Girls	Both
N 39	N 75	N 9	N 9	N 18	N 68	N 70	N 138
0-8	0-8	0-4	0-8	0-8	0-10	0-8	0-10
0	0	0	0	0	0	0	0
0	0	0	0	0	0	0	0
0	0	0	2.5	0	0	0	0
0.5	1.0	0.4	1.4	0.9	1.2	0.9	1.0
1.7	2.4	1.3	2.8	2.2	2.8	2.1	2.4

SEVEN YEAR OLD LONGITUDINAL GROUP

Girls	Both	Boys	Girls	Both	Boys	Girls	Both
N 39	N 75	N 9	N 9	N 18	N 68	N 70	N 138
0-13	0-13	0-9	0-10	0-10	0-9	0-13	0-13
0	0	0	0	0	0	0	0
0	0	0	0	0	0	0	0
0	0	2.0	0	0	0	0	0
0.5	0.5	1.4	1.1	1.3	0.8	0.8	0.8
2.3	2.0	3.0	3.1	3.1	2.2	2.5	2.3

SEVEN YEAR OLD CONTROL GROUP

Girls	Both	Boys	Girls	Both	Boys	Girls	Both
N 15	N 34	N 4	N 8	N 12	N 38	N 35	N 73
0-9	0-9	0-8	0-0	0-8	0-9	0-10	0-10
0	0	0	0	0	0	0	0
0	0	0	0	0	0	0	0
0	0	6.0	0	0	0	0	0
0.9	0.8	2.0	0	0.7	1.1	0.7	0.9
2.5	2.2	3.5	0	2.2	2.7	2.4	2.6

EIGHT YEAR OLD LONGITUDINAL GROUP

Girls	Both	Boys	Girls	Both	Boys	Girls	Both
N 39	N 75	N 9	N 9	N 18	N 68	N 70	N 138
0-6	0-9	0-5	0-0	0-5	0-9	0-10	0-10
0	0	0	0	0	0	0	0
0	0	0	0	0	0	0	0
0	0	0	0	0	0	0	0

	Superior (125 I.Q. and up)			Bright (110-124 I.Q.)			

EIGHT YEAR OLD LONGITUDINAL GROUP (Continued)

Mean	0	1.4	0.8	0.6	1.3	0.9	0.6
SD	0	2.3	1.8	1.4	2.8	2.2	1.9

NINE YEAR OLD LONGITUDINAL GROUP

	Boys N 6	Girls N 7	Both N 13	Boys N 17	Girls N 15	Both N 32	Boys N 36
Range	0-6	0-6	0-6	0-5	0-14	0-14	0-5
Q_1	0	0	0	0	0	0	0
Mdn	0	2.0	0	0	0	0	0
Q_3	1.5	4.0	3.5	1.5	4.0	2.2	0
Mean	1.0	2.1	1.6	0.9	1.9	1.4	0.4
SD	2.2	2.2	2.3	1.7	3.8	2.9	1.3

TEN YEAR OLD LONGITUDINAL GROUP

	Boys N 6	Girls N 7	Both N 13	Boys N 17	Girls N 15	Both N 32	Boys N 36
Range	0-9	0-3	0-9	0-8	0-15	0-15	0-6
Q_1	0	0	0	0	0	0	0
Mdn	0	0	0	0	0	0	0
Q_3	8.2	3.0	3.0	3.0	4.0	3.0	0
Mean	2.8	0.9	1.8	1.3	2.6	1.9	0.6
SD	4.0	1.4	3.1	5.8	4.6	3.6	1.6

ELEVEN YEAR OLD LONGITUDINAL GROUP

	Boys N 6	Girls N 7	Both N 13	Boys N 17	Girls N 15	Both N 32	Boys N 36
Range	0-3	0-4	0-4	0-11	0-24	0-24	0-5
Q_1	0	0	0	0	0	0	0
Mdn	0	0	0	0	0	0	0
Q_3	3.0	3.0	3.0	1.0	1.0	1.5	0
Mean	1.0	1.1	1.1	1.5	2.9	2.2	0.4
SD	1.4	1.6	1.5	3.3	6.8	5.2	1.3

ELEVEN YEAR OLD CONTROL GROUP

	Boys N 3	Girls N 5	Both N 8	Boys N 7	Girls N 11	Both N 18	Boys N 22
Range	0-0	0-0	0-0	0-6	0-3	0-6	0-7
Q_1	0	0	0	0	0	0	0
Mdn	0	0	0	0	0	0	0
Q_3	0	0	0	4.0	0	4.0	4.5
Mean	0	0	0	1.4	1.2	1.3	1.6
SD	0	0	0	2.3	2.0	2.1	2.7

Average (90-109 I.Q.)		Dull (89 I.Q. and below)			Total (74-140 I.Q.)		

EIGHT YEAR OLD LONGITUDINAL GROUP (Continued)

Girls	Both	Boys	Girls	Both	Boys	Girls	Both
0.2	0.4	0.6	0	0.3	0.6	0.5	0.6
1.1	1.5	1.6	0	1.2	1.7	1.7	1.7

NINE YEAR OLD LONGITUDINAL GROUP

Girls	Both	Boys	Girls	Both	Boys	Girls	Both
N 39	N 75	N 9	N 9	N 18	N 68	N 70	N 138
0-5	0-5	0-0	0-0	0-0	0-6	0-14	0-14
0	0	0	0	0	0	0	0
0	0	0	0	0	0	0	0
0	0	0	0	0	0	0	0
0.4	0.4	0	0	0	0.6	0.8	0.7
1.3	1.2	0	0	0	1.5	2.2	1.8

TEN YEAR OLD LONGITUDINAL GROUP

Girls	Both	Boys	Girls	Both	Boys	Girls	Both
N 39	N 75	N 9	N 9	N 18	N 68	N 70	N 138
0-5	0-6	0-0	0-5	0-5	0-9	0-15	0-15
0	0	0	0	0	0	0	0
0	0	0	0	0	0	0	0
0	0	0	0	0	0	0	0
0.4	0.5	0	0.6	0.3	0.9	0.9	0.9
1.2	1.4	0	1.6	1.2	2.2	2.5	2.3

ELEVEN YEAR OLD LONGITUDINAL GROUP

Girls	Both	Boys	Girls	Both	Boys	Girls	Both
N 39	N 75	N 9	N 9	N 18	N 68	N 70	N 138
0-8	0-8	0-0	0-3	0-3	0-11	0-24	0-24
0	0	0	0	0	0	0	0
0	0	0	0	0	0	0	0
0	0	0	0	0	0	0	0
0.6	0.5	0	0.3	0.2	0.7	1.1	0.9
1.6	1.4	0	.9	.7	2.0	3.5	2.8

ELEVEN YEAR OLD CONTROL GROUP

Girls	Both	Boys	Girls	Both	Boys	Girls	Both
N 18	N 40	N 8	N 6	N 14	N 40	N 40	N 80
0-15	0-15	0-7	0-0	0-7	0-7	0-15	0-15
0	0	0	0	0	0	0	0
0	0	0	0	0	0	0	0
5.0	4.8	2.2	0	0	2.2	0	0
2.4	2.0	1.2	0	0.7	1.4	1.4	1.4
4.1	3.4	2.4	0	1.9	2.5	3.1	2.7

TABLE G

F% OR PERCENTAGE OF FORM RESPONSES
GIVEN TO THE RORSCHACH CARDS BY LONGITUDINAL AND CONTROL GROUPS

(Read across pages 128 and 129.)

	Superior (125 I.Q. and up)			Bright (110-124 I.Q.)			

SIX YEAR OLD LONGITUDINAL GROUP

	Boys N 6	Girls N 7	Both N 13	Boys N 17	Girls N 15	Both N 32	Boys N 36
Range	43-71	14-69	14-71	27-92	0-86	0-92	6-86
Q_1	49.0	19.0	27.0	45.5	14.0	31.5	30.8
Mdn	54.5	27.0	54.0	50.0	38.0	50.0	43.5
Q_3	64.2	67.0	64.5	64.0	57.0	59.2	52.8
Mn	56.0	40.7	47.8	53.9	38.5	46.7	44.7
SD	8.8	22.4	19.1	15.6	24.8	21.6	17.4

SEVEN YEAR OLD LONGITUDINAL GROUP

	Boys N 6	Girls N 7	Both N 13	Boys N 17	Girls N 15	Both N 32	Boys N 36
Range	21-81	14-59	14-81	23-77	18-75	18-77	0-90
Q_1	24.0	30.0	27.5	44.5	36.0	42.5	35.0
Mdn	55.0	56.0	56.0	50.0	47.0	50.0	49.0
Q_3	79.5	59.0	63.5	63.5	62.0	62.8	60.8
Mn	52.7	45.0	48.5	52.8	48.7	50.9	48.9
SD	24.6	16.4	20.9	12.3	15.4	13.8	20.1

SEVEN YEAR OLD CONTROL GROUP

	Boys N 6	Girls N 3	Both N 9	Boys N 9	Girls N 9	Both N 18	Boys N 19
Range	20-61	28-50	20-61	25-83	8-69	8-83	14-91
Q_1	29.8	28.0	30.5	38.5	30.0	34.5	25.0
Mdn	55.0	43.0	50.0	63.0	43.0	46.0	58.0
Q_3	57.2	50.0	55.5	75.5	67.0	66.0	73.0
Mn	66.8	40.3	44.6	56.7	41.2	48.9	50.4
SD	14.9	9.2	13.6	19.1	17.8	20.2	24.1

EIGHT YEAR OLD LONGITUDINAL GROUP

	Boys N 6	Girls N 7	Both N 13	Boys N 17	Girls N 15	Both N 32	Boys N 36
Range	32-61	19-75	19-75	29-88	25-76	25-88	8-73
Q_1	37.5	29.0	33.5	39.5	43.0	43.0	39.2
Mdn	44.0	44.0	44.0	46.0	50.0	48.5	48.0
Q_3	52.8	71.0	60.5	63.0	59.0	61.2	58.0

TABLE G (Continued)

OF ELEMENTARY SCHOOL CHILDREN FROM SIX THROUGH ELEVEN YEARS OF AGE REPORTED ACCORDING TO INTELLIGENCE LEVELS AND SEX

(Read across pages 128 and 129.)

Average (90-109 I.Q.)		Dull (75-89 I.Q.)			Total (74-140 I.Q.)		

SIX YEAR OLD LONGITUDINAL GROUP

Girls	Both	Boys	Girls	Both	Boys	Girls	Both
N 39	N 75	N 9	N 9	N 18	N 68	N 70	N 138
5-90	5-90	21-90	8-89	21-90	6-92	0-90	0-92
29.0	30.0	36.0	21.5	33.0	39.0	25.8	31.0
39.0	40.0	50.0	50.0	50.0	50.0	39.0	44.5
58.0	53.0	70.5	56.0	61.0	56.5	58.0	58.0
42.3	43.5	52.0	44.3	48.2	49.0	41.6	45.2
20.7	18.5	20.5	23.4	22.6	17.7	21.6	19.5

SEVEN YEAR OLD LONGITUDINAL GROUP

Girls	Both	Boys	Girls	Both	Boys	Girls	Both
N 39	N 75	N 9	N 9	N 18	N 68	N 70	N 138
18-100	0-100	17-86	10-80	10-86	0-90	10-100	0-100
33.0	35.0	43.5	45.0	47.5	42.0	37.5	38.0
47.0.	48.0	70.0	58.0	63.0	50.0	50.0	50.0
62.0	61.0	81.0	65.5	78.5	66.8	62.0	64.0
49.8	49.4	62.9	53.4	58.2	52.0	49.6	50.8
20.4	19.5	22.2	18.8	21.3	20.1	18.4	18.6

SEVEN YEAR OLD CONTROL GROUP

Girls	Both	Boys	Girls	Both	Boys	Girls	Both
N 15	N 34	N 4	N 8	N 12	N 38	N 35	N 73
8-77	8-91	8-54	31-80	8-80	8-91	8-80	8-91
31.0	29.0	9.0	37.0	32.2	28.0	33.0	31.0
56.0	55.5	31.0	53.5	42.0	55.0	44.0	50.0
70.0	70.0	53.0	79.0	60.8	64.8	69.0	67.0
49.9	50.2	31.0	56.2	47.8	49.3	48.3	48.8
21.4	22.5	21.1	19.4	23.2	22.2	20.4	21.8

EIGHT YEAR OLD LONGITUDINAL GROUP

Girls	Both	Boys	Girls	Both	Boys	Girls	Both
N 39	N 75	N 9	N 9	N 18	N 68	N 70	N 138
20-100	8-100	16-84	27-91	16-91	8-88	19-100	8-100
33.0	36.0	37.5	34.0	38.2	39.2	37.5	39.0
47.0	47.0	48.0	45.0	47.0	47.0	47.0	47.0
58.0	58.0	59.5	60.5	57.2	58.0	58.0	58.0

	Superior (125 I.Q. and up)			Bright (110-124 I.Q.)			

EIGHT YEAR OLD LONGITUDINAL GROUP (Continued)

	Boys	Girls	Both	Boys	Girls	Both	Boys
Mn	44.8	47.6	46.3	50.9	51.5	51.2	48.7
SD	9.3	20.0	16.0	16.2	12.1	14.3	15.6

NINE YEAR OLD LONGITUDINAL GROUP

	Boys N 6	Girls N 7	Both N 13	Boys N 17	Girls N 15	Both N 32	Boys N 36
Range	36-53	15-86	15-86	22-76	34-88	22-88	14-88
Q_1	41.2	27.0	37.0	41.5	40.0	40.2	37.2
Mdn	44.5	64.0	45.0	56.0	46.0	51.5	43.0
Q_3	50.8	67.0	65.5	61.0	62.0	62.0	56.5
Mn	45.2	52.0	48.8	52.8	51.1	52.0	46.9
SD	5.4	23.8	18.1	13.2	14.2	13.6	17.0

TEN YEAR OLD LONGITUDINAL GROUP

	Boys N 6	Girls N 7	Both N 13	Boys N 17	Girls N 15	Both N 32	Boys N 36
Range	29-46	33-73	29-73	20-77	18-75	18-77	6-79
Q_1	32.0	35.0	34.0	31.0	38.0	36.2	29.0
Mdn	40.0	47.0	41.0	43.0	47.0	46.5	42.0
Q_3	45.2	71.0	51.5	59.5	56.0	57.8	47.8
Mn	38.8	50.6	45.2	45.9	47.9	46.8	40.2
SD	6.1	15.4	13.4	17.9	14.4	16.2	16.2

ELEVEN YEAR OLD LONGITUDINAL GROUP

	Boys N 6	Girls N 7	Both N 13	Boys N 17	Girls N 15	Both N 32	Boys N 36
Range	22-59	32-78	22-78	16-83	16-87	16-87	8-75
Q_1	24.5	33.0	32.5	32.5	30.0	32.5	33.5
Mdn	36.5	38.0	38.0	40.0	42.0	41.5	41.5
Q_3	46.2	59.0	56.0	55.0	54.0	53.5	50.0
Mn	38.0	46.9	42.8	43.6	44.3	46.8	41.2
SD	11.3	16.0	14.7	17.0	17.8	17.2	15.2

ELEVEN YEAR OLD CONTROL GROUP

	Boys N 3	Girls N 5	Both N 8	Boys N 7	Girls N 11	Both N 18	Boys N 22
Range	28-47	32-61	28-61	17-56	35-65	17-65	14-76
Q_1	28.0	35.0	33.5	41.0	38.0	39.5	38.8
Mdn	38.0	50.0	42.5	49.0	43.0	47.5	51.5
Q_3	47.0	60.5	57.5	51.0	52.0	51.2	63.2
Mn	37.7	48.2	44.2	44.4	45.9	45.3	49.3
SD	7.8	11.6	11.5	12.0	8.8	10.2	14.7

Average (90-109 I.Q.)		Dull (75-89 I.Q.)			Total (74-140 I.Q.)		

EIGHT YEAR OLD LONGITUDINAL GROUP (Continued)

47.3	48.0	48.8	48.7	48.7	48.9	48.4	48.6
18.5	16.5	17.9	19.2	18.7	15.9	17.2	16.0

NINE YEAR OLD LONGITUDINAL GROUP

Girls	Both	Boys	Girls	Both	Boys	Girls	Both
N 39	N 75	N 9	N 9	N 18	N 68	N 70	N 138
18-87	14-88	29-79	33-67	29-79	14-88	15-88	14-88
36.0	36.0	39.5	41.0	40.5	39.0	38.0	38.0
47.0	45.0	55.0	50.0	54.0	45.5	47.5	46.5
61.0	61.0	61.5	64.5	63.5	58.0	63.0	62.0
47.9	47.4	52.6	51.7	52.1	48.9	49.5	49.2
17.5	16.7	14.1	11.7	13.1	15.6	16.6	15.6

TEN YEAR OLD LONGITUDINAL GROUP

Girls	Both	Boys	Girls	Both	Boys	Girls	Both
N 39	N 75	N 9	N 9	N 18	N 68	N 70	N 138
20-84	6-84	42-89	31-61	31-89	6-89	18-84	6-89
35.0	32.0	44.5	26.5	40.8	33.0	35.8	34.5
42.0	42.0	50.0	43.0	48.5	43.5	43.0	43.0
50.0	50.0	64.5	52.0	55.0	51.5	53.2	52.0
43.8	42.0	54.2	39.9	47.1	43.4	44.7	44.1
14.8	15.0	11.8	15.1	15.4	16.5	14.7	15.1

ELEVEN YEAR OLD LONGITUDINAL GROUP

Girls	Both	Boys	Girls	Both	Boys	Girls	Both
N 39	N 75	N 9	N 9	N 18	N 68	N 70	N 138
6-73	6-75	29-83	27-55	27-83	8-83	6-87	6-87
29.0	30.0	34.0	29.0	31.2	33.2	30.0	31.8
37.0	40.0	41.0	33.0	40.0	40.0	38.0	40.0
50.0	50.0	57.0	51.0	47.8	47.8	52.0	50.0
38.6	39.8	46.3	39.4	42.9	42.2	40.7	41.5
16.4	15.3	16.2	10.7	14.3	15.9	15.9	15.9

ELEVEN YEAR OLD CONTROL GROUP

Girls	Both	Boys	Girls	Both	Boys	Girls	Both
N 18	N 40	N 8	N 6	N 14	N 40	N 40	N 80
16-69	14-76	27-75	19-82	19-82	14-76	16-82	14-82
34.5	38.2	38.8	31.0	35.8	38.2	37.2	38.0
47.0	47.5	52.0	46.0	48.0	48.5	47.0	47.5
60.2	60.0	66.8	69.2	66.2	57.0	59.8	58.5
45.9	47.8	51.5	48.8	50.4	48.0	46.6	47.3
15.9	15.4	15.3	20.3	17.5	14.5	14.6	14.0

M OR FREQUENCY OF MOVEMENT RESPONSES
GIVEN TO THE RORSCHACH CARDS BY LONGITUDINAL AND CONTROL GROUPS

(Read across pages 132 and 133.)

	Superior (125 I.Q. and up)			Bright (110-124 I.Q.)			

SIX YEAR OLD LONGITUDINAL GROUP

	Boys N 6	Girls N 7	Both N 13	Boys N 17	Girls N 15	Both N 32	Boys N 36
Range	1-4	0-3	0-4	0-3	0-6	0-6	0-4
Q_1	1.0	0	1.0	0	0	0	0
Mdn	2.0	2.0	2.0	1.0	1.0	1.0	1.0
Q_3	4.0	2.0	3.0	1.5	3.0	2.0	1.0
Mean	2.3	1.6	1.9	0.9	1.5	1.2	0.8

SEVEN YEAR OLD LONGITUDINAL GROUP

	Boys N 6	Girls N 7	Both N 13	Boys N 17	Girls N 15	Both N 32	Boys N 36
Range	0-6	1-4	0-6	0-5	0-4	0-5	0-3
Q_1	0.8	1.0	1.0	0.5	0	0	0
Mdn	1.0	2.0	1.5	1.0	1.0	1.0	1.0
Q_3	3.8	2.0	2.4	2.0	1.0	2.0	1.0
Mean	2.0	2.0	2.0	1.6	0.8	1.2	0.9

SEVEN YEAR OLD CONTROL GROUP

	Boys N 6	Girls N 3	Both N 9	Boys N 9	Girls N 9	Both N 18	Boys N 19
Range	0-7	1-4	0-7	0-4	0-4	0-4	0-5
Q_1	0.8	1.0	1.0	0	1.0	0	0
Mdn	2.5	1.0	1.0	1.0	1.0	1.0	1.0
Q_3	4.8	4.0	4.0	2.5	3.5	3.0	1.0
Mean	2.8	2.0	2.6	1.2	1.9	1.6	1.1

EIGHT YEAR OLD LONGITUDINAL GROUP

	Boys N 6	Girls N 7	Both N 13	Boys N 17	Girls N 15	Both N 32	Boys N 36
Range	2-5	2-7	2-7	0-8	0-5	0-8	0-5
Q_1	2.0	3.0	2.0	1.0	1.0	1.0	0
Mdn	2.5	3.0	3.0	2.0	2.0	2.0	1.0
Q_3	4.0	5.0	5.0	3.5	3.0	3.0	3.0
Mean	3.2	3.9	3.5	2.2	2.3	2.2	1.5

TABLE H (Continued)

OF ELEMENTARY SCHOOL CHILDREN FROM SIX THROUGH ELEVEN YEARS OF AGE
REPORTED ACCORDING TO INTELLIGENCE LEVELS AND SEX

(Read across pages 132 and 133.)

Average (90-109 I.Q.)		Dull (75-89 I.Q.)			Total (74-140 I.Q.)		

SIX YEAR OLD LONGITUDINAL GROUP

Girls	Both	Boys	Girls	Both	Boys	Girls	Both
N 39	N 75	N 9	N 9	N 18	N 68	N 70	N 138
0-6	0-6	0-1	0-1	0-1	0-4	0-6	0-6
0	0	0	0	0	0	0	0
1.0	1.0	0	0	0	1.0	1.0	1.0
2.0	2.0	1.0	1.0	1.0	1.0	2.0	2.0
1.4	1.1	0.3	0.3	0.3	0.9	1.3	1.1

SEVEN YEAR OLD LONGITUDINAL GROUP

Girls	Both	Boys	Girls	Both	Boys	Girls	Both
N 39	N 75	N 9	N 9	N 18	N 68	N 70	N 138
0-5	0-5	0-2	0-3	0-3	0-6	0-5	0-6
0	0	0	0	0	0	0	0
1.0	1.0	0	0	0	1.0	1.0	1.0
2.0	2.0	1.5	1.0	1.0	2.0	2.0	2.0
1.1	1.0	0.6	0.6	0.6	1.1	1.1	1.1

SEVEN YEAR OLD CONTROL GROUP

Girls	Both	Boys	Girls	Both	Boys	Girls	Both
N 15	N 34	N 4	N 8	N 12	N 38	N 35	N 73
0-5	0-5	0-3	0-3	0-3	0-7	0-5	0-7
0	0	0	0.2	0	0	0	0
1.0	1.0	1.0	1.0	1.0	1.0	1.0	1.0
1.0	1.0	2.8	2.8	2.8	2.0	2.0	2.0
1.3	1.2	1.2	1.4	1.3	1.4	1.5	1.4

EIGHT YEAR OLD LONGITUDINAL GROUP

Girls	Both	Boys	Girls	Both	Boys	Girls	Both
N 39	N 75	N 9	N 9	N 18	N 68	N 70	N 138
0-7	0-7	0-5	0-5	0-5	0-8	0-7	0-8
0	0	0	0	0	0	0	0
2.0	1.0	2.0	0	1.5	1.5	2.0	2.0
3.0	3.0	3.0	2.0	2.2	3.0	3.0	3.0
2.0	1.7	1.7	1.1	1.4	1.8	2.1	1.8

	Superior (125 I.Q. and up)			Bright (110-124 I.Q.)			

NINE YEAR OLD LONGITUDINAL GROUP

	Boys N 6	Girls N 7	Both N 13	Boys N 17	Girls N 15	Both N 32	Boys N 36
Range	0-9	0-5	0-9	0-7	0-7	0-7	0-6
Q_1	1.5	2.0	2.0	1.0	1.0	1.0	0.2
Mdn	4.0	3.0	3.0	3.0	2.0	2.5	1.0
Q_3	8.2	5.0	5.0	4.0	4.0	4.0	3.0
Mean	4.5	3.0	3.7	2.8	2.9	2.8	1.8

TEN YEAR OLD LONGITUDINAL GROUP

	Boys N 6	Girls N 7	Both N 13	Boys N 17	Girls N 15	Both N 32	Boys N 36
Range	2-6	2-6	2-6	0-25	0-6	0-25	0-6
Q_1	2.8	3.0	3.0	1.0	1.0	1.0	1.0
Mdn	3.5	4.0	3.5	2.0	3.0	3.0	2.0
Q_3	5.2	4.0	4.5	3.5	4.0	4.0	3.8
Mean	3.8	3.7	3.8	3.6	2.9	3.3	2.1

ELEVEN YEAR OLD LONGITUDINAL GROUP

	Boys N 6	Girls N 7	Both N 13	Boys N 17	Girls N 15	Both N 32	Boys N 36
Range	3-14	3-9	3-14	0-24	0-8	0-24	0-8
Q_1	4.2	3.0	3.0	2.0	2.0	2.0	1.0
Mdn	7.0	3.0	5.0	3.0	3.0	3.0	2.0
Q_3	8.8	5.0	7.0	4.0	6.0	5.0	3.0
Mean	7.0	4.1	5.5	3.9	3.5	3.9	2.4

ELEVEN YEAR OLD CONTROL GROUP

	Boys N 3	Girls N 5	Both N 8	Boys N 7	Girls N 11	Both N 18	Boys N 22
Range	2-9	0-6	0-9	1-8	0-6	0-8	0-6
Q_1	2.0	1.0	2.0	1.0	1.0	1.0	0
Mdn	7.0	3.0	3.5	2.0	2.0	2.0	1.5
Q_3	9.0	5.0	6.8	7.0	3.0	3.2	3.0
Mean	6.0	3.0	4.1	3.1	2.4	2.7	1.8

| Average (90-109 I.Q.) | | Dull (75-89 I.Q.) | | | Total (74-140 I.Q.) | | |

NINE YEAR OLD LONGITUDINAL GROUP

Girls	Both	Boys	Girls	Both	Boys	Girls	Both
N 39	N 75	N 9	N 9	N 18	N 68	N 70	N 138
0-7	0-7	0-3	0-3	0-3	0-9	0-7	0-9
1.0	1.0	0	0.5	0	1.0	1.0	1.0
2.0	2.0	1.0	2.0	1.0	2.0	2.0	2.0
3.0	3.0	2.5	3.0	3.0	3.0	3.0	3.0
2.2	2.0	1.2	1.9	1.5	2.2	2.4	2.3

TEN YEAR OLD LONGITUDINAL GROUP

Girls	Both	Boys	Girls	Both	Boys	Girls	Both
N 39	N 75	N 9	N 9	N 18	N 68	N 70	N 138
0-9	0-9	0-4	0-3	0-4	0-25	0-9	0-25
1.0	1.0	0.5	0	0	1.0	1.0	1.0
2.0	2.0	2.0	2.0	2.0	2.0	2.0	2.0
3.0	3.0	2.5	2.5	2.2	3.0	3.2	3.0
2.4	2.2	1.7	1.4	1.6	2.6	2.5	2.6

ELEVEN YEAR OLD LONGITUDINAL GROUP

Girls	Both	Boys	Girls	Both	Boys	Girls	Both
N 39	N 75	N 9	N 9	N 18	N 68	N 70	N 138
0-10	0-10	0-3	0-3	0-3	0-24	0-10	0-24
1.0	1.0	1.0	0	0.8	1.0	1.0	1.0
2.0	2.0	3.0	1.0	2.0	2.5	2.0	2.0
4.0	4.0	3.0	2.0	3.0	4.0	4.0	4.0
2.8	2.6	2.1	1.2	1.7	3.6	2.9	3.3

ELEVEN YEAR OLD CONTROL GROUP

Girls	Both	Boys	Girls	Both	Boys	Girls	Both
N 18	N 40	N 8	N 6	N 14	N 40	N 40	N 80
0-8	0-8	0-3	0-4	0-4	0-9	0-8	0-9
1.0	1.0	0.2	0	0	1.0	1.0	1.0
3.0	2.0	2.0	0.5	1.5	2.0	2.0	2.0
3.5	3.0	2.0	2.5	2.0	3.0	3.0	3.0
2.9	2.3	1.5	1.2	1.4	2.8	2.5	2.7

TABLE I

FM OR FREQUENCY OF ANIMAL MOVEMENT RESPONSES
GIVEN TO THE RORSCHACH CARDS BY LONGITUDINAL AND CONTROL GROUPS

(Read across pages 136 and 137.)

	Superior (125 I.Q. and up)			Bright (110-124 I.Q.)			

SIX YEAR OLD LONGITUDINAL GROUP

	Boys N 6	Girls N 7	Both N 13	Boys N 17	Girls N 15	Both N 32	Boys N 36
Range	1-11	1-7	1-11	1-12	0-8	0-12	0-11
Q_1	1.8	1.0	1.0	1.5	0	1.0	1.0
Mdn	3.0	2.0	3.0	3.0	2.0	2.5	3.0
Q_3	6.5	4.0	4.5	5.0	5.0	5.0	4.8
Mean	4.3	2.7	3.5	3.9	2.9	3.4	3.0

SEVEN YEAR OLD LONGITUDINAL GROUP

	Boys N 6	Girls N 7	Both N 13	Boys N 17	Girls N 15	Both N 32	Boys N 36
Range	1-7	1-9	1-9	0-12	1-9	0-12	0-9
Q_1	1.8	2.0	2.0	1.5	2.0	2.0	2.0
Mdn	3.0	4.0	4.0	3.0	4.0	3.5	3.0
Q_3	6.2	5.0	5.5	5.0	7.0	5.8	5.8
Mean	3.7	4.0	3.8	3.9	4.3	4.1	3.8

SEVEN YEAR OLD CONTROL GROUP

	Boys N 6	Girls N 3	Both N 9	Boys N 9	Girls N 9	Both N 18	Boys N 19
Range	1-8	1-4	1-8	0-6	1-7	0-7	0-8
Q_1	1.8	1.0	1.5	0	2.5	1.8	1.0
Mdn	4.5	4.0	4.0	3.0	4.0	3.5	2.0
Q_3	7.8	4.0	6.5	4.5	5.0	5.0	5.0
Mean	4.5	3.0	4.0	2.7	3.9	3.3	3.3

EIGHT YEAR OLD LONGITUDINAL GROUP

	Boys N 6	Girls N 7	Both N 13	Boys N 17	Girls N 15	Both N 32	Boys N 36
Range	3-10	1-6	1-10	0-7	2-8	0-8	0-10
Q_1	3.0	2.0	3.0	2.0	3.0	3.0	3.0
Mdn	8.0	4.0	4.0	4.0	4.0	4.0	4.0
Q_3	9.2	6.0	8.0	6.0	7.0	6.0	5.0
Mean	6.8	3.9	5.2	4.0	4.8	4.4	4.2

TABLE I (Continued)

OF ELEMENTARY SCHOOL CHILDREN FROM SIX THROUGH ELEVEN YEARS OF AGE
REPORTED ACCORDING TO INTELLIGENCE LEVELS AND SEX

(Read across pages 136 and 137.)

Average (90-109 I.Q.)		Dull (75-89 I.Q.)			Total (74-140 I.Q.)		

SIX YEAR OLD LONGITUDINAL GROUP

Girls	Both	Boys	Girls	Both	Boys	Girls	Both
N 39	N 75	N 9	N 9	N 18	N 68	N 70	N 138
0-6	0-11	0-8	0-8	0-8	0-12	0-8	0-12
0	1.0	0.5	0.5	0.8	1.0	1.0	1.0
3.0	3.0	2.0	2.0	2.0	3.0	2.5	3.0
5.0	5.0	4.0	4.0	4.0	5.0	5.0	5.0
2.8	2.9	2.6	2.7	2.6	3.3	2.8	3.0

SEVEN YEAR OLD LONGITUDINAL GROUP

Girls	Both	Boys	Girls	Both	Boys	Girls	Both
N 39	N 75	N 9	N 9	N 18	N 68	N 70	N 138
0-8	0-9	0-3	0-6	0-6	0-12	0-9	0-12
2.0	2.0	0.5	1.5	1.0	2.0	2.0	2.0
4.0	3.0	2.0	4.0	2.0	3.0	4.0	3.0
6.0	5.0	2.5	4.5	4.0	5.0	6.0	5.0
3.8	3.8	1.6	3.1	2.3	3.6	3.9	3.8

SEVEN YEAR OLD CONTROL GROUP

Girls	Both	Boys	Girls	Both	Boys	Girls	Both
N 15	N 34	N 4	N 8	N 12	N 38	N 35	N 73
1-10	0-10	1-8	0-7	0-8	0-8	0-10	0-10
1.0	1.0	1.0	0	0.2	1.0	1.0	1.0
2.0	2.0	1.5	1.5	1.5	2.5	3.0	3.0
5.0	5.0	6.5	3.0	3.0	5.2	4.0	5.0
3.2	3.1	3.0	2.0	2.3	3.4	3.2	3.3

EIGHT YEAR OLD LONGITUDINAL GROUP

Girls	Both	Boys	Girls	Both	Boys	Girls	Both
N 39	N 75	N 9	N 9	N 18	N 68	N 70	N 138
0-9	0-10	0-8	1-8	0-8	0-10	0-9	0-10
3.0	3.0	1.5	2.0	2.0	3.0	3.0	3.0
4.0	4.0	3.0	5.0	4.0	4.0	4.0	4.0
6.0	6.0	4.5	7.0	5.5	5.8	6.0	6.0
4.4	4.3	3.2	4.4	2.8	4.7	4.8	4.8

(Read across pages 138 and 139.)

TABLE I (Continued)

	Superior (125 I.Q. and up)			Bright (110-124 I.Q.)			

NINE YEAR OLD LONGITUDINAL GROUP

	Boys N 6	Girls N 7	Both N 13	Boys N 17	Girls N 15	Both N 32	Boys N 36
Range	5-12	2-8	2-12	1-13	2-8	1-13	1-10
Q_1	5.8	5.0	5.0	3.5	4.0	4.0	3.0
Mdn	7.5	7.0	7.0	6.0	5.0	5.5	4.5
Q_3	9.8	7.0	8.0	5.0	6.0	7.0	7.0
Mean	7.8	5.9	6.8	5.6	5.0	5.3	5.2

TEN YEAR OLD LONGITUDINAL GROUP

	Boys N 6	Girls N 7	Both N 13	Boys N 17	Girls N 15	Both N 32	Boys N 36
Range	5-15	3-13	3-15	1-24	3-13	1-24	3-12
Q_1	6.5	4.0	5.0	4.5	4.0	4.2	5.0
Mdn	8.0	5.0	7.0	8.0	7.0	7.5	6.0
Q_3	13.8	11.0	12.0	9.5	10.0	9.8	9.0
Mean	9.3	6.7	7.9	7.8	7.1	7.5	6.8

ELEVEN YEAR OLD LONGITUDINAL GROUP

	Boys N 6	Girls N 7	Both N 13	Boys N 17	Girls N 15	Both N 32	Boys N 36
Range	4-24	4-15	4-24	1-23	3-13	1-23	2-17
Q_1	10.0	4.0	5.0	3.0	6.0	4.2	4.0
Mdn	12.5	8.0	11.0	7.0	8.0	8.0	6.0
Q_3	17.2	11.0	14.0	12.0	8.0	9.8	9.0
Mean	13.2	8.1	10.5	9.5	7.5	8.6	6.8

ELEVEN YEAR OLD CONTROL GROUP

	Boys N 3	Girls N 5	Both N 8	Boys N 7	Girls N 11	Both N 18	Boys N 22
Range	4-10	3-8	3-10	4-16	2-18	2-18	0-11
Q_1	4.0	3.5	4.0	5.0	3.0	4.0	3.0
Mdn	4.0	4.0	4.0	6.0	5.0	5.0	4.0
Q_3	10.0	7.5	7.8	7.0	7.0	7.0	8.2
Mean	6.0	5.2	5.5	7.1	6.2	6.6	6.1

TABLE I (Continued)
(Read across pages 138 and 139.)

Average (90-109 I.Q.)		Dull (75-89 I.Q.)			Total (74-140 I.Q.)		

NINE YEAR OLD LONGITUDINAL GROUP

Girls	Both	Boys	Girls	Both	Boys	Girls	Both
N 39	N 75	N 9	N 9	N 18	N 68	N 70	N 138
1-11	1-11	0-10	3-9	0-10	0-13	1-9	0-13
3.0	3.0	2.5	3.0	3.0	3.0	3.0	3.0
5.0	5.0	4.0	4.0	4.0	5.0	5.0	5.0
6.0	7.0	7.0	7.5	7.2	7.0	6.2	7.0
4.8	5.0	4.7	5.1	4.9	5.9	5.4	5.7

TEN YEAR OLD LONGITUDINAL GROUP

Girls	Both	Boys	Girls	Both	Boys	Girls	Both
N 39	N 75	N 9	N 9	N 18	N 68	N 70	N 138
1-13	1-13	1-12	5-14	1-14	1-24	1-14	1-24
5.0	5.0	2.5	5.5	4.8	5.0	5.0	5.0
6.0	6.0	5.0	7.0	6.0	6.5	7.0	7.0
8.0	8.0	6.5	11.5	7.5	9.0	8.0	9.0
6.5	6.6	5.1	8.2	6.7	7.9	7.6	7.8

ELEVEN YEAR OLD LONGITUDINAL GROUP

Girls	Both	Boys	Girls	Both	Boys	Girls	Both
N 39	N 75	N 9	N 9	N 18	N 68	N 70	N 138
2-20	2-20	1-12	2-16	1-16	1-24	2-20	1-24
5.0	4.0	3.5	4.0	3.5	4.0	5.0	4.0
7.0	6.0	5.0	9.0	7.0	7.0	7.0	7.0
9.0	9.0	9.0	11.0	9.2	10.8	9.0	9.0
7.0	6.9	6.3	7.9	7.1	9.2	7.9	8.1

ELEVEN YEAR OLD CONTROL GROUP

Girls	Both	Boys	Girls	Both	Boys	Girls	Both
N 18	N 40	N 8	N 6	N 14	N 40	N 40	N 80
1-12	0-12	1-9	3-13	1-13	0-16	1-18	0-18
3.0	3.0	1.0	3.8	2.5	3.0	3.2	3.0
5.0	4.5	3.5	6.0	4.5	4.0	5.0	5.0
6.2	7.0	7.5	9.2	8.0	7.8	7.0	7.0
5.2	5.7	6.1	6.7	6.4	6.3	5.7	6.0

mOR FREQUENCY OF INANIMATE MOVEMENT RESPONSES GIVEN TO THE RORSCHACH CARDS BY LONGITUDINAL AND CONTROL GROUPS

(Read across pages 140 and 141.)

	Superior (125 I.Q. and up)			Bright (110-124 I.Q.)			

SIX YEAR OLD LONGITUDINAL GROUP

	Boys N 6	Girls N 7	Both N 13	Boys N 17	Girls N 15	Both N 32	Boys N 36
Range	0-1	0-1	0-1	0-2	0-3	0-3	0-3
Q_1	0	0	0	0	0	0	0
Mdn	0	0	0	0	0	0	0
Q_3	1.0	1.0	1.0	1.0	0	0.8	1.0
Mean	0.3	0.3	0.3	0.4	0.4	0.4	0.4

SEVEN YEAR OLD LONGITUDINAL GROUP

	Boys N 6	Girls N 7	Both N 13	Boys N 17	Girls N 15	Both N 32	Boys N 36
Range	0-0	0-1	0-1	0-2	0-2	0-2	0-5
Q_1	0	0	0	0	0	0	0
Mdn	0	1.0	0	0	0	0	0
Q_3	0	1.0	1.0	0	1.0	0	1.0
Mean	0	0.6	0.3	0.2	0.3	0.3	0.5

SEVEN YEAR OLD CONTROL GROUP

	Boys N 6	Girls N 3	Both N 9	Boys N 9	Girls N 9	Both N 18	Boys N 19
Range	0-2	0-1	0-2	0-0	0-2	0-2	0-3
Q_1	0	0	0	0	0	0	0
Mdn	1.0	0	1.0	0	0	0	0
Q_3	1.2	1.0	1.5	0	1.0	0	0
Mean	0.8	0.3	0.7	0	0.4	0.2	0.3

EIGHT YEAR OLD LONGITUDINAL GROUP

	Boys N 6	Girls N 7	Both N 13	Boys N 17	Girls N 15	Both N 32	Boys N 36
Range	0-1	0-1	0-1	0-2	0-3	0-3	0-2
Q_1	0	0	0	0	0	0	0
Mdn	0	0	0	0	0	0	0
Q_3	0.2	1.0	1.0	0.5	1.0	0.8	0.8
Mean	0.2	0.4	0.3	0.4	0.4	0.4	0.3

OF ELEMENTARY SCHOOL CHILDREN FROM SIX THROUGH ELEVEN YEARS OF AGE
REPORTED ACCORDING TO INTELLIGENCE LEVELS AND SEX

(Read across pages 140 and 141.)

Average (90-109 I.Q.)		Dull (75-89 I.Q.)			Total (74-140 I.Q.)		

SIX YEAR OLD LONGITUDINAL GROUP

Girls	Both	Boys	Girls	Both	Boys	Girls	Both
N 39	N 75	N 9	N 9	N 18	N 68	N 70	N 138
0-3	0-3	0-1	0-1	0-1	0-3	0-3	0-3
0	0	0	0	0	0	0	0
0	0	0	0	0	0	0	0
0	0	0	0	0	1.0	0	0
0.2	0.3	0.1	0.1	0.1	0.4	0.2	0.3

SEVEN YEAR OLD LONGITUDINAL GROUP

Girls	Both	Boys	Girls	Both	Boys	Girls	Both
N 39	N 75	N 9	N 9	N 18	N 68	N 70	N 138
0-1	0-5	0-1	0-0	0-1	0-5	0-2	0-5
0	0	0	0	0	0	0	0
0	0	0	0	0	0	0	0
0	0	0	0	0	0	0	0
0	0.3	0.1	0	0.1	0.4	0.2	0.2

SEVEN YEAR OLD CONTROL GROUP

Girls	Both	Boys	Girls	Both	Boys	Girls	Both
N 15	N 34	N 4	N 8	N 12	N 38	N 35	N 73
0-2	0-3	0-1	0-1	0-1	0-3	0-2	0-3
0	0	0.2	0	0	0	0	0
0	0	1.0	0	0	0	0	0
0	0	1.0	0	1.0	1.0	0	1.0
0.3	0.3	0.8	0.1	0.3	0.4	0.3	0.3

EIGHT YEAR OLD LONGITUDINAL GROUP

Girls	Both	Boys	Girls	Both	Boys	Girls	Both
N 39	N 75	N 9	N 9	N 18	N 68	N 70	N 138
0-2	0-2	0-1	0-2	0-2	0-2	0-3	0-3
0	0	0	0	0	0	0	0
0	0	0	0	0	0	0	0
0	0	1.0	0.5	1.0	1.0	0	0.2
0.2	0.2	0.4	0.3	0.4	0.3	0.3	0.3

	Superior (125 I.Q. and up)			Bright (110-124 I.Q.)			

NINE YEAR OLD LONGITUDINAL GROUP

	Boys N 6	Girls N 7	Both N 13	Boys N 17	Girls N 15	Both N 32	Boys N 36
Range	0-3	0-2	0-2	0-4	0-2	0-4	0-2
Q_1	0	0	0	0	0	0	0
Mdn	1.5	0	0	0	0	0	0
Q_3	2.2	1.0	1.0	1.5	1.0	1.0	0
Mean	1.3	0.4	0.8	0.8	0.3	0.6	0.3

TEN YEAR OLD LONGITUDINAL GROUP

	Boys N 6	Girls N 7	Both N 13	Boys N 17	Girls N 15	Both N 32	Boys N 36
Range	0-2	0-3	0-3	0-4	0-2	0-4	0-3
Q_1	1.0	0	0	0	0	0	0
Mdn	1.0	1.0	1.0	0	0	0	0
Q_3	1.2	3.0	2.0	1.5	0	1.0	1.0
Mean	1.0	1.3	1.2	0.7	0.3	0.5	0.7

ELEVEN YEAR OLD LONGITUDINAL GROUP

	Boys N 6	Girls N 7	Both N 13	Boys N 17	Girls N 15	Both N 32	Boys N 36
Range	0-2	0-3	0-3	0-7	0-2	0-7	0-4
Q_1	0	0	0	0	0	0	0
Mdn	0.5	0	1.0	0.5	0	0	0
Q_3	2.0	2.0	2.0	1.5	1.0	1.0	1.0
Mean	0.8	1.3	1.1	1.3	0.4	0.9	0.8

ELEVEN YEAR OLD CONTROL GROUP

	Boys N 3	Girls N 5	Both N 8	Boys N 7	Girls N 11	Both N 18	Boys N 22
Range	1-4	0-2	0-4	0-8	0-2	0-8	0-3
Q_1	1.0	0.5	1.0	0	0	0	0
Mdn	2.0	2.0	2.0	0	0	0	0
Q_3	4.0	2.0	2.0	0	1.0	1.0	1.0
Mean	2.3	1.4	1.8	1.1	0.6	0.8	0.7

Average (90-109 I.Q.)		Dull (75-89 I.Q.)			Total (74-140 I.Q.)		

NINE YEAR OLD LONGITUDINAL GROUP

Girls N 39	Both N 75	Boys N 9	Girls N 9	Both N 18	Boys N 68	Girls N 70	Both N 138
0-2	0-2	0-1	0-1	0-1	0-4	0-2	0-4
0	0	0	0	0	0	0	0
0	0	0	0	0	0	0	0
0	0	1.0	0	1.0	1.0	0	1.0
0.2	0.2	0.4	0.1	0.3	0.5	0.2	0.3

TEN YEAR OLD LONGITUDINAL GROUP

Girls N 39	Both N 75	Boys N 9	Girls N 9	Both N 18	Boys N 68	Girls N 70	Both N 138
0-2	0-3	0-1	0-1	0-1	0-4	0-3	0-4
0	0	0	0	0	0	0	0
0	0	0	0	0	0	0	0
0	1.0	0.5	0.5	0.2	1.0	0	1.0
0.2	0.4	0.2	0.2	0.2	0.7	0.3	0.5

ELEVEN YEAR OLD LONGITUDINAL GROUP

Girls N 39	Both N 75	Boys N 9	Girls N 9	Both N 18	Boys N 68	Girls N 70	Both N 138
0-2	0-4	0-4	0-0	0-4	0-7	0-3	0-7
0	0	0	0	0	0	0	0
0	0	0	0	0	0	0	0
0	1.0	1.0	0	0	1.0	0.2	1.0
0.2	0.5	0.7	0	0.3	0.8	0.7	0.5

ELEVEN YEAR OLD CONTROL GROUP

Girls N 18	Both N 40	Boys N 8	Girls N 6	Both N 14	Boys N 40	Girls N 40	Both N 80
0-5	0-5	0-2	0-1	0-2	0-8	0-5	0-8
0	0	0	0	0	0	0	0
1.0	1.0	0	0	0	0	0.5	0
2.0	1.0	2.0	0.2	1.2	1.0	1.0	1.0
0.2	0.9	0.8	0.2	0.5	0.9	0.7	0.8

CF OR FREQUENCY OF BRIGHT COLOR WITH INDEFINITE FORM RESPONSES GIVEN TO THE RORSCHACH CARDS BY LONGITUDINAL AND CONTROL GROUPS

(Read across pages 144 and 145.)

	Superior (125 I.Q. and up			Bright (110-124 I.Q.)			

SIX YEAR OLD LONGITUDINAL GROUP

	Boys N 6	Girls N 7	Both N 13	Boys N 17	Girls N 15	Both N 32	Boys N 36
Range	0-3	0-2	0-3	0-4	0-5	0-5	0-4
Q_1	0	1.0	0.5	0	0	0	0
Mdn	1.0	2.0	1.0	1.0	1.0	1.0	1.0
Q_3	2.2	5.0	3.5	2.0	2.0	2.0	2.0
Mean	1.2	2.4	1.8	1.1	1.3	1.2	1.1

SEVEN YEAR OLD LONGITUDINAL GROUP

	Boys N 6	Girls N 7	Both N 13	Boys N 17	Girls N 15	Both N 32	Boys N 36
Range	0-4	0-3	0-4	0-3	0-4	0-4	0-5
Q_1	0	0	0	0	0	0	0
Mdn	0.5	0	0	1.0	0	0	1.0
Q_3	1.8	2.0	2.0	2.0	1.0	1.8	1.0
Mean	1.0	1.0	1.0	1.0	0.8	0.9	1.0

SEVEN YEAR OLD CONTROL GROUP

	Boys N 6	Girls N 3	Both N 9	Boys N 9	Girls N 9	Both N 18	Boys N 19
Range	0-3	1-2	0-3	0-4	0-3	0-4	0-3
Q_1	0	2.0	0.5	0	0	0	0
Mdn	1.5	2.0	2.0	3.0	0	1.0	0
Q_3	3.0	2.0	2.5	3.5	2.0	2.2	1.0
Mean	1.5	2.0	1.7	1.8	0.9	1.3	0.7

EIGHT YEAR OLD LONGITUDINAL GROUP

	Boys N 6	Girls N 7	Both N 13	Boys N 17	Girls N 15	Both N 32	Boys N 36
Range	0-5	0-3	0-5	0-2	0-3	0-3	0-5
Q_1	0	0	0	0	0	0	0
Mdn	1.5	2.0	2.0	0	0	0	1.0
Q_3	2.8	3.0	2.5	1.0	1.0	1.0	2.8
Mean	1.7	1.6	1.6	0.4	0.5	0.4	1.4

OF ELEMENTARY SCHOOL CHILDREN FROM SIX THROUGH ELEVEN YEARS OF AGE REPORTED ACCORDING TO INTELLIGENCE LEVELS AND SEX

(Read across pages 144 and 145.)

Average (90-109 I.Q.)		Dull (75-89 I.Q.)			Total (74-140 I.Q.)		

SIX YEAR OLD LONGITUDINAL GROUP

Girls N 39	Both N 75	Boys N 9	Girls N 9	Both N 18	Boys N 68	Girls N 70	Both N 138
0-4	0-4	0-3	0-3	0-3	0-4	0-5	0-5
0	0	0	0	0	0	0	0
1.0	1.0	0	1.0	0	0	1.0	1.0
1.0	2.0	1.0	1.0	1.0	1.0	2.0	1.0
1.0	1.0	0.6	0.8	0.7	1.0	1.2	1.1

SEVEN YEAR OLD LONGITUDINAL GROUP

Girls N 39	Both N 75	Boys N 9	Girls N 9	Both N 18	Boys N 68	Girls N 70	Both N 138
0-4	0-5	0-2	0-2	0-2	0-5	0-4	0-5
0	0	0	0	0	0	0	0
0	1.0	0	0	0	1.0	0	0
1.0	1.0	0.5	0.5	0.25	1.0	1.0	1.0
0.7	0.8	0.3	0.3	0.3	0.9	0.7	0.8

SEVEN YEAR OLD CONTROL GROUP

Girls N 15	Both N 34	Boys N 4	Girls N 8	Both N 12	Boys N 38	Girls N 35	Both N 73
0-3	0-3	0-1	0-3	0-3	0-4	0-3	0-4
0	0	1.0	0	0	0	0	0
1.0	0.5	1.0	0	1.0	1.0	1.0	1.0
2.0	1.0	1.0	1.0	1.0	1.2	2.0	2.0
1.0	0.8	1.0	0.6	0.8	1.1	1.0	1.1

EIGHT YEAR OLD LONGITUDINAL GROUP

Girls N 39	Both N 75	Boys N 9	Girls N 9	Both N 18	Boys N 68	Girls N 70	Both N 138
0-5	0-5	0-3	0-2	0-3	0-5	0-5	0-5
0	0	0	0	0	0	0	0
0	1.0	0	0	0	0.5	0	0
1.0	2.0	0.5	1.0	1.0	2.0	2.0	2.0
0.9	1.2	0.4	0.6	0.5	1.1	0.8	0.9

TABLE K (Continued)
(Read across pages 146 and 147.)

	Superior (125 I.Q. and up)			Bright (110-124 I.Q.)			

NINE YEAR OLD LONGITUDINAL GROUP

	Boys N 6	Girls N 7	Both N 13	Boys N 17	Girls N 15	Both N 32	Boys N 36
Range	0-2	0-3	0-3	0-2	0-5	0-5	0-6
Q_1	0	0	0	0	0	0	0
Mdn	1.5	0	0	1.0	1.0	1.0	1.0
Q_3	2.0	2.0	2.0	1.5	1.0	1.0	1.8
Mean	1.2	0.7	0.9	1.0	0.9	0.9	1.1

TEN YEAR OLD LONGITUDINAL GROUP

	Boys N 6	Girls N 7	Both N 13	Boys N 17	Girls N 15	Both N 32	Boys N 36
Range	0-2	0-2	0-2	0-6	0-4	0-6	0-3
Q_1	0	0	0	0	0	0	0
Mdn	0.5	1.0	1.0	1.0	0	0	1.0
Q_3	1.2	1.0	1.0	2.0	1.0	1.8	1.0
Mean	0.7	0.9	0.8	1.1	0.7	0.9	0.8

ELEVEN YEAR OLD LONGITUDINAL GROUP

	Boys N 6	Girls N 7	Both N 13	Boys N 17	Girls N 15	Both N 32	Boys N 36
Range	0-5	0-2	0-5	0-5	0-3	0-5	0-4
Q_1	0	0	0	0	0	0	0
Mdn	1.0	1.0	1.0	0	0	0	1.0
Q_3	2.0	2.0	2.0	1.0	1.0	1.0	1.0
Mean	1.3	1.1	1.2	0.8	0.6	0.7	0.8

ELEVEN YEAR OLD CONTROL GROUP

	Boys N 3	Girls N 5	Both N 8	Boys N 7	Girls N 11	Both N 18	Boys N 22
Range	0-3	0-4	0-4	0-3	0-6	0-6	0-4
Q_1	0	0	0	0	0	0	0
Mdn	3.0	1.0	1.5	0	2.0	1.0	1.0
Q_3	3.0	3.0	3.0	1.0	3.0	2.2	1.0
Mean	2.0	1.4	1.6	0.6	1.9	1.4	0.9

Average (90-109 I.Q.)		Dull (75-89 I.Q.)			Total (74-140 I.Q.)		

NINE YEAR OLD LONGITUDINAL GROUP

Girls N 39	Both N 75	Boys N 9	Girls N 9	Both N 18	Boys N 68	Girls N 70	Both N 138
0-4	0-6	0-1	0-2	0-2	0-6	0-5	0-6
0	0	0	0	0	0	0	0
0	0	0	0	0	1.0	0	0.5
2.0	2.0	1.0	0	1.0	1.8	1.0	1.0
0.8	0.9	1.1	0.2	0.7	1.1	0.7	0.9

TEN YEAR OLD LONGITUDINAL GROUP

Girls N 39	Both N 75	Boys N 9	Girls N 9	Both N 18	Boys N 68	Girls N 70	Both N 138
0-5	0-5	0-1	0-4	0-4	0-6	0-5	0-6
0	0	0	0	0	0	0	0
0	0	0	0	0	0	0	1.0
1.0	1.0	1.0	1.5	1.0	1.0	1.0	1.0
0.8	0.8	0.3	0.8	0.6	0.8	0.8	0.9

ELEVEN YEAR OLD LONGITUDINAL GROUP

Girls N 39	Both N 75	Boys N 9	Girls N 9	Both N 18	Boys N 68	Girls N 70	Both N 138
0-5	0-5	0-1	0-3	0-3	0-5	0-5	0-5
0	0	0	0	0	0	0	0
0	0	1.0	0	0	0.5	0	0
2.0	1.0	1.0	1.5	1.0	1.0	2.0	1.0
0.8	0.9	0.6	0.7	0.6	0.8	0.9	1.0

ELEVEN YEAR OLD CONTROL GROUP

Girls N 18	Both N 40	Boys N 8	Girls N 6	Both N 14	Boys N 40	Girls N 40	Both N 80
0-5	0-5	0-6	0-5	0-6	0-6	0-6	0-6
0	0	1.0	0	0.8	0	0	0
1.0	1.0	2.5	2.5	2.5	1.0	1.0	1.0
2.0	2.0	4.5	4.2	4.2	2.0	2.0	2.0
1.1	1.0	2.6	2.3	2.5	1.3	1.6	1.4

TABLE L

K OR FREQUENCY OF SHADING AS DIFFUSION RESPONSES
GIVEN TO RORSCHACH CARDS BY LONGITUDINAL AND CONTROL GROUPS

(Read across pages 148 and 149.)

	Superior (125 I.Q. and up)			Bright (110-124 I.Q.)			

SIX YEAR OLD LONGITUDINAL GROUP

	Boys N 6	Girls N 7	Both N 13	Boys N 17	Girls N 15	Both N 32	Boys N 36
Range	0-1	0-2	0-2	0-3	0-1	0-3	0-5
Q_1	0	0	0	0	0	0	0
Mdn	0	0	0	0	0	0	0
Q_3	0.2	1.0	0.5	1.0	1.0	1.0	1.0
Mean	0.2	0.4	0.3	0.9	0.4	0.7	0.9

SEVEN YEAR OLD LONGITUDINAL GROUP

	Boys N 6	Girls N 7	Both N 13	Boys N 17	Girls N 15	Both N 32	Boys N 36
Range	0-0	0-1	0-1	0-1	0-3	0-3	0-2
Q_1	0	0	0	0	0	0	0
Mdn	0	0	0	0	0	0	0
Q_3	0	1.0	0	1.0	1.0	1.0	0
Mean	0	0.3	0.2	0.7	0.7	0.7	0.2

SEVEN YEAR OLD CONTROL GROUP

	Boys N 6	Girls N 3	Both N 9	Boys N 9	Girls N 9	Both N 18	Boys N 19
Range	0-2	0-0	0-2	0-1	0-1	0-1	0-2
Q_1	0.8	0	0	0	0	0	0
Mdn	1.0	0	1.0	0	0	0	1.0
Q_3	1.2	0	1.0	0	0	0	1.0
Mean	1.0	0	0.7	0.1	0.1	0.1	0.6

EIGHT YEAR OLD LONGITUDINAL GROUP

	Boys N 6	Girls N 7	Both N 13	Boys N 17	Girls N 15	Both N 32	Boys N 36
Range	0-1	0-1	0-1	0-1	0-4	0-4	0-1
Q_1	0	0	0	0	0	0	0
Mdn	0	0	0	0	0	0	0
Q_3	0.2	1.0	0.5	0.5	1.0	0.8	0.8
Mean	0.2	0.3	0.2	0.4	0.8	1.2	0.3

TABLE L (Continued)

OF ELEMENTARY SCHOOL CHILDREN FROM SIX THROUGH ELEVEN YEARS OF AGE
REPORTED ACCORDING TO INTELLIGENCE LEVELS AND SEX

(Read across pages 148 and 149.)

Average (90-109 I.Q.)		Dull (75-89 I.Q.)			Total (74-140 I.Q.)		

SIX YEAR OLD LONGITUDINAL GROUP

Girls	Both	Boys	Girls	Both	Boys	Girls	Both
N 39	N 75	N 9	N 9	N 18	N 68	N 70	N 138
0-5	0-5	0-2	0-1	0-2	0-5	0-5	0-5
0	0	0	0	0	0	0	0
0	0	0.	0	0	0	0	0
0	1.0	1.0	0.5	1.0	1.0	0.2	1.0
0.5	0.7	0.4	0.2	0.3	0.7	0.4	0.6

SEVEN YEAR OLD LONGITUDINAL GROUP

Girls	Both	Boys	Girls	Both	Boys	Girls	Both
N 39	N 75	N 9	N 9	N 18	N 68	N 70	N 138
0-3	0-3	0-2	0-0	0-2	0-2	0-3	0-3
0	0	0	0	0	0	0	0
0	0	0	0	0	0	0	0
0	0	2.0	0	0.2	0	0	0
0.2	0.2	0.8	0	0.4	0.3	0.2	0.3

SEVEN YEAR OLD CONTROL GROUP

Girls	Both	Boys	Girls	Both	Boys	Girls	Both
N 15	N 34	N 4	N 8	N 12	N 38	N 35	N 73
0-1	0-2	0-3	0-4	0-4	0-3	0-4	0-4
0	0	0	0	0	0	0	0
0	0	0.5	0	0	0	0	0
0	1.0	2.5	0.8	1.0	1.0	0	1.0
0.1	0.4	1.0	0.6	0.8	0.6	0.2	0.4

EIGHT YEAR OLD LONGITUDINAL GROUP

Girls	Both	Boys	Girls	Both	Boys	Girls	Both
N 39	N 75	N 9	N 9	N 18	N 68	N 70	N 138
0-1	0-1	0-1	0-0	0-1	0-1	0-4	0-4
0	0	0	0	0	0	0	0
0	0	0	0	0	0	0	0
0	0	1.0	0	0	0.8	0	0
0	0.2	0.3	0	0.2	0.3	0.2	0.2

TABLE L (Continued)

(Read across pages 150 and 151.)

	Superior (125 I.Q. and up)			Bright (110-124 I.Q.)			

NINE YEAR OLD LONGITUDINAL GROUP

	Boys N 6	Girls N 7	Both N 13	Boys N 17	Girls N 15	Both N 32	Boys N 36
Range	0-2	0-2	0-2	0-2	0-3	0-3	0-3
Q_1	0	0	0	0	0	0	0
Mdn	0	0	0	0	0	0	0
Q_3	0.5	2.0	1.0	0.5	0	0	0.8
Mean	0.3	0.6	0.5	0.7	0.7	0.7	0.4

TEN YEAR OLD LONGITUDINAL GROUP

	Boys N 6	Girls N 7	Both N 13	Boys N 17	Girls N 15	Both N 32	Boys N 36
Range	0-2	0-2	0-2	0-2	0-3	0-3	0-2
Q_1	0	0	0	0	0	0	0
Mdn	0	0	0	0	0	0	0
Q_3	0.5	2.0	1.0	1.0	1.0	1.0	0
Mean	0.3	0.6	0.5	0.7	0.9	1.6	0.3

ELEVEN YEAR OLD LONGITUDINAL GROUP

	Boys N 6	Girls N 7	Both N 13	Boys N 17	Girls N 15	Both N 32	Boys N 36
Range	0-2	0-2	0-2	0-2	0-2	0-2	0-1
Q_1	0	0	0	0	0	0	0
Mdn	0	0	0	0	0	0	0
Q_3	0.5	1.0	0.5	0.5	1.0	0.8	0
Mean	0.3	0.4	0.4	0.7	1.1	1.8	0.1

ELEVEN YEAR OLD CONTROL GROUP

	Boys N 3	Girls N 5	Both N 8	Boys N 7	Girls N 11	Both N 18	Boys N 22
Range	0-0	0-1	0-1	0-0	0-2	0-2	0-1
Q_1	0	0	0	0	0	0	0
Mdn	0	0	0	0	0	0	0
Q_3	0	0.5	0	0	0	0	0
Mean	0	0.2	0.1	0.7	0.3	0.4	0.1

TABLE L (Continued)
(Read across pages 150 and 151.)

| Average (90-109 I.Q.) | | Dull (75-89 I.Q.) | | | Total (74-140 I.Q.) | | |

NINE YEAR OLD LONGITUDINAL GROUP

Girls	Both	Boys	Girls	Both	Boys	Girls	Both
N 39	N 75	N 9	N 9	N 18	N 68	N 70	N 138
0-2	0-3	0-1	0-1	0-1	0-3	0-3	0-3
0	0	0	0	0	0	0	0
0	0	0	0	0	0	0	0
0	0	1.0	0	0.2	0.8	0	0
0.2	0.2	0.3	0.1	0.2	0.4	0.2	0.3

TEN YEAR OLD LONGITUDINAL GROUP

Girls	Both	Boys	Girls	Both	Boys	Girls	Both
N 39	N 75	N 9	N 9	N 18	N 68	N 70	N 138
0-3	0-3	0-1	0-0	0-1	0-2	0-3	0-3
0	0	0	0	0	0	0	0
0	0	0	0	0	0	0	0
0	0	0.5	0	0	0	0	0
0.1	0.2	0.2	0	0.1	0.4	0.2	0.3

ELEVEN YEAR OLD LONGITUDINAL GROUP

Girls	Both	Boys	Girls	Both	Boys	Girls	Both
N 39	N 75	N 9	N 9	N 18	N 68	N 70	N 138
0-2	0-2	0-1	0-0	0-1	0-2	0-2	0-2
0	0	0	0	0	0	0	0
0	0	0	0	0	0	0	0
0	0	0	0	0	0	0	0
0.2	0.2	0.1	0	0.1	0.2	0.3	0.3

ELEVEN YEAR OLD CONTROL GROUP

Girls	Both	Boys	Girls	Both	Boys	Girls	Both
N 18	N 40	N 8	N 6	N 14	N 40	N 40	N 80
0-2	0-2	0-2	0-0	0-2	0-2	0-2	0-2
0	0	0	0	0	0	0	0
0	0	0	0	0	0	0	0
0	0	0	0	0	0	0	0
0.3	0.2	0.1	0	0.1	0.2	0.2	0.2

TABLE M

FK OR FREQUENCY OF SHADING AS VISTA RESPONSES
GIVEN TO THE RORSCHACH CARDS BY LONGITUDINAL AND CONTROL GROUPS

(Read across pages 152 and 153.)

	Superior (125 I.Q. and up)			Bright (110-124 I.Q.)			

SIX YEAR OLD LONGITUDINAL GROUP

	Boys N 6	Girls N 7	Both N 13	Boys N 17	Girls N 15	Both N 32	Boys N 36
Range	0-1	0-0	0-1	0-3	0-0	0-3	0-1
Q_1	0	0	0	0	0	0	0
Mdn	0.5	0	0	0	0	0	0
Q_3	1.0	0	0.5	0	0	0	0
Mean	0.5	0	0.2	0.2	0	0.3	0

SEVEN YEAR OLD LONGITUDINAL GROUP

	Boys N 6	Girls N 7	Both N 13	Boys N 17	Girls N 15	Both N 32	Boys N 36
Range	0-0	0-0	0-0	0-0	0-0	0-0	0-1
Q_1	0	0	0	0	0	0	0
Mdn	0	0	0	0	0	0	0
Q_3	0	0	0	0	0	0	0
Mean	0	0	0	0	0	0	0.1

SEVEN YEAR OLD CONTROL GROUP

	Boys N 6	Girls N 3	Both N 9	Boys N 9	Girls N 9	Both N 18	Boys N 19
Range	0-0	0-1	0-1	0-1	0-1	0-1	0-1
Q_1	0	0	0	0	0	0	0
Mdn	0	0	0	0	0	0	0
Q_3	0	1.0	0	0	0	0	0
Mean	0.2	0.3	0.1	0.1	0.1	0.1	0.1

EIGHT YEAR OLD LONGITUDINAL GROUP

	Boys N 6	Girls N 7	Both N 13	Boys N 17	Girls N 15	Both N 32	Boys N 35
Range	0-0	0-1	0-1	0-0	0-1	0-1	0-2
Q_1	0	0	0	0	0	0	0
Mdn	0	0	0	0	0	0	0
Q_3	0	0	0	0	0	0	0
Mean	0	0.1	0.1	0.1	0.2	0.3	0.3

OF ELEMENTARY SCHOOL CHILDREN SIX THROUGH ELEVEN YEARS OF AGE
REPORTED ACCORDING TO INTELLIGENCE LEVELS AND SEX

(Read across pages 152 and 153.)

Average (90-109 I.Q.)		Dull (75-89 I.Q.)			Total (74-140 I.Q.)		

SIX YEAR OLD LONGITUDINAL GROUP

Girls N 39	Both N 75	Boys N 9	Girls N 9	Both N 18	Boys N 68	Girls N 70	Both N 138
0-1	0-1	0-0	0-0	0-0	0-3	0-1	0-3
0	0	0	0	0	0	0	0
0	0	0	0	0	0	0	0
0	0	0	0	0	0	0	0
0.1	0.1	0	0	0	0.1	0	0.1

SEVEN YEAR OLD LONGITUDINAL GROUP

Girls N 39	Both N 75	Boys N 9	Girls N 9	Both N 18	Boys N 68	Girls N 70	Both N 138
0-1	0-1	0-1	0-0	0-1	0-1	0-1	0-1
0	0	0	0	0	0	0	0
0	0	0	0	0	0	0	0
0	0	0	0	0	0	0	0
0.1	0.1	0.1	0	0.1	0.1	0	0.1

SEVEN YEAR OLD CONTROL GROUP

Girls N 15	Both N 34	Boys N 4	Girls N 8	Both N 12	Boys N 38	Girls N 35	Both N 73
0-2	0-2	0-0	0-0	0-0	0-1	0-2	0-2
0	0	0	0	0	0	0	0
0	0	0	0	0	0	0	0
0	0	0	0	0	0	0	0
0.3	0.2	0	0	0	0.1	0.2	0.1

EIGHT YEAR OLD LONGITUDINAL GROUP

Girls N 39	Both N 75	Boys N 9	Girls N 9	Both N 18	Boys N 68	Girls N 70	Both N 138
0-1	0-2	0-0	0-0	0-0	0-2	0-1	0-2
0	0	0	0	0	0	0	0
0	0	0	0	0	0	0	0
0	0	0	0	0	0	0	0
0.0	0.2	0	0	0	0.2	0.1	0.1

| | Superior (125 I.Q. and up) | | | Bright (110-124 I.Q.) | | | |

NINE YEAR OLD LONGITUDINAL GROUP

	Boys N 6	Girls N 7	Both N 13	Boys N 17	Girls N 15	Both N 32	Boys N 36
Range	0-0	0-2	0-2	0-0	0-1	0-1	0-2
Q_1	0	0	0	0	0	0	0
Mdn	0	0	0	0	0	0	0
Q_3	0	0	0	0	0	0	0
Mean	0	0.3	0.2	0	0.1	0.1	0.1

TEN YEAR OLD LONGITUDINAL GROUP

	Boys N 6	Girls N 7	Both N 13	Boys N 17	Girls N 15	Both N 32	Boys N 36
Range	0-2	0-1	0-2	0-5	0-2	0-5	0-2
Q_1	0	0	0	0	0	0	0
Mdn	0	0	0	0	0	0	0
Q_3	0	1.0	0.5	0	0	0	0
Mean	0.3	0.4	0.4	0.4	0.3	0.3	0.2

ELEVEN YEAR OLD LONGITUDINAL GROUP

	Boys N 6	Girls N 7	Both N 13	Boys N 17	Girls N 15	Both N 32	Boys N 36
Range	0-2	0-2	0-2	0-3	0-2	0-3	0-3
Q_1	0	0	0	0	0	0	0
Mdn	0	0	0	0	0	0	0
Q_3	0.5	0	0	1.0	0	1.0	1.0
Mean	0.3	0.3	0.3	0.6	0.3	0.4	0.5

ELEVEN YEAR OLD CONTROL GROUP

	Boys N 3	Girls N 5	Both N 8	Boys N 7	Girls N 11	Both N 18	Boys N 22
Range	0-0	0-1	0-1	0-3	0-1	0-3	0-1
Q_1	0	0	0	0	0	0	0
Mdn	0	0	0	0	0	0	0
Q_3	0	0.5	0	1.0	1.0	1.0	0
Mean	0	0.2	0.1	0.6	0.4	0.4	0.2

Average (90-109 I.Q.)		Dull (75-89 I.Q.)			Total (74-140 I.Q.)		

NINE YEAR OLD LONGITUDINAL GROUP

Girls N 39	Both N 75	Boys N 9	Girls N 9	Both N 18	Boys N 68	Girls N 70	Both N 138
0-2	0-2	0-0	0-1	0-1	0-2	0-2	0-2
0	0	0	0	0	0	0	0
0	0	0	0	0	0	0	0
0	0	0	0	0	0	0	0
0.1	0.1	0	0.1	0.1	0.1	0.1	0.1

TEN YEAR OLD LONGITUDINAL GROUP

Girls N 39	Both N 75	Boys N 9	Girls N 9	Both N 18	Boys N 68	Girls N 70	Both N 138
0-2	0-2	0-0	0-0	0-0	0-5	0-2	0-5
0	0	0	0	0	0	0	0
0	0	0	0	0	0	0	0
0	0	0	0	0	0	0	0
0.1	0.2	0	0	0	0.3	0.2	0.2

ELEVEN YEAR OLD LONGITUDINAL GROUP

Girls N 39	Both N 75	Boys N 9	Girls N 9	Both N 18	Boys N 68	Girls N 70	Both N 138
0-3	0-3	0-0	0-0	0-0	0-3	0-3	0-3
0	0	0	0	0	0	0	0
0	0	0	0	0	0	0	0
0	1.0	0	0	0	0.8	0	0
0.3	0.4	0	0	0	0.4	0.3	0.4

ELEVEN YEAR OLD CONTROL GROUP

Girls N 18	Both N 40	Boys N 8	Girls N 6	Both N 14	Boys N 40	Girls N 40	Both N 80
0-1	0-1	0-0	0-0	0-0	0-6	0-1	0-6
0	0	0	0	0	0	0	0
0	0	0	0	0	0	0	0
0	0	1.0	0	0.2	0	0	0
0.2	0.2	1.0	0	0.6	0.4	0.2	0.3

TABLE N

c OR FREQUENCY OF SHADING AS TEXTURE RESPONSES
GIVEN TO THE RORSCHACH CARDS BY LONGITUDINAL AND CONTROL GROUPS

(Read across pages 156 and 157.)

	Superior (125 I.Q. and up)			Bright (110-124 I.Q.)			

SIX YEAR OLD LONGITUDINAL GROUP

	Boys N 6	Girls N 7	Both N 13	Boys N 17	Girls N 15	Both N 32	Boys N 36
Range	0-1	0-2	0-2	0-5	0-2	0-5	0-2
Q₁	0	0	0	0	0	0	0
Mdn	0.5	0	0	0	0	0	0
Q₃	1.0	0	1.0	1.0	1.0	1.0	0
Mean	0.5	0.3	0.4	0.6	0.5	0.6	0.2

SEVEN YEAR OLD LONGITUDINAL GROUP

	Boys N 6	Girls N 7	Both N 13	Boys N 17	Girls N 15	Both N 32	Boys N 36
Range	0-2	0-1	0-2	0-1	0-3	0-3	0-1
Q₁	0	0	0	0	0	0	0
Mdn	0	0	0	0	0	0	0
Q₃	1.2	0	0	0	1.0	1.0	0
Mean	0.5	0.1	0.3	0.2	0.7	0.4	0.4

SEVEN YEAR OLD CONTROL GROUP

	Boys N 6	Girls N 3	Both N 9	Boys N 9	Girls N 9	Both N 18	Boys N 19
Range	0-4	0-1	0-4	0-1	0-2	0-2	0-1
Q₁	0	0	0	0	0	0	0
Mdn	0	0	0	0	0	0	0
Q₃	2.5	1.0	1.5	0	1.0	0.2	1.0
Mean	1.0	0.3	0.8	0.1	0.4	0.3	0.3

EIGHT YEAR OLD LONGITUDINAL GROUP

	Boys N 6	Girls N 7	Both N 13	Boys N 17	Girls N 15	Both N 32	Boys N 36
Range	0-2	0-1	0-2	0-2	0-3	0-3	0-4
Q₁	0	0	0	0	0	0	0
Mdn	0.5	0	0	0	1.0	1.0	0
Q₃	1.2	1.0	1.0	1.0	2.0	1.0	0
Mean	0.7	0.3	0.5	0.4	1.1	0.8	0.3

OF ELEMENTARY SCHOOL CHILDREN FROM SIX THROUGH ELEVEN YEARS OF AGE
REPORTED ACCORDING TO INTELLIGENCE LEVELS AND SEX

(Read across pages 156 and 157.)

Average (90–109 I.Q.)		Dull (75–89 I.Q.)			Total (74–140 I.Q.)		

SIX YEAR OLD LONGITUDINAL GROUP

Girls	Both	Boys	Girls	Both	Boys	Girls	Both
N 39	N 75	N 9	N 9	N 18	N 68	N 70	N 138
0-1	0-2	0-5	0-1	0-5	0-5	0-2	0-5
0	0	0	0	0	0	0	0
0	0	0	0	0	0	0	0
0	0	0	0	0	0	0	0
0.2	0.2	0.7	0.1	0.4	0.4	0.2	0.3

SEVEN YEAR OLD LONGITUDINAL GROUP

Girls	Both	Boys	Girls	Both	Boys	Girls	Both
N 39	N 75	N 9	N 9	N 18	N 68	N 70	N 138
0-2	0-2	0-1	0-1	0-1	0-2	0-3	0-3
0	0	0	0	0	0	0	0
0	0	0	0	0	0	0	0
0	0	0	0	0	0	0.2	0
0.3	0.2	0.1	0.1	0.1	0.2	0.3	0.3

SEVEN YEAR OLD CONTROL GROUP

Girls	Both	Boys	Girls	Both	Boys	Girls	Both
N 15	N 34	N 4	N 8	N 12	N 38	N 35	N 73
0-1	0-1	0-0	0-1	0-1	0-4	0-2	0-4
0	0	0	0	0	0	0	0
0	0	0	0	0	0	0	0
0	0	0	0.8	0	0.2	0	0
0.1	0.2	0	0.2	0.2	0.3	0.2	0.3

EIGHT YEAR OLD LONGITUDINAL GROUP

Girls	Both	Boys	Girls	Both	Boys	Girls	Both
N 39	N 75	N 9	N 9	N 18	N 68	N 70	N 138
0-3	0-4	0-1	0-1	0-1	0-4	0-3	0-4
0	0	0	0	0	0	0	0
0	0	0	0	0	0	0	0
1.0	0	0	0.5	0	1.8	1.0	1.0
0.3	0.3	0.1	0.2	0.2	0.3	0.5	0.4

(Read across pages 158 and 159.)

	Superior (125 I.Q. and up)			Bright (110-124 I.Q.)			

NINE YEAR OLD LONGITUDINAL GROUP

	Boys N 6	Girls N 7	Both N 13	Boys N 17	Girls N 15	Both N 32	Boys N 36
Range	0-1	0-3	0-3	0-2	0-5	0-5	0-2
Q_1	0	0	0	0	0	0	0
Mdn	1.0	2.0	1.0	1.0	1.0	1.0	0
Q_3	1.0	2.0	2.0	1.0	2.0	1.0	1.0
Mean	0.7	1.3	1.0	0.7	1.2	0.9	0.6

TEN YEAR OLD LONGITUDINAL GROUP

	Boys N 6	Girls N 7	Both N 13	Boys N 17	Girls N 15	Both N 32	Boys N 36
Range	0-3	0-4	0-4	0-4	0-4	0-4	0-4
Q_1	0.8	1.0	1.0	0	0	0	0
Mdn	2.0	1.0	1.0	1.0	1.0	1.0	1.0
Q_3	2.2	1.0	2.0	2.0	2.0	2.0	1.0
Mean	1.8	1.3	1.5	1.2	1.3	1.3	0.9

ELEVEN YEAR OLD LONGITUDINAL GROUP

	Boys N 6	Girls N 7	Both N 13	Boys N 17	Girls N 15	Both N 32	Boys N 36
Range	0-1	0-4	0-4	0-4	0-5	0-5	0-4
Q_1	0	0	0	0.5	1.0	1.0	0
Mdn	1.0	1.0	1.0	1.0	1.0	1.0	1.0
Q_3	1.0	2.0	1.5	2.0	2.0	2.0	2.0
Mean	1.3	1.4	1.4	1.3	1.5	1.4	1.2

ELEVEN YEAR OLD CONTROL GROUP

	Boys N 3	Girls N 5	Both N 8	Boys N 7	Girls N 11	Both N 18	Boys N 22
Range	0-2	0-5	0-5	0-2	0-3	0-3	0-3
Q_1	0	0	0	0	0	0	0
Mdn	1.0	2.0	1.0	1.0	1.0	1.0	1.0
Q_3	2.0	4.0	2.8	2.0	1.0	1.2	2.0
Mean	1.0	1.8	1.5	0.9	0.8	0.8	1.0

(Read across pages 158 and 159.)

TABLE N (Continued)

| Average (90-109 I.Q.) | | Dull (75-89 I.Q.) | | | Total (74-140 I.Q.) | | |

NINE YEAR OLD LONGITUDINAL GROUP

Girls N 39	Both N 75	Boys N 9	Girls N 9	Both N 18	Boys N 68	Girls N 70	Both N 138
0-2	0-2	0-1	0-1	0-1	0-2	0-5	0-5
0	0	0	0	0	0	0	0
0	0	0	0	0	0	0	0
1.0	1.0	0	0	0	1.0	1.0	1.0
0.5	0.6	0.1	0.1	0.1	0.6	0.7	0.6

TEN YEAR OLD LONGITUDINAL GROUP

Girls N 39	Both N 75	Boys N 9	Girls N 9	Both N 18	Boys N 68	Girls N 70	Both N 138
0-4	0-4	0-1	0-2	0-2	0-4	0-4	0-4
0	0	0	0	0	0	0	0
0	0	0	0	0	1.0	0	1.0
1.0	1.0	1.0	0.5	1.0	2.0	1.0	1.0
0.5	0.7	0.3	0.3	0.3	1.0	0.7	0.9

ELEVEN YEAR OLD LONGITUDINAL GROUP

Girls N 39	Both N 75	Boys N 9	Girls N 9	Both N 18	Boys N 68	Girls N 70	Both N 138
0-3	0-4	0-3	0-3	0-3	0-4	0-5	0-5
0	0	0	0	0	0	0	0
1.0	1.0	1.0	0	0	1.0	1.0	1.0
1.0	2.0	2.0	2.0	1.5	2.0	2.0	2.0
0.9	1.1	1.0	0.8	0.9	1.2	1.1	1.4

ELEVEN YEAR OLD CONTROL GROUP

Girls N 18	Both N 40	Boys N 8	Girls N 6	Both N 14	Boys N 40	Girls N 40	Both N 80
0-4	0-4	0-1	0-1	0-1	0-3	0-5	0-5
0	0	0	0	0	0	0	0
0	0.5	0	0	0	1.0	0	0
1.0	1.8	1.0	0.2	1.0	1.8	1.0	1.0
0.7	0.9	0.4	0.2	0.3	0.9	0.8	0.9

C' OR FREQUENCY OF ACHROMATIC SURFACE COLOR RESPONSES
GIVEN TO THE RORSCHACH CARDS BY LONGITUDINAL AND CONTROL GROUPS

(Read across pages 160 and 161.)

	Superior (125 I.Q. and up)			Bright (110-124 I.Q.)			

SIX YEAR OLD LONGITUDINAL GROUP

	Boys N 6	Girls N 7	Both N 13	Boys N 17	Girls N 15	Both N 32	Boys N 36
Range	0-2	0-4	0-4	0-2	0-6	0-6	0-3
Q_1	0	0	0	0	0	0	0
Mdn	0	0	0	0	1.0	0	0
Q_3	1.2	3.0	1.5	1.0	1.0	1.0	1.0
Mean	0.5	1.0	0.8	0.4	1.3	0.8	0.5

SEVEN YEAR OLD LONGITUDINAL GROUP

	Boys N 6	Girls N 7	Both N 13	Boys N 17	Girls N 15	Both N 32	Boys N 36
Range	0-1	0-1	0-1	0-2	0-3	0-3	0-4
Q_1	0	0	0	0	0	0	0
Mdn	0	0	0	0	0	1.0	0
Q_3	1.0	1.0	1.0	0	0	1.0	1.0
Mean	0.3	0.3	0.3	0.5	0.3	0.4	0.4

SEVEN YEAR OLD CONTROL GROUP

	Boys N 6	Girls N 3	Both N 9	Boys N 9	Girls N 9	Both N 18	Boys N 19
Range	0-1	0-0	0-1	0-2	0-1	0-2	0-3
Q_1	0	0	0	0	0	0	0
Mdn	0	0	0	0	0	0	0
Q_3	0.2	0	0	0.5	1.0	1.0	0
Mean	0.2	0	0.1	0.3	0.4	0.4	0.3

EIGHT YEAR OLD LONGITUDINAL GROUP

	Boys N 6	Girls N 7	Both N 13	Boys N 17	Girls N 15	Both N 32	Boys N 36
Range	0-0	0-0	0-0	0-2	0-2	0-2	0-3
Q_1	0	0	0	0	0	0	0
Mdn	0	0	0	0	0	0	0
Q_3	0	0	0	1.0	0	0	0
Mean	0	0	0	0.3	0.1	0.2	0.3

OF ELEMENTARY SCHOOL CHILDREN FROM SIX THROUGH ELEVEN YEARS OF AGE REPORTED ACCORDING TO INTELLIGENCE LEVELS AND SEX

(Read across pages 160 and 161.)

Average (90-109 I.Q.)		Dull (75-89 I.Q.)			Total (74-140 I.Q.)		

SIX YEAR OLD LONGITUDINAL GROUP

Girls	Both	Boys	Girls	Both	Boys	Girls	Both
N 39	N 75	N 9	N 9	N 18	N 68	N 70	N 138
0-4	0-4	0-4	0-5	0-5	0-4	0-6	0-6
0	0	0	0	0	0	0	0
0	0	0	0	0	0	0	0
1.0	1.0	1.0	1.0	1.0	0	1.0	1.0
0.7	0.6	0.8	0.8	0.8	0.5	0.9	0.7

SEVEN YEAR OLD LONGITUDINAL GROUP

Girls	Both	Boys	Girls	Both	Boys	Girls	Both
N 39	N 75	N 9	N 9	N 18	N 68	N 70	N 138
0-2	0-4	0-4	0-6	0-6	0-4	0-6	0-6
0	0	0	0	0	0	0	0
0	0	1.0	0	0	0	0	0
0	0	2.0	0.5	1.0	1.0	0	1.0
0.2	0.3	1.1	0.8	0.9	0.5	0.3	0.4

SEVEN YEAR OLD CONTROL GROUP

Girls	Both	Boys	Girls	Both	Boys	Girls	Both
N 15	N 34	N 4	N 8	N 12	N 38	N 35	N 73
0-4	0-4	0-2	0-2	0-2	0-3	0-4	0-4
0	0	0.2	0	0	0	0	0
0	0	1.0	0	0	0	0	0
1.0	1.0	1.8	0	1.0	1.0	1.0	1.0
0.5	0.4	1.0	0.2	0.5	0.4	0.4	0.5

EIGHT YEAR OLD LONGITUDINAL GROUP

Girls	Both	Boys	Girls	Both	Boys	Girls	Both
N 39	N 75	N 9	N 9	N 18	N 68	N 70	N 138
0-2	0-3	0-3	0-1	0-3	0-3	0-2	0-3
0	0	0	0	0	0	0	0
0	0	0	0	0	0	0	0
0	0	2.0	0	0.2	0	0	0
0.2	0.2	0.8	0.1	0.4	0.4	0.1	0.2

TABLE O (Continued)

(Read across pages 162 and 163.)

	Superior (125 I.Q. and up)			Bright (110-124 I.Q.)			

NINE YEAR OLD LONGITUDINAL GROUP

	Boys N 6	Girls N 7	Both N 13	Boys N 17	Girls N 15	Both N 32	Boys N 36
Range	0-1	0-1	0-1	0-2	0-3	0-3	0-2
Q_1	0	0	0	0	0	0	0
Mdn	0.5	0	0	0	0	0	0
Q_3	1.0	0	0	0	1.0	0	0
Mean	0.5	0.1	0.3	0.2	0.5	0.3	0.2

TEN YEAR OLD LONGITUDINAL GROUP

	Boys N 6	Girls N 7	Both N 13	Boys N 17	Girls N 15	Both N 32	Boys N 36
Range	0-0	0-2	0-2	0-3	0-1	0-3	0-2
Q_1	0	0	0	0	0	0	0
Mdn	0	0	0	0	0	0	0
Q_3	0	0	0	1.0	0	1.0	0
Mean	0	0.3	0.2	0.6	0.2	0.4	0.2

ELEVEN YEAR OLD LONGITUDINAL GROUP

	Boys N 6	Girls N 7	Both N 13	Boys N 17	Girls N 15	Both N 32	Boys N 36
Range	0-1	0-1	0-1	0-2	0-1	0-2	0-2
Q_1	0	0	0	0	0	0	0
Mdn	0	0	0	0	0	0	0
Q_3	0.2	0	0	1.0	0	0	0
Mean	0.2	0.1	0.2	0.4	0.1	0.2	0.2

ELEVEN YEAR OLD CONTROL GROUP

	Boys N 3	Girls N 5	Both N 8	Boys N 7	Girls N 11	Both N 18	Boys N 22
Range	0-0	0-0	0-0	0-5	0-3	0-5	0-2
Q_1	0	0	0	0	0	0	0
Mdn	0	0	0	1.0	0	0	0
Q_3	0	0	0	3.0	0	1.2	0
Mean	0	0	0	1.6	0.4	0.8	0.2

Average (90-109 I.Q.)		Dull (75-89 I.Q.)			Total (74-140 I.Q.)		

NINE YEAR OLD LONGITUDINAL GROUP

Girls	Both	Boys	Girls	Both	Boys	Girls	Both
N 39	N 75	N 9	N 9	N 18	N 68	N 70	N 138
0-1	0-2	0-1	0-1	0-1	0-2	0-3	0-3
0	0	0	0	0	0	0	0
0	0	0	0	0	0	0	0
0	0	1.0	0	0.2	0	0	0
0.1	0.2	0.3	0.1	0.2	0.3	0.2	0.2

TEN YEAR OLD LONGITUDINAL GROUP

Girls	Both	Boys	Girls	Both	Boys	Girls	Both
N 39	N 75	N 9	N 9	N 18	N 68	N 70	N 138
0-1	0-2	0-2	0-1	0-2	0-3	0-2	0-3
0	0	0	0	0	0	0	0
0	0	0	0	0	0	0	0
0	0	0.5	0	0	0	0	0
0.05	0.1	0.3	0.1	0.2	0.3	0.1	0.2

ELEVEN YEAR OLD LONGITUDINAL GROUP

Girls	Both	Boys	Girls	Both	Boys	Girls	Both
N 39	N 75	N 9	N 9	N 18	N 68	N 70	N 138
0-1	0-2	0-3	0-1	0-3	0-3	0-1	0-3
0	0	0	0	0	0	0	0
0	0	0	0	0	0	0	0
0	0	1.0	0	0	0	0	0
0	0.2	0.6	0.1	0.3	0.3	0.1	0.2

ELEVEN YEAR OLD CONTROL GROUP

Girls	Both	Boys	Girls	Both	Boys	Girls	Both
N 18	N 40	N 8	N 6	N 14	N 40	N 40	N 80
0-2	0-2	0-1	0-1	0-1	0-5	0-3	0-5
0	0	0	0	0	0	0	0
0	0	0	0	0	0	0	0
0	0	0.8	0.2	0.2	0.8	0	0
0.1	0.2	0.2	0.2	0.2	0.4	0.2	0.3

FC OR FREQUENCY OF DEFINITE FORM WITH BRIGHT COLOR RESPONSES
GIVEN TO THE RORSCHACH CARDS BY LONGITUDINAL AND CONTROL GROUPS

(Read across pages 164 and 165.)

	Superior (125 I.Q. and up)			Bright (110-124 I.Q.)			

SIX YEAR OLD LONGITUDINAL GROUP

	Boys N 6	Girls N 7	Both N 13	Boys N 17	Girls N 15	Both N 32	Boys N 36
Range	0-3	0-1	0-3	0-3	0-5	0-5	0-6
Q_1	0	0	0	0	0	0	0
Mdn	1.0	1.0	1.0	1.0	1.0	1.0	1.0
Q_3	2.2	1.0	1.5	1.0	2.0	1.8	2.0
Mean	1.2	0.7	0.9	0.8	1.9	1.3	1.2

SEVEN YEAR OLD LONGITUDINAL GROUP

	Boys N 6	Girls N 7	Both N 13	Boys N 17	Girls N 15	Both N 32	Boys N 36
Range	0-2	0-3	0-3	0-4	0-6	0-6	0-4
Q_1	0	1.0	0	0	0	0	0
Mdn	0	1.0	1.0	0	1.0	0	1.0
Q_3	2.0	2.0	2.0	1.0	2.0	1.8	2.0
Mean	0.7	1.4	1.2	0.7	1.1	0.9	1.1

SEVEN YEAR OLD CONTROL GROUP

	Boys N 6	Girls N 3	Both N 9	Boys N 9	Girls N 9	Both N 18	Boys N 19
Range	0-4	0-1	0-4	0-2	0-3	0-3	0-6
Q_1	0	0	0	0	0	0	0
Mdn	1.0	1.0	1.0	1.0	1.0	1.0	1.0
Q_3	1.8	1.0	1.0	1.5	2.0	2.0	2.0
Mean	1.2	0.7	1.0	0.9	1.0	0.9	1.3

EIGHT YEAR OLD LONGITUDINAL GROUP

	Boys N 6	Girls N 7	Both N 13	Boys N 17	Girls N 15	Both N 32	Boys N 36
Range	0-6	0-11	0-11	0-6	0-5	0-6	0-6
Q_1	2.5	1.0	1.0	0	0	0	0
Mdn	1.0	3.0	1.0	1.0	1.0	1.0	0.5
Q_3	0.8	4.0	4.0	2.0	3.0	2.8	2.0
Mean	1.7	3.7	2.8	1.6	1.7	1.7	1.2

OF ELEMENTARY SCHOOL CHILDREN FROM SIX THROUGH ELEVEN YEARS OF AGE
REPORTED ACCORDING TO INTELLIGENCE LEVELS AND SEX

(Read across pages 164 and 165.)

Average (90-109 I.Q.)		Dull (75-89 I.Q.)			Total (74-140 I.Q.)		

SIX YEAR OLD LONGITUDINAL GROUP

Girls	Both	Boys	Girls	Both	Boys	Girls	Both
N 39	N 75	N 9	N 9	N 18	N 68	N 70	N 138
0-7	0-7	0-2	0-3	0-3	1-6	0-7	0-7
0	0	0	0	0	0	0	0
1.0	1.0	0	1.0	0	1.0	1.0	1.0
2.0	2.0	0.5	2.0	1.2	2.0	2.0	2.0
1.2	1.2	0.3	1.0	0.7	1.0	1.3	1.1

SEVEN YEAR OLD LONGITUDINAL GROUP

Girls	Both	Boys	Girls	Both	Boys	Girls	Both
N 39	N 75	N 9	N 9	N 18	N 68	N 70	N 138
0-7	0-7	0-6	0-3	0-6	0-6	0-7	0-7
0	0	0	0	0	0	0	0
1.0	1.0	0	1.0	0.5	0	1.0	1.0
1.0	1.0	3.5	1.0	1.5	2.0	1.0	2.0
0.8	1.0	1.6	0.8	1.2	1.0	0.9	0.9

SEVEN YEAR OLD CONTROL GROUP

Girls	Both	Boys	Girls	Both	Boys	Girls	Both
N 15	N 34	N 4	N 8	N 12	N 38	N 35	N 73
0-5	0-6	0-1	0-3	0-3	0-6	0-5	0-6
0	0	0.2	0.2	0.2	0	0	0
1.0	1.0	1.0	1.5	1.0	1.0	1.0	1.0
1.0	1.2	1.0	2.0	2.0	1.0	2.0	1.5
1.1	1.2	0.8	1.4	1.2	1.1	1.1	1.1

EIGHT YEAR OLD LONGITUDINAL GROUP

Girls	Both	Boys	Girls	Both	Boys	Girls	Both
N 39	N 75	N 9	N 9	N 18	N 68	N 70	N 138
0-4	0-6	0-3	0-3	0-3	0-6	0-11	0-11
0	0	0	0	0	0	0	0
1.0	1.0	1.0	1.0	1.0	1.0	1.0	1.0
1.0	2.0	1.5	2.5	2.0	2.0	2.2	2.0
1.0	1.1	0.9	1.1	1.0	1.3	1.4	1.3

| | Superior (125 I.Q. and up) | | | Bright (110-124 I.Q.) | | | |

NINE YEAR OLD LONGITUDINAL GROUP

	Boys N 6	Girls N 7	Both N 13	Boys N 17	Girls N 15	Both N 32	Boys N 36
Range	1-2	0-4	0-4	0-5	0-6	0-6	0-4
Q_1	1.0	1.0	1.0	1.0	0	1.0	0
Mdn	1.0	1.0	1.0	2.0	2.0	2.0	1.0
Q_3	2.0	3.0	2.5	2.0	3.0	2.0	2.0
Mean	1.3	1.9	1.6	1.6	2.1	1.8	1.3

TEN YEAR OLD LONGITUDINAL GROUP

	Boys N 6	Girls N 7	Both N 13	Boys N 17	Girls N 15	Both N 32	Boys N 36
Range	0-3	0-10	0-10	1-7	0-10	0-10	0-5
Q_1	0.8	0	0.5	1.0	0	1.0	0
Mdn	2.0	2.0	2.0	2.0	2.0	2.0	1.0
Q_3	3.0	4.0	3.5	2.5	5.0	3.0	2.0
Mean	1.8	1.9	1.8	2.2	2.8	2.5	1.6

ELEVEN YEAR OLD LONGITUDINAL GROUP

	Boys N 6	Girls N 7	Both N 13	Boys N 17	Girls N 15	Both N 32	Boys N 36
Range	1-6	0-13	0-13	0-6	0-8	0-8	0-7
Q_1	1.0	1.0	1.0	1.0	0	1.0	0
Mdn	1.5	2.0	2.0	2.0	1.0	1.0	1.0
Q_3	3.0	4.0	3.5	2.5	3.0	3.0	2.0
Mean	2.2	3.6	2.9	1.8	1.8	1.8	1.6

ELEVEN YEAR OLD CONTROL GROUP

	Boys N 3	Girls N 5	Both N 8	Boys N 7	Girls N 11	Both N 18	Boys N 22
Range	1-5	0-3	0-5	0-5	0-3	0-5	0-4
Q_1	1.0	0	0.2	0	0	0	0
Mdn	1.0	1.0	1.0	1.0	1.0	1.0	0.5
Q_3	5.0	2.0	2.5	3.0	2.0	2.2	1.2
Mean	2.3	1.0	1.5	1.6	1.2	1.3	0.9

TABLE P (Continued)
(Read across pages 166 and 167.)

Average (90-109 I.Q.)		Dull (75-89 I.Q.)			Total (74-140 I.Q.)		

NINE YEAR OLD LONGITUDINAL GROUP

Girls N 39	Both N 75	Boys N 9	Girls N 9	Both N 18	Boys N 68	Girls N 70	Both N 138
0-5	0-5	0-5	0-3	0-5	0-5	0-6	0-6
0	0	0.5	0	0	1.0	0	0
1.0	1.0	1.0	1.0	1.0	1.0	1.0	1.0
2.0	2.0	2.5	2.5	2.2	2.0	3.0	2.0
1.3	1.3	1.7	1.1	1.4	1.4	1.5	1.4

TEN YEAR OLD LONGITUDINAL GROUP

Girls N 39	Both N 75	Boys N 9	Girls N 9	Both N 18	Boys N 68	Girls N 70	Both N 138
0-6	0-6	0-7	0-2	0-7	0-7	0-10	0-10
1.0	0	0.5	0	0	1.0	0	0.8
2.0	1.0	1.0	0	0.5	1.0	2.0	1.0
2.0	2.0	2.0	0.5	2.0	2.0	2.2	2.0
1.7	1.6	1.8	0.3	1.1	1.8	1.8	1.9

ELEVEN YEAR OLD LONGITUDINAL GROUP

Girls N 39	Both N 75	Boys N 9	Girls N 9	Both N 18	Boys N 68	Girls N 70	Both N 138
0-7	0-7	1-4	0-5	0-5	0-7	0-13	0-13
1.0	0	1.0	0	1.0	1.0	1.0	1.0
1.0	1.0	2.0	1.0	1.0	2.0	1.0	1.0
2.0	2.0	3.0	2.0	3.0	2.0	3.0	3.0
1.6	1.6	2.1	1.2	1.7	1.8	1.8	2.0

ELEVEN YEAR OLD CONTROL GROUP

Girls N 18	Both N 40	Boys N 8	Girls N 6	Both N 14	Boys N 40	Girls N 40	Both N 80
0-2	0-4	0-7	0-2	0-7	0-7	0-3	0-7
0	0	0	0	0	0	0	0
0	0	0.5	0	0	1.0	1.0	1.0
1.0	1.0	3.5	1.2	2.0	2.0	1.0	1.8
0.6	0.8	1.8	0.5	1.2	1.3	0.8	1.0

C OR FREQUENCY OF COLOR RESPONSES
GIVEN TO THE RORSCHACH CARDS BY LONGITUDINAL AND CONTROL GROUPS

(Read across pages 168 and 169.)

	Superior (125 I.Q. and up)			Bright (110-124 I.Q.)			

SIX YEAR OLD LONGITUDINAL GROUP

	Boys N 6	Girls N 7	Both N 13	Boys N 17	Girls N 15	Both N 32	Boys N 36
Range	0-6	0-1	0-6	0-2	0-3	0-3	0-5
Q_1	0	0	0	0	0	0	0
Mdn	0.5	0	0	0	0	0	0
Q_3	4.8	0	1.0	0.5	1.0	1.0	1.0
Mean	1.3	0.1	0.7	0.4	0.6	0.5	0.8

SEVEN YEAR OLD LONGITUDINAL GROUP

	Boys N 6	Girls N 7	Both N 13	Boys N 17	Girls N 15	Both N 32	Boys N 36
Range	0-3	0-1	0-3	0-3	0-1	0-3	0-2
Q_1	0	0	0	0	0	0	0
Mdn	0	0	0	0	0	0	0
Q_3	2.2	0	0	0	0	0	0
Mean	0.5	0.1	0.3	0.3	0.2	0.2	0.1

SEVEN YEAR OLD CONTROL GROUP

	Boys N 6	Girls N 3	Both N 9	Boys N 9	Girls N 9	Both N 18	Boys N 19
Range	0-1	0-0	0-1	0-1	0-0	0-1	0-1
Q_1	0	0	0	0	0	0	0
Mdn	1.0	0	0	0	0	0	0
Q_3	1.0	0	1.0	0	0	0	1.0
Mean	0.7	0	0.4	0.1	0	0.1	0.3

EIGHT YEAR OLD LONGITUDINAL GROUP

	Boys N 6	Girls N 7	Both N 13	Boys N 17	Girls N 15	Both N 32	Boys N 36
Range	0-1	0-0	0-1	0-1	0-1	0-1	0-2
Q_1	0	0	0	0	0	0	0
Mdn	0	0	0	0	0	0	0
Q_3	0.8	0	0	0	0	0	0
Mean	0.2	0	0.1	0.1	0.1	0.1	0.1

OF ELEMENTARY SCHOOL CHILDREN FROM SIX THROUGH ELEVEN YEARS OF AGE
REPORTED ACCORDING TO INTELLIGENCE LEVELS AND SEX

(Read across pages 168 and 169.)

Average			Dull			Total		
(90-109 I.Q.)			(75-89 I.Q.)			(74-140 I.Q.)		

SIX YEAR OLD LONGITUDINAL GROUP

Girls	Both	Boys	Girls	Both	Boys	Girls	Both
N 39	N 75	N 9	N 9	N 18	N 68	N 70	N 138
0-4	0-5	0-5	0-2	0-5	0-6	0-4	0-6
0	0	0	0	0	0	0	0
0	0	0	0	0	0	0	0
1.0	1.0	3.0	2.0	2.0	1.0	1.0	1.0
0.7	0.8	1.2	0.8	1.0	0.8	0.7	0.7

SEVEN YEAR OLD LONGITUDINAL GROUP

Girls	Both	Boys	Girls	Both	Boys	Girls	Both
N 39	N 75	N 9	N 9	N 18	N 68	N 70	N 138
0-4	0-4	0-3	0-1	0-3	0-3	0-4	0-4
0	0	0	0	0	0	0	0
0	0	0	0	0	0	0	0
0	0	0	0	0	0	0	0
0.3	0.2	0.3	0.1	0.2	0.2	0.2	0.2

SEVEN YEAR OLD CONTROL GROUP

Girls	Both	Boys	Girls	Both	Boys	Girls	Both
N 15	N 34	N 4	N 8	N 12	N 38	N 35	N 73
0-2	0-2	0-2	0-1	0-2	0-2	0-2	0-2
0	0	0.2	0	0	0	0	0
0	0	1.0	0	0	0	0	0
1.0	1.0	1.8	0.8	1.0	1.0	0	1.0
0.4	0.4	0.8	0.2	0.4	0.4	0.2	0.3

EIGHT YEAR OLD LONGITUDINAL GROUP

Girls	Both	Boys	Girls	Both	Boys	Girls	Both
N 39	N 75	N 9	N 9	N 18	N 68	N 70	N 138
0-2	0-2	0-1	0-2	0-2	0-2	0-2	0-2
0	0	0	0	0	0	0	0
0	0	0	0	0	0	0	0
0	0	1.0	0.5	1.0	0	0	0
0.3	0.2	0.3	0.3	0.3	0.2	0.2	0.2

TABLE Q (Continued)
(Read across pages 170 and 171.)

<table>
<tr><td></td><td colspan="3">Superior
(125 I.Q. and up)</td><td colspan="3">Bright
(110-124 I.Q.)</td><td></td></tr>
</table>

NINE YEAR OLD LONGITUDINAL GROUP

	Boys N 6	Girls N 7	Both N 13	Boys N 17	Girls N 15	Both N 32	Boys N 36
Range	0-2	0-0	0-2	0-1	0-1	0-1	0-3
Q_1	0	0	0	0	0	0	0
Mdn	0	0	0	0	0	0	0
Q_3	1.8	0	0	0	0	0	0
Mean	0.5	0	0.2	0.7	0.1	0.1	0.3

TEN YEAR OLD LONGITUDINAL GROUP

	Boys N 6	Girls N 7	Both N 13	Boys N 17	Girls N 15	Both N 32	Boys N 36
Range	0-0	0-0	0-0	0-3	0-0	0-3	0-2
Q_1	0	0	0	0	0	0	0
Mdn	0	0	0	0	0	0	0
Q_3	0	0	0	0	0	0	0
Mean	0	0	0	0.2	0	0.1	0.2

ELEVEN YEAR OLD LONGITUDINAL GROUP

	Boys N 6	Girls N 7	Both N 13	Boys N 17	Girls N 15	Both N 32	Boys N 36
Range	0-0	0-0	0-0	0-0	0-0	0-0	0-2
Q_1	0	0	0	0	0	0	0
Mdn	0	0	0	0	0	0	0
Q_3	0	0	0	0	0	0	0
Mean	0	0	0	0	0	0	0.1

ELEVEN YEAR OLD CONTROL GROUP

	Boys N 3	Girls N 5	Both N 8	Boys N 7	Girls N 11	Both N 18	Boys N 22
Range	0-0	0-1	0-1	0-5	0-1	0-5	0-1
Q_1	0	0	0	0	0	0	0
Mdn	0	0	0	0	0	0	0
Q_3	0	0.5	0	0	1.0	0.2	0
Mean	0	0.2	0.1	0.7	0.3	0.4	0

(Read across pages 170 and 171.)

Average (90-109 I.Q.)		Dull (75-89 I.Q.)			Total (74-140 I.Q.)		

NINE YEAR OLD LONGITUDINAL GROUP

Girls N 39	Both N 75	Boys N 9	Girls N 9	Both N 18	Boys N 68	Girls N 70	Both N 138
0-2	0-3	0-1	0-4	0-4	0-3	0-4	0-4
0	0	0	0	0	0	0	0
0	0	0	0	0	0	0	0
0	0	0	1.0	0	0	0	0
0.2	0.2	0.1	0.7	0.4	0.2	0.2	0.2

TEN YEAR OLD LONGITUDINAL GROUP

Girls N 39	Both N 75	Boys N 9	Girls N 9	Both N 18	Boys N 68	Girls N 70	Both N 138
0-3	0-3	0-0	0-1	0-1	0-3	0-3	0-3
0	0	0	0	0	0	0	0
0	0	0	0	0	0	0	0
0	0	0	0	0	0	0	0
0.2	0.2	0	0.1	0.1	0.2	0.1	0.2

ELEVEN YEAR OLD LONGITUDINAL GROUP

Girls N 39	Both N 75	Boys N 9	Girls N 9	Both N 18	Boys N 68	Girls N 70	Both N 138
0-1	0-2	0-1	0-1	0-1	0-2	0-1	0-2
0	0	0	0	0	0	0	0
0	0	0	0	0	0	0	0
0	0	0	0	0	0	0	0
0	0.1	0.1	0.1	0	0.1	0	0.1

ELEVEN YEAR OLD CONTROL GROUP

Girls N 18	Both N 40	Boys N 8	Girls N 6	Both N 14	Boys N 40	Girls N 40	Both N 80
0-1	0-1	0-3	0-0	0-3	0-5	0-1	0-5
0	0	0	0	0	0	0	0
0	0	0.5	0	0	0	0	0
0	0	2.8	0	1.2	0	0	0
0.1	0.1	1.1	0	0.6	0.4	0.2	0.3

TABLE R

A%, OR PERCENTAGE OF ANIMAL RESPONSES
GIVEN TO THE RORSCHACH CARDS BY LONGITUDINAL AND CONTROL GROUPS

(Read across pages 172 and 173.)

	Superior (125 I.Q. and up)			Bright (110-124 I.Q.)			

SIX YEAR OLD LONGITUDINAL GROUP

	Boys N 6	Girls N 7	Both N 13	Boys N 17	Girls N 15	Both N 32	Boys N 36
Range	35-67	19-56	19-67	20-100	18-64	18-100	13-100
Q_1	38.0	33.0	35.5	35.0	33.0	33.8	33.0
Mdn	46.5	44.0	44.0	55.0	48.0	50.0	43.5
Q_3	59.5	54.0	56.5	59.0	57.0	57.8	53.8
Mn	48.5	41.3	44.6	50.9	44.3	47.8	45.6
SD	11.0	12.0	12.1	21.2	13.3	18.0	19.7

SEVEN YEAR OLD LONGITUDINAL GROUP

	Boys N 6	Girls N 7	Both N 13	Boys N 17	Girls N 15	Both N 32	Boys N 36
Range	33-64	37-80	33-80	16-83	19-100	16-100	24-92
Q_1	39.0	47.0	43.0	36.0	38.0	38.2	44.0
Mdn	55.5	55.0	55.0	50.0	60.0	54.0	53.5
Q_3	59.5	70.0	59.5	71.5	78.0	73.0	67.0
Mn	51.2	57.0	54.3	51.4	58.6	54.8	55.5
SD	10.8	13.7	12.8	18.4	22.0	20.2	17.2

SEVEN YEAR OLD CONTROL GROUP

	Boys N 6	Girls N 3	Both N 9	Boys N 9	Girls N 9	Both N 18	Boys N 19
Range	40-53	28-79	28-79	30-89	17-70	17-89	25-100
Q_1	40.8	28.0	40.0	28.5	32.5	31.5	40.0
Mdn	44.5	40.0	44.0	35.0	39.0	36.0	60.0
Q_3	48.5	79.0	50.0	43.0	42.0	42.0	64.0
Mn	45.0	49.0	46.3	49.6	43.0	46.3	54.6
SD	4.3	21.8	13.2	16.3	17.1	17.2	18.9

EIGHT YEAR OLD LONGITUDINAL GROUP

	Boys N 6	Girls N 7	Both N 13	Boys N 17	Girls N 15	Both N 32	Boys N 36
Range	41-62	30-58	30-62	32-92	21-80	21-92	22-100
Q_1	42.5	36.0	42.0	38.0	33.0	35.2	40.5
Mdn	48.5	54.0	51.0	54.0	53.0	53.5	53.5
Q_3	56.8	56.0	55.0	71.0	69.0	70.5	72.5

OF ELEMENTARY SCHOOL CHILDREN FROM SIX THROUGH ELEVEN YEARS OF AGE
REPORTED ACCORDING TO INTELLIGENCE LEVELS AND SEX

(Read across pages 172 and 173.)

Average (90-109 I.Q.)		Dull (75-89 I.Q.)			Total (74-140 I.Q.)		

SIX YEAR OLD LONGITUDINAL GROUP

Girls	Both	Boys	Girls	Both	Boys	Girls	Both
N 39	N 75	N 9	N 9	N 18	N 68	N 70	N 138
0-81	0-100	17-100	37-100	17-100	13-100	0-100	0-100
33.0	33.0	27.0	44.5	35.5	33.5	33.0	33.0
42.0	42.0	57.0	67.0	60.5	47.5	47.5	47.0
55.0	55.0	85.0	81.5	81.5	59.5	57.0	57.0
44.1	44.6	55.2	64.1	59.7	48.5	46.2	47.3
17.1	17.8	28.7	20.7	25.6	21.5	17.4	18.8

SEVEN YEAR OLD LONGITUDINAL GROUP

Girls	Both	Boys	Girls	Both	Boys	Girls	Both
N 39	N 75	N 9	N 9	N 18	N 68	N 70	N 138
19-100	19-100	41-90	43-100	41-100	16-92	19-100	16-100
43.0	44.0	44.0	53.0	48.5	42.2	44.8	43.8
59.0	56.0	55.0	64.0	62.5	54.5	60.5	56.0
69.0	68.0	72.5	90.0	81.8	66.8	73.5	69.2
57.8	56.7	58.9	69.7	64.3	54.5	59.4	57.0
22.1	19.2	15.9	18.5	18.3	17.3	20.7	18.7

SEVEN YEAR OLD CONTROL GROUP

Girls	Both	Boys	Girls	Both	Boys	Girls	Both
N 15	N 34	N 4	N 8	N 12	N 38	N 35	N 73
8-100	8-100	17-59	11-100	11-100	17-100	8-100	8-100
39.0	39.8	18.5	30.0	24.0	40.0	36.0	38.5
60.0	60.0	33.0	53.0	44.5	44.5	47.0	45.0
63.0	64.0	55.0	88.0	72.0	61.2	69.0	62.0
54.3	54.5	35.5	56.5	49.5	49.9	51.5	50.6
22.1	20.0	16.4	29.3	27.5	17.3	23.7	21.0

EIGHT YEAR OLD LONGITUDINAL GROUP

Girls	Both	Boys	Girls	Both	Boys	Girls	Both
N 39	N 75	N 9	N 9	N 18	N 68	N 70	N 138
26-100	22-100	27-82	47-100	27-100	22-100	21-100	21-100
47.0	46.0	36.0	54.5	42.8	41.0	46.8	42.8
58.0	54.0	45.0	65.0	60.0	52.5	56.5	54.0
73.0	73.0	74.5	81.0	80.0	73.8	71.0	71.0

	Superior (125 I.Q. and up)			Bright (110-124 I.Q.)			

EIGHT YEAR OLD LONGITUDINAL GROUP (Continued)

	Superior Boys	Superior Girls	Superior Both	Bright Boys	Bright Girls	Bright Both	Boys
Mn	49.7	48.4	49.0	56.5	51.8	54.3	54.8
SD	7.2	10.1	8.9	18.7	18.4	18.5	17.9

NINE YEAR OLD LONGITUDINAL GROUP

	Boys N 6	Girls N 7	Both N 13	Boys N 17	Girls N 15	Both N 32	Boys N 36
Range	38–59	37–55	37–59	25–93	19–76	19–93	21–88
Q_1	40.2	39.0	39.5	40.5	40.0	40.2	44.2
Mdn	45.5	44.0	44.0	51.0	51.0	49.5	48.5
Q_3	56.0	53.0	54.0	60.0	65.0	59.0	63.8
Mn	47.3	45.0	46.1	52.1	50.8	51.5	43.9
SD	7.9	6.7	7.4	17.5	14.8	16.1	16.2

TEN YEAR OLD LONGITUDINAL GROUP

	Boys N 6	Girls N 7	Both N 13	Boys N 17	Girls N 15	Both N 32	Boys N 36
Range	38–71	38–66	38–71	18–93	22–71	18–93	26–93
Q_1	44.0	42.0	42.5	47.0	52.0	48.0	44.0
Mdn	51.0	44.0	46.0	56.0	58.0	56.0	54.5
Q_3	64.2	48.0	58.0	67.0	64.0	61.8	61.8
Mn	53.2	46.4	49.5	52.9	55.5	54.2	53.6
SD	10.9	8.5	10.2	15.2	9.9	12.9	15.3

ELEVEN YEAR OLD LONGITUDINAL GROUP

	Boys N 6	Girls N 7	Both N 13	Boys N 17	Girls N 15	Both N 32	Boys N 36
Range	27–68	38–65	27–68	31–91	23–70	23–91	27–85
Q_1	42.0	41.0	41.5	43.0	44.0	43.2	42.5
Mdn	49.0	43.0	48.0	48.0	52.0	50.5	52.5
Q_3	60.5	49.0	53.5	56.5	59.0	58.8	58.0
Mn	49.7	46.6	48.0	50.4	51.6	50.9	52.1
SD	12.5	8.3	10.6	13.6	11.9	12.7	13.8

ELEVEN YEAR OLD CONTROL GROUP

	Boys N 3	Girls N 5	Both N 8	Boys N 7	Girls N 11	Both N 18	Boys N 22
Range	33–53	30–56	30–56	21–82	0–68	0–82	19–89
Q_1	33.0	31.5	33.0	38.0	19.0	26.2	44.8
Mdn	39.0	36.0	37.5	67.0	41.0	50.0	53.5
Q_3	53.0	51.0	51.2	72.0	52.0	67.0	65.2
Mn	41.7	40.2	40.8	56.9	38.2	45.4	52.3
SD	8.4	9.6	9.2	19.2	20.0	22.1	15.8

Average (90-109 I.Q.)		Dull (75-89 I.Q.)			Total (74-140 I.Q.)		

EIGHT YEAR OLD LONGITUDINAL GROUP (Continued)

| 60.0 | 57.5 | 51.9 | 69.3 | 60.6 | 54.4 | 58.3 | 56.4 |
| 19.8 | 18.4 | 19.0 | 16.3 | 19.9 | 18.0 | 18.7 | 17.8 |

NINE YEAR OLD LONGITUDINAL GROUP

Girls	Both	Boys	Girls	Both	Boys	Girls	Both
N 39	N 75	N 9	N 9	N 18	N 68	N 70	N 138
27-93	21-93	46-76	43-100	43-100	21-93	19-100	19-100
48.0	45.0	51.5	45.0	46.0	43.2	44.8	44.0
55.0	54.0	65.0	57.0	64.5	50.5	53.5	52.5
65.0	64.0	70.5	83.5	74.2	63.8	65.0	64.0
57.9	56.0	62.4	64.9	63.8	54.0	56.0	55.0
16.8	16.0	10.1	20.1	16.1	16.0	16.5	15.8

TEN YEAR OLD LONGITUDINAL GROUP

Girls	Both	Boys	Girls	Both	Boys	Girls	Both
N 39	N 75	N 9	N 9	N 18	N 68	N 70	N 138
32-100	26-100	43-75	50-94	43-94	18-93	22-100	18-100
47.0	46.0	54.0	55.0	56.0	46.2	47.8	47.0
58.0	55.0	64.0	68.0	65.5	55.5	57.5	56.0
68.0	65.0	70.5	82.5	70.2	62.8	67.0	66.0
58.8	56.3	62.3	68.3	65.3	54.6	58.1	56.4
15.3	15.0	9.8	14.6	12.9	14.9	14.2	13.6

ELEVEN YEAR OLD LONGITUDINAL GROUP

Girls	Both	Boys	Girls	Both	Boys	Girls	Both
N 39	N 75	N 9	N 9	N 18	N 68	N 70	N 138
30-83	27-85	39-81	58-95	39-95	27-91	23-95	23-95
43.0	43.0	42.5	66.0	53.8	43.2	43.8	43.8
53.0	53.0	54.0	67.0	66.0	52.5	57.5	53.0
63.0	61.0	71.0	73.0	73.0	58.0	53.5	62.0
54.4	53.3	57.3	70.2	63.8	52.2	55.1	53.6
14.2	13.6	14.4	9.7	14.0	14.1	13.8	13.6

ELEVEN YEAR OLD CONTROL GROUP

Girls	Both	Boys	Girls	Both	Boys	Girls	Both
N 18	N 40	N 8	N 6	N 14	N 40	N 40	N 80
26-74	19-89	20-71	33-76	20-76	19-89	0-76	0-89
33.8	37.5	31.2	34.5	34.5	38.2	33.0	34.2
44.0	47.5	43.0	58.0	52.0	52.0	44.0	47.5
58.8	62.5	54.8	73.0	61.2	65.8	57.8	58.0
45.5	49.2	43.9	55.3	48.8	50.6	44.3	47.5
14.3	15.6	15.4	16.5	16.8	16.9	16.9	16.5

TABLE S

H% OR PERCENTAGE OF HUMAN RESPONSES GIVEN TO THE RORSCHACH CARDS BY LONGITUDINAL AND CONTROL GROUPS

(Read across pages 176 and 177.)

	Superior (125 I.Q. and up)			Bright (110-124 I.Q.)			

SIX YEAR OLD LONGITUDINAL GROUP

	Boys N 6	Girls N 7	Both N 13	Boys N 17	Girls N 15	Both N 32	Boys N 36
Range	6-25	0-25	0-25	0-25	0-29	0-29	0-38
Q_1	9.0	8.0	9.0	2.5	8.0	5.5	4.0
Mdn	12.5	14.0	14.0	8.0	19.0	8.5	8.5
Q_3	24.2	22.0	23.0	9.5	22.0	20.0	16.2
Mean	15.0	14.1	14.5	8.3	16.3	12.0	10.1
SD	5.6	8.2	7.8	7.3	8.3	8.6	9.0

SEVEN YEAR OLD LONGITUDINAL GROUP

	Boys N 6	Girls N 7	Both N 13	Boys N 17	Girls N 15	Both N 32	Boys N 36
Range	0-22	10-29	0-29	0-36	0-29	0-36	0-35
Q_1	6.0	10.0	10.0	6.5	6.0	6.2	6.0
Mdn	13.0	14.0	14.0	10.0	10.0	10.0	9.0
Q_3	18.2	23.0	21.0	17.5	17.0	17.0	15.8
Mean	12.2	17.0	14.8	13.1	12.0	12.2	10.7
SD	5.4	6.5	7.2	9.7	7.8	8.8	8.6

SEVEN YEAR OLD CONTROL GROUP

	Boys N 6	Girls N 3	Both N 9	Boys N 9	Girls N 9	Both N 18	Boys N 19
Range	0-29	7-28	0-29	0-31	0-46	0-46	0-26
Q_1	5.2	7.0	7.0	3.5	7.0	6.8	6.0
Mdn	12.0	10.0	10.0	9.0	18.0	12.5	10.0
Q_3	22.2	28.0	24.0	17.0	27.0	20.2	17.0
Mean	15.0	13.2	13.8	11.1	18.6	14.8	11.0
SD	9.4	9.2	9.4	9.2	13.2	12.1	7.7

EIGHT YEAR OLD LONGITUDINAL GROUP

	Boys N 6	Girls N 7	Both N 13	Boys N 17	Girls N 15	Both N 32	Boys N 36
Range	13-21	16-30	13-30	0-30	0-24	0-30	0-29
Q_1	13.8	19.0	15.0	7.0	11.0	10.2	4.2
Mdn	16.0	21.0	20.0	14.0	17.0	14.0	11.0
Q_3	21.0	29.0	23.0	22.0	20.0	20.8	6.0

OF ELEMENTARY SCHOOL CHILDREN FROM SIX THROUGH ELEVEN YEARS OF AGE REPORTED ACCORDING TO INTELLIGENCE LEVELS AND SEX

(Read across pages 176 and 177.)

Average (90-109 I.Q.)		Dull (75-89 I.Q.)			Total (74-140 I.Q.)		

SIX YEAR OLD LONGITUDINAL GROUP

Girls	Both	Boys	Girls	Both	Boys	Girls	Both
N 39	N 75	N 9	N 9	N 18	N 68	N 70	N 138
0-53	0-53	0-20	0-20	0-20	0-38	0-53	0-53
11.0	7.0	0	4.0	0	5.0	10.0	6.0
16.0	13.0	4.0	10.0	8.5	8.5	15.5	11.0
20.0	18.0	14.5	16.5	16.2	14.8	20.0	19.0
17.6	14.0	6.7	10.4	8.6	9.6	16.0	12.9
12.4	10.6	7.5	6.7	7.4	8.6	10.0	9.6

SEVEN YEAR OLD LONGITUDINAL GROUP

Girls	Both	Boys	Girls	Both	Boys	Girls	Both
N 39	N 75	N 9	N 9	N 18	N 68	N 70	N 138
0-43	0-43	0-50	0-38	0-50	0-50	0-43	0-50
9.0	6.0	0	0	0	6.0	8.0	6.0
13.0	11.0	7.0	10.0	9.5	9.5	13.0	11.0
17.0	16.0	15.0	27.0	18.0	17.0	18.0	17.0
13.5	12.1	11.3	14.0	12.7	11.5	13.4	12.5
8.8	8.5	14.8	13.3	14.3	10.0	9.0	9.2

SEVEN YEAR OLD CONTROL GROUP

Girls	Both	Boys	Girls	Both	Boys	Girls	Both
N 15	N 34	N 4	N 8	N 12	N 38	N 35	N 73
0-36	0-36	0-21	0-30	0-30	0-31	0-46	0-46
8.0	6.8	0	10.2	2.0	5.5	8.0	7.0
15.0	12.0	7.5	18.0	17.5	10.0	17.0	13.0
20.0	17.8	19.5	21.5	20.8	17.8	21.0	20.0
14.9	12.7	9.0	16.6	14.1	11.2	16.3	13.6
9.1	8.4	9.2	8.5	9.4	8.5	10.5	10.0

EIGHT YEAR OLD LONGITUDINAL GROUP

Girls	Both	Boys	Girls	Both	Boys	Girls	Both
N 39	N 75	N 9	N 9	N 18	N 68	N 70	N 138
0-36	0-36	0-33	0-23	0-33	0-33	0-36	0-36
13.0	19.0	2.0	0	0	5.0	10.8	7.0
15.0	23.0	15.0	6.0	9.0	14.0	15.5	15.0
14.0	21.0	20.0	15.0	17.8	20.5	22.0	21.0

TABLE S (Continued)
(Read across pages 178 and 179.)

	Superior (125 I.Q. and up)			Bright (110-124 I.Q.)			

EIGHT YEAR OLD LONGITUDINAL GROUP (Continued)

Mean	16.8	22.8	20.1	14.4	15.3	14.8	12.1
SD	3.3	4.9	5.2	8.6	6.6	7.6	9.1

NINE YEAR OLD LONGITUDINAL GROUP

	Boys N 6	Girls N 7	Both N 13	Boys N 17	Girls N 15	Both N 32	Boys N 36
Range	6-36	14-35	6-36	0-30	3-40	0-40	0-40
Q_1	8.2	15.0	14.5	7.5	13.0	11.2	6.5
Mdn	24.5	23.0	24.0	15.0	16.0	15.0	11.0
Q_3	27.8	25.0	25.0	23.5	27.0	24.0	16.0
Mean	20.8	22.1	21.5	15.0	19.1	16.9	13.0
SD	10.3	6.6	8.5	9.1	10.0	9.6	9.2

TEN YEAR OLD LONGITUDINAL GROUP

	Boys N 6	Girls N 7	Both N 13	Boys N 17	Girls N 15	Both N 32	Boys N 36
Range	8-27	16-36	8-36	0-42	6-29	0-42	0-44
Q_1	8.8	17.0	13.5	8.5	12.0	10.5	6.0
Mdn	16.5	19.0	19.0	14.0	14.0	14.0	11.0
Q_3	22.5	32.0	29.0	21.5	20.0	20.0	18.5
Mean	16.5	24.0	20.5	15.9	16.9	16.3	13.4
SD	5.3	8.0	8.4	11.4	6.8	9.6	9.8

ELEVEN YEAR OLD LONGITUDINAL GROUP

	Boys N 6	Girls N 7	Both N 13	Boys N 17	Girls N 15	Both N 32	Boys N 36
Range	9-26	12-35	9-35	0-38	0-32	0-38	0-48
Q_1	12.0	16.0	15.0	9.0	12.0	11.2	5.2
Mdn	19.0	23.0	22.0	14.0	18.0	14.0	12.0
Q_3	23.5	27.0	25.0	21.0	25.0	23.2	20.8
Mean	18.5	22.7	20.8	16.0	18.3	17.1	14.4
SD	6.0	6.9	6.8	10.0	9.1	9.6	11.7

ELEVEN YEAR OLD CONTROL GROUP

	Boys N 3	Girls N 5	Both N 8	Boys N 7	Girls N 11	Both N 18	Boys N 22
Range	18-25	0-21	0-25	11-29	0-17	0-29	0-36
Q_1	18.0	8.5	17.2	12.0	7.0	8.5	5.2
Mdn	20.0	18.0	18.5	17.0	14.0	14.5	15.5
Q_3	25.0	20.0	20.8	17.0	16.0	17.0	22.2
Mean	21.0	15.0	17.2	16.4	11.5	13.4	14.4
SD	2.9	7.6	7.8	5.7	5.8	6.3	10.5

178

Average (90-109 I.Q.)		Dull (75-89 I.Q.)			Total (74-140 I.Q.)		

EIGHT YEAR OLD LONGITUDINAL GROUP (Continued)

15.4	13.8	14.7	7.9	11.3	13.4	15.1	14.3
9.8	9.3	12.8	8.1	11.4	9.5	9.0	9.0

NINE YEAR OLD LONGITUDINAL GROUP

Girls	Both	Boys	Girls	Both	Boys	Girls	Both
N 39	N 75	N 9	N 9	N 18	N 68	N 70	N 138
0-45	0-45	0-14	0-25	0-25	0-40	0-45	0-45
9.0	8.0	5.5	2.5	4.8	7.2	10.0	9.0
19.0	12.0	12.0	11.0	11.5	12.0	17.0	14.0
25.0	22.0	13.0	17.5	13.2	20.2	25.0	23.0
17.2	15.2	9.7	10.4	10.0	13.7	17.2	15.5
10.3	9.7	5.5	8.1	6.7	9.4	9.8	9.4

TEN YEAR OLD LONGITUDINAL GROUP

Girls	Both	Boys	Girls	Both	Boys	Girls	Both
N 39	N 75	N 9	N 9	N 18	N 68	N 70	N 138
0-38	0-44	0-25	0-19	0-25	0-44	0-38	0-44
8.0	7.0	7.0	5.0	6.8	7.0	11.0	8.0
17.0	15.0	11.0	12.0	11.5	13.0	16.5	15.0
20.0	20.0	18.0	16.0	16.0	20.5	20.0	20.0
15.5	14.5	12.8	10.1	11.4	14.2	15.9	15.1
8.6	9.0	6.3	6.6	6.6	9.9	8.4	8.9

ELEVEN YEAR OLD LONGITUDINAL GROUP

Girls	Both	Boys	Girls	Both	Boys	Girls	Both
N 39	N 75	N 9	N 9	N 18	N 68	N 70	N 138
0-46	0-48	2-18	0-18	0-18	0-48	0-46	0-48
8.0	8.0	5.5	5.5	5.8	7.0	9.8	8.8
16.0	14.0	12.0	11.0	11.5	13.5	16.5	14.0
21.0	21.0	17.0	17.5	17.0	19.5	22.0	20.0
16.0	15.2	11.3	11.2	11.3	14.8	16.5	15.6
9.2	10.5	5.5	6.1	5.9	10.5	9.3	9.6

ELEVEN YEAR OLD CONTROL GROUP

Girls	Both	Boys	Girls	Both	Boys	Girls	Both
N 18	N 40	N 8	N 6	N 14	N 40	N 40	N 80
0-39	0-39	2-14	0-18	0-18	0-36	0-39	0-39
12.0	7.0	5.0	0	1.5	7.2	7.0	7.0
15.0	15.0	9.5	4.0	8.0	14.0	15.0	14.0
22.0	22.0	13.8	16.5	14.0	21.8	18.8	19.8
17.4	15.7	9.2	7.0	8.3	14.2	13.9	14.1
9.7	10.3	4.3	7.6	6.0	9.0	9.0	8.7

P OR NUMBER OF KLOPFER POPULAR RESPONSES
GIVEN TO THE RORSCHACH CARDS BY LONGITUDINAL AND CONTROL GROUPS

(Read across pages 180 and 181.)

	Superior (125 I.Q. and up)			Bright (110-124 I.Q.)			

SIX YEAR OLD LONGITUDINAL GROUP

	Boys N 6	Girls N 7	Both N 13	Boys N 17	Girls N 15	Both N 32	Boys N 36
Range	2-8	3-6	2-8	0-6	0-8	0-8	1-7
Q_1	3.5	3.0	3.5	1.5	2.0	2.0	2.0
Mdn	4.5	5.0	5.0	3.0	3.0	3.0	3.0
Q_3	5.8	6.0	5.5	5.0	4.0	5.0	4.0
Mean	4.7	4.6	4.6	3.3	3.3	3.3	3.2

SEVEN YEAR OLD LONGITUDINAL GROUP

	Boys N 6	Girls N 7	Both N 13	Boys N 17	Girls N 15	Both N 32	Boys N 36
Range	3-7	4-7	3-7	2-7	1-8	1-8	0-7
Q_1	3.0	4.0	4.0	2.5	3.0	3.0	3.0
Mdn	4.0	4.0	4.0	3.0	4.0	3.5	3.0
Q_3	5.5	7.0	7.0	5.0	5.0	5.0	4.0
Mean	4.3	5.1	4.8	3.6	4.1	3.9	3.5

SEVEN YEAR OLD CONTROL GROUP

	Boys N 6	Girls N 3	Both N 9	Boys N 9	Girls N 9	Both N 18	Boys N 19
Range	1-7	2-5	1-7	1-6	1-6	1-6	2-6
Q_1	1.0	2.0	1.5	2.0	3.0	2.8	2.0
Mdn	4.5	4.0	4.0	4.0	3.0	3.5	3.0
Q_3	5.5	5.0	5.0	5.5	5.0	5.2	4.0
Mean	3.8	3.7	3.8	3.7	3.7	3.7	3.1

EIGHT YEAR OLD LONGITUDINAL GROUP

	Boys N 6	Girls N 7	Both N 13	Boys N 17	Girls N 15	Both N 32	Boys N 36
Range	5-8	4-8	4-8	2-7	3-10	2-10	2-9
Q_1	5.0	5.0	5.0	3.0	5.0	4.0	3.2
Mdn	7.0	6.0	6.0	5.0	6.0	5.0	5.0
Q_3	8.0	9.0	8.0	5.0	7.0	6.0	6.0
Mean	6.7	6.0	6.3	4.6	5.7	5.1	4.9

OF ELEMENTARY SCHOOL CHILDREN FROM SIX THROUGH ELEVEN YEARS OF AGE
REPORTED ACCORDING TO INTELLIGENCE LEVELS AND SEX

(Read across pages 180 and 181.)

Average (90-109 I.Q.)		Dull (75-89 I.Q.)			Total (74-140 I.Q.)		

SIX YEAR OLD LONGITUDINAL GROUP

Girls	Both	Boys	Girls	Both	Boys	Girls	Both
N 39	N 75	N 9	N 9	N 18	N 68	N 70	N 138
0-7	0-7	0-5	1-5	0-5	0-8	0-8	0-8
2.0	2.0	1.0	1.0	1.0	2.0	2.0	2.0
3.0	3.0	3.0	2.0	2.0	3.0	3.0	3.0
4.0	4.0	3.5	3.5	3.2	5.0	4.0	4.0
3.1	3.2	2.4	2.2	2.3	3.3	3.2	3.2

SEVEN YEAR OLD LONGITUDINAL GROUP

Girls	Both	Boys	Girls	Both	Boys	Girls	Both
N 39	N 75	N 9	N 9	N 18	N 68	N 70	N 138
1-7	0-7	1-5	1-6	1-6	0-7	1-8	0-8
3.0	3.0	2.0	2.0	2.0	2.2	3.0	3.0
4.0	4.0	2.0	3.0	3.0	3.0	4.0	4.0
5.0	5.0	4.0	4.0	4.0	5.0	5.0	5.0
3.9	3.7	2.8	3.1	3.0	3.5	4.0	3.8

SEVEN YEAR OLD CONTROL GROUP

Girls	Both	Boys	Girls	Both	Boys	Girls	Both
N 15	N 34	N 4	N 8	N 12	N 38	N 35	N 73
2-6	2-6	1-6	1-4	1-6	1-7	1-6	1-7
3.0	2.0	1.5	3.0	2.2	2.0	3.0	2.0
3.0	3.0	3.5	3.0	3.0	3.0	3.0	3.0
5.0	4.0	5.5	3.0	3.8	4.2	4.0	4.0
3.5	3.3	3.5	2.8	3.0	3.4	3.4	3.4

EIGHT YEAR OLD LONGITUDINAL GROUP

Girls	Both	Boys	Girls	Both	Boys	Girls	Both
N 39	N 75	N 9	N 9	N 18	N 68	N 70	N 138
1-8	1-9	2-5	1-7	1-7	2-9	1-10	1-10
3.0	4.0	2.5	2.0	2.0	3.0	4.0	3.8
5.0	5.0	3.0	3.0	3.0	5.0	5.0	5.0
6.0	6.0	4.0	6.5	4.2	6.0	6.0	6.0
4.6	4.8	3.2	3.8	3.5	4.7	4.9	4.8

	Superior (125 I.Q. and up)			Bright (110-124 I.Q.)			

NINE YEAR OLD LONGITUDINAL GROUP

	Boys N 6	Girls N 7	Both N 13	Boys N 17	Girls N 15	Both N 32	Boys N 36
Range	4-8	4-7	4-8	3-8	3-9	3-9	2-9
Q_1	5.5	5.0	5.5	4.0	4.0	4.0	4.0
Mdn	6.5	6.0	6.0	5.0	6.0	5.0	5.0
Q_3	8.0	7.0	7.0	5.5	8.0	7.0	6.8
Mean	6.5	6.0	6.2	5.0	6.1	5.5	5.0

TEN YEAR OLD LONGITUDINAL GROUP

	Boys N 6	Girls N 7	Both N 13	Boys N 17	Girls N 15	Both N 32	Boys N 36
Range	6-9	3-8	3-9	2-10	3-9	2-10	1-8
Q_1	6.8	4.0	6.0	5.0	5.0	5.0	5.0
Mdn	7.5	7.0	7.0	6.0	6.0	6.0	6.0
Q_3	9.0	7.0	8.0	8.0	8.0	8.0	7.0
Mean	7.7	6.0	6.8	6.1	6.3	6.2	5.6

ELEVEN YEAR OLD LONGITUDINAL GROUP

	Boys N 6	Girls N 7	Both N 13	Boys N 17	Girls N 15	Both N 32	Boys N 36
Range	7-10	4-9	4-10	3-10	4-10	3-10	2-9
Q_1	7.8	5.0	6.0	5.0	5.0	5.0	4.2
Mdn	8.0	7.0	8.0	7.0	7.0	7.0	7.0
Q_3	9.2	8.0	8.5	8.0	8.0	8.0	7.0
Mean	8.3	6.4	7.3	6.4	6.8	6.6	5.8

ELEVEN YEAR OLD CONTROL GROUP

	Boys N 3	Girls N 5	Both N 8	Boys N 7	Girls N 11	Both N 18	Boys N 22
Range	4-6	2-6	2-6	2-8	2-8	2-8	2-9
Q_1	4.0	2.5	3.2	2.0	4.0	3.0	3.0
Mdn	4.0	4.0	3.0	3.0	5.0	5.0	4.5
Q_3	6.0	6.0	6.0	5.0	6.0	6.0	5.0
Mean	4.7	4.2	4.4	3.9	5.1	4.6	4.6

Average (90-109 I.Q.)		Dull (75-89 I.Q.)			Total (74-140 I.Q.)		

NINE YEAR OLD LONGITUDINAL GROUP

Girls	Both	Boys	Girls	Both	Boys	Girls	Both
N 39	N 75	N 9	N 9	N 18	N 68	N 70	N 138
2-8	2-9	3-7	2-7	2-7	2-9	2-9	2-9
4.0	4.0	3.5	3.0	3.0	4.0	4.0	4.0
5.0	5.0	4.0	4.0	4.0	5.0	5.5	5.0
7.0	7.0	5.0	6.0	6.0	6.0	7.0	7.0
5.2	5.1	4.3	4.3	4.3	5.0	5.4	5.2

TEN YEAR OLD LONGITUDINAL GROUP

Girls	Both	Boys	Girls	Both	Boys	Girls	Both
N 39	N 75	N 9	N 9	N 18	N 68	N 70	N 138
1-9	1-9	3-7	0-8	0-8	1-10	0-10	0-10
4.0	5.0	3.0	4.0	3.8	5.0	4.0	4.8
6.0	6.0	4.0	4.0	4.0	6.0	6.0	6.0
7.0	7.0	6.0	7.0	6.2	7.0	7.0	7.0
5.6	5.6	4.6	4.8	4.7	5.8	5.7	5.7

ELEVEN YEAR OLD LONGITUDINAL GROUP

Girls	Both	Boys	Girls	Both	Boys	Girls	Both
N 39	N 75	N 9	N 9	N 18	N 68	N 70	N 138
3-9	2-9	4-9	1-10	1-10	2-10	1-10	1-10
4.0	4.0	4.0	4.0	4.0	5.0	5.0	5.0
7.0	7.0	6.0	5.0	5.0	6.0	6.0	6.0
7.0	7.0	7.0	7.0	7.0	7.0	6.0	7.0
6.0	5.9	5.8	5.3	5.6	6.1	6.1	6.1

ELEVEN YEAR OLD CONTROL GROUP

Girls	Both	Boys	Girls	Both	Boys	Girls	Both
N 18	N 40	N 8	N 6	N 14	N 40	N 40	N 80
1-7	1-9	2-7	2-6	2-7	2-9	1-8	1-9
3.8	3.2	2.2	2.8	2.8	3.0	3.0	3.0
5.0	5.0	4.5	3.0	3.5	4.0	5.0	5.0
6.0	5.8	5.8	5.2	5.2	5.0	6.0	6.0
4.6	4.6	4.2	3.7	4.0	4.4	4.6	4.5

Bibliography

It is impossible to list accurately the many and varied sources from which the contents of this book have been derived. In the decade and a half of reading, investigation, and thinking, the author has drawn inspiration and information from innumerable articles, books, and other less tangible sources. Attendance at workshops and lectures given by such experts in the field as Klopfer, Beck, Hertz, and Piotrowski, has been an additional source of inspiration and drive to complete this study.

Any attempt on this author's part to compile a bibliography, even if it could be done with accuracy, would be merely carrying coals to New Castle, since the reader has access to many excellent compilations. Such a one is found in the second volume of *Developments in the Rorschach Technique* by Klopfer and others, published in 1956 by the World Book Company. This bibliography is recommended especially to those who are looking for literature dealing with children's Rorschachs. To those interested in other specific aspects of Rorschach investigation, the division of the ponderous bibliography into topics of current interest will prove a welcome expediency.